Sex, Lies
and
The
Dirty

Sex, Lies
and
The Dirty

A Memoir
Nik Richie

FERAL HOUSE

Feral House
1240 W. Sims Way
Suite 124
Port Townsend, WA 98368
feralhouse.com

Cover by Sean Tejaratchi
Book design by Gregg Einhorn

ISBN 978-1936239597

Printed in the United States of America

10 9 8 7 6 5 4 3 2 1

Acknowledgements

Myself.
Without me, none of this would have been possible.

Contents

Vegas; Hard Rock   *9*

A Call From Justin Levine   *21*

Exposure   *23*

Origins (Part 1)   *27*

Dolce Vendetta   *37*

Split   *45*

Lohan   *48*

Chuck   *52*

Three   *56*

Pleasanton   *60*

Carrie Prejean; Perez Hilton   *64*

Scooby Snack   *68*

Escorts & Porta-Potties   *73*

Ginger   *76*

Origins (Part 2)   *84*

Posts   *97*

31   *100*

Colors   *107*

Vegas; Lavo   *112*

Shayne   *118*

Media   *129*

Optima   *134*

Meeting the Family   *138*

Origins (Part 3)   *144*

Ben Quayle   *153*

$11M   *156*

Dr. Phil   *158*

Origins (Part 4)   *171*

20/20 (Part 1)   *181*

Deposition   *184*

Broadcast   *193*

20/20 (Part 2)   *195*

Anderson: Episode 1   *197*

Verdict   *199*

Anderson: Episode 2   *201*

Billboards   *206*

Origins (Part 5)   *208*

The Tour   *221*

The Catalyst   *225*

To Press   *227*

Exit   *230*

Niktionary   *233*

Vegas; Hard Rock

Audrina Patridge ends up fucking us.

Our original plan is to do a 4th of July weekend out in Vegas for branding purposes, but because I haven't gone public yet as Nik Richie, we need to put a face on the event. Someone that we can put on flyers and people will recognize. Tony Wang[1], who is our contact, tells us we should reach out to a celebrity to host this thing, recommending that we get a cast member from *The Hills*[2] because everyone is watching that fucking show. There's also the issue of the $25,000 the Hard Rock wants to charge us for being there or using their venue or whatever. If we pull in a celeb to host, Tony explains, the Hard Rock will waive that.

The decision doesn't take long. We don't want a dude to host and Lauren Conrad costs fifty grand, so Audrina is our best option. We agree to fly her and her four friends out (first class), pay for their rooms at the hotel (suites), and Audrina's $15,000 appearance fee.

I'm glad we manage to book a celeb for the event and save a few grand, but I have to admit that I don't know much about Audrina outside of the following two things:

1) She's on a popular TV show, and although she has a terrible refund gap[3] I could probably fuck her and feel okay about it.

2) From guys I know that have fucked her, she gets really wet—like obnoxiously wet. So wet that you can't feel anything and you need five paper towels just to wipe your dick off. I realize this shouldn't be a point of issue, but it's disgusting from what I've been told. Like she's got a drooling Labrador inside her cervix.

Despite the rumors, I'm still leaning toward fucking her should the

---

1 Committed suicide in 2011.

2 Scripted reality show that aired from 2006 to 2010 on MTV. Preceded by *Laguna Beach*.

3 The huge gap between a woman's fake breasts that is so huge they should ask their doctor for a refund.

opportunity arise. If it doesn't, I'm cool with just meeting her and getting a contact out of the deal. It's whatever. I'm optimistic about things. We buy a bunch of extra merchandise to give away to coincide with the Audrina appearance: T-shirts, trucker hats, and panties that have *The Dirty* logo on the ass. Everything is in line for a successful weekend.

Five days before the event is when we get the call.

It's Audrina's management telling us, "Audrina's not doing it. She doesn't want to go to Vegas."

It comes off a little shady because, again, Audrina is getting paid to show up at Body English, drink for free, and take a few photos. Not very difficult in the grand scheme of things. That's the excuse they give us though: "She's not doing it. She doesn't want to go."

And I'm thinking, *Seriously, who doesn't want to get paid to go to Vegas?*

So I'm fucking livid because Audrina is canceling five days before the event (and not even with a decent excuse), and because she's doing it so short-notice that makes it next to impossible to book another celeb to fill the slot. We're also back on the hook to pay $25,000 to the Hard Rock. Fortunately, we have a backup plan.

Who needs Audrina when you've got *Dirty* Celebs?

◆◆◆

Leper and Alien are from Dallas.

G-Girl is from Scottsdale.

We're flying all three of them out to Vegas for the event, but it's tough to even get these girls on an airplane because they're all alcoholics and drug addicts. Anything they can put in their body to lose their sense of reality, they're on it, and you can tell G-Girl is taking all sorts of crazy pre-scription shit on top of whatever bottle she can get those engorged lips around. Leper and Alien would suck a hobo's cock if they thought Crown Royal was going to shoot out, but that's not really saying much since it's a well-known fact they dabble in porn and pay-for-play[4]. Pictures don't lie.

They're blonde and tan and slutty and rarely sober, and though I'm inclined to disagree, the general consensus is that they're all "totally

---

4 Prostitution.

fuckable." So these girls, these *Dirty* Celebs[5], as we refer to them, are meant to replace Audrina Patridge to an extent. The idea is that we're going to hire ten photographers to follow them around like paparazzi, and that this will draw attention to them in a way that will have people associating *Dirty* Celebs with chicks like Paris Hilton who are always out partying. Add a bunch of alcohol and whatever drugs they wind up taking, and it should yield some interesting footage. Something tangible.

These girls can be the thing that Nik Richie can't: a public image, a face to the idea. No matter how often they say "don't look at me" or "stop talking about me," it's bullshit. They're some of the biggest fame-chasers[6] out there, and the fact that they're coming out to Vegas confirms that in my mind.

Meanwhile, on the Audrina Patridge front, the Hard Rock gets back with us and verifies that her *I don't want to go to Vegas* excuse was a crock of shit. Apparently, she (or her management) thought we wanted her to wear the *Dirty* panties at the Rehab pool party, and then there was another line of bullshit about how she got booked somewhere else for a higher rate.

I make a mental note to blast her on the site later.

No time to think about that now. The girls are in Vegas and already Alien is trying to fuck me.

◆ ◆ ◆

Someone from my idiot staff tells Alien that I'm the guy.

Not directly, but they give her my room number which is basically the same thing. Even a drunk like her can find a room number. How she actually gets in is still a mystery to me. All I know is that around three in the afternoon, Alien is in my bedroom taking her clothes off, saying, "Eat my pussy. Eat my pussy," in her weird Dallas accent, slurring hard on airplane booze and whatever else she's on.

Her skin smells like urine and spray tan, and she's pushing me onto the bed. Pushing hard. Aggressive. And I'm saying "No." Confused. Caught off-guard because for the better part of a year I've called this chick out for

5 A person, usually a woman, that is featured on the site so often and so prominently that they become well-known amongst the users, and by extension, throughout the nightlife scene as a whole. A *Dirty* Celeb becomes official when they're given a moniker by Nik Richie. Traditionally, this is a name that references or alludes to their worst physical feature.
6 An individual whose goal in life is to become famous. Typically, this person will have no remarkable talent or skill.

being a drunk-slut-cokehead piece of shit, putting her on blast[7], boosting my own popularity at her expense. Now she's throwing herself at me. Wanting me. Holding me down on the hotel bed.

This is how Alien and I meet: her saying, "Eat my pussy, Nik." Small tits hanging out. She presses them to my face, my mouth. Those smell like urine, too, and my lips curl over my teeth. Curl tight. Her fingers wrap around my wrist, spelling G-L-A-M in blue and red ink. One letter per finger. They clamp down and lock. My face turns left…right…back again, avoiding her lips. Her breath smells like liquor and shit, and she's saying it again. Alien says, "Eat my cunt," like every disparaging thing I ever wrote about her was my weird way of flirting.

I say, "No, I'm not the guy. I'm not the guy," trying to push back, and when she reaches down to grab my cock, I'm able to shift my weight and throw her off. Alien is so fucked-up though that she thinks I'm playing into her aggressive bullshit, smiling messy pink gloss. Drunk. She can't even comprehend rejection. Can't process a guy not wanting to fuck her, maybe because whatever is kicking around in her system won't let her. I'm not sure.

"Seriously, I'm not him," and then I pull Alien off of the bed, walking her out of the suite and locking the door behind her.

That's only the beginning; I can feel it.

It's about to get so much worse.

◆ ◆ ◆

At Body English inside the Hard Rock, G–Girl, Leper, and Alien are getting photo-bombed at the press wall, doing what they do best: smiling, posing, hair-flipping, and that thing where they bring their faces in like they're about to kiss, but then they freeze less than an inch from touching. Teasing. The cameras love them. Alien does one of her signature poses, flipping the bird and kissing the print of her middle finger while G-Girl and Leper bounce their tits for the photographers. Huge, fake tits that someone else paid for, and now the crowd is stopping to see what all the fuss is about. Tan, blonde girls flaunting themselves and each other. Advertising. Modeling. Fame-chasing.

Kiss. Wink. Flash.

Everyone's watching.

Audrina Patridge shows up to the event—not to host or to meet any of

---

7 Putting someone in the spotlight and/or exposing them; talking crap about someone.

us, mind you. She's just there, drinking with friends and hanging out. So I despise Audrina now because she not only pulled out of the deal at the last minute, but then she showed up anyway acting like a fucking tough chick. She keeps throwing little bitchy glares our way.

Of course, I can't say anything directly because Nik Richie isn't supposed to be here. There's rumors going around that I am, and after that shit with Alien showing up to my room, I've got Duane Bell (my black security guy) tailing me through the club, just in case some idiot from my staff decides to out me again. I'm mostly here to make sure the event goes smoothly and keep everyone on task.

We've got the center stage at Body English: bottles of Grey Goose and people taking photos of Leper and Alien making out on one of the maroon leather couches. Hip-hop music thumping. Cameras flashing, and not just from the photographers now. People are either crowding up to get a shirt or pair of underwear, or they're trying to get a shot of Leper shoving her tongue into Alien's mouth, sucking on it while Alien reaches over to grab G-Girl's tit. It feels like the club and everyone in it stops to watch these girls, because it's not casual or a couple of chicks kissing for attention. These are drunk strippers, so coked-out they're probably not even aware they're being watched, photographed, adored. They have no idea how much this is going to help out the business.

◆ ◆ ◆

After–party. My suite.

The staff is all here along with a bunch of random girls, and in a way you could call this a celebration since the event did what we intended it to do. Mostly due to Leper, Alien, and G-Girl, we've left our mark on Vegas, got a ton of footage, and most importantly, got people talking about *The Dirty*[8]. In hindsight, Audrina dropping out was a bit of a blessing. Body English is buzzing over *The Dirty*, not *The Dirty* and "that chick from *The Hills*.'

So everyone's here now: drinking, partying, socializing.

I'm a little bit more at ease now that the event is behind us and I don't need Duane to tail me anymore, but every once in a while I'll catch a look. Nothing hostile. It's more like recognition. Like they know who I really am. Slowly, everyone in the room is figuring out that I'm the guy. The secret spreads. It circulates through loose talk and lowered inhibitions, finally getting to the wrong girls. The fame-chasers.

---

8 www.thedirty.com

This manifests when I go to take a piss. G-Girl follows me into the bathroom, locking the door behind her. I'm pissing and she takes her top off. She's hammered—almost blackout drunk with her tits hanging out now, and they're spray-tanned in a way where her nipples have been painted over. I'm pissing, looking at two huge lumps of tan meat, then Leper and Alien are at the bathroom door.

They're pounding, yelling in their drunken Texas accents, "I'm gonna kick your ass, you fuckin' slut-bag whore!"

I'm pissing, and G-Girl folds onto the floor. Tits spilling everywhere, and they're still out there pounding. Pounding and yelling. I shake, tuck my Greg[9] away and zip up. G-Girl's eyes are fluttering. She's barely conscious, fading, so I open the door and let Leper and Alien see her laying on the bathroom tiles. Drunk and harmless.

I shrug at the two of them, saying, "Hey, I'm just taking a piss. I don't know what her deal is." Then I have one of my guys, Tristan, mop G-Girl off the floor and take her away. Her tits are still hanging out, and for all I know she probably thinks she's walking off with me.

I'm left standing with Alien and Leper.

They're on way too many drugs and they know who I am now.

◆ ◆ ◆

Leper decides she's going to let Alien have me because, apparently, she called dibs or something like that. They're respecting the dibs rule because they're best friends. Never mind the fact that I haven't the slightest fucking interest in Alien—that I actually think Leper isn't bad-looking (the +2's[10] and Dallas blue eyes do it for me). Because this crazy bitch called dibs, I'm stuck with her throwing herself at me again while Duane ushers everyone out of the suite. It's four in the morning, and all I want to do is sleep because we've got to do this all over again tomorrow (later today, actually) at Rehab.

Alien is telling me, "I just want to talk."

And I'm like, "Talk? About what?"

"About…my life," she says. "The site. Nothing's going to happen."

"Fine," I say.

---

9 Slang vernacular for "penis."

10 Refers to: fake breasts. The idea is that by having them they automatically add two points to the traditional one to ten scale of attractiveness. For instance, if you were a six you'd automatically be an eight.

Then we're in my bedroom, and I'm under the clean cool sheets, trying to drift off while Alien meanders in the room. She's staring. Just looking at me. Not talking. Alien tries to get into bed with me and I say "No."

She says, "I just want to talk," and she stinks even worse than this afternoon. It's piss and old spray tan. It's sweat and liquor that has dried to her skin, and her face is wrecked. Smeared. And I close my eyes to not see it, thinking, *go away…just go the fuck away*, but I can still feel her getting closer. The smell intensifies: the liquor and drugs and piss seeping through her pores, and I say "No, it's not happening."

Alien gets out of the bed, and for a second—one thrilling moment—I think it might be that easy. She'll walk off and leave me alone. I'll deal with her shit for one more day and never have to see her again.

She says, "I'm going to kill myself. You're going to watch me kill myself if you don't fuck me right now."

I open my eyes. I look at her.

"I have a daughter," she says. "I'm going to kill myself."

So the choice is: I can either take one for the team by fucking this whore, or I could yell for Duane and have him come in and get rid of her.

Then I'm thinking, *There's no fucking way she's going to jump*, but that's when Alien opens the balcony door and throws one of her legs over the ledge. We're on the sixth floor. It's just high up enough that she could survive the fall if she doesn't land on her head.

She's sitting there, looking at me, saying, "I have a daughter."

I pause, thinking, then I tell her, "Jump."

I say it again. Firmer this time. "Jump."

Alien challenges, "You really want to me jump? I'll jump."

I say, "Kill yourself. I don't fucking care. You're worthless to me."

I'm thinking, *Fuck, this better work.*

I say it again. "Jump." And she's so out of her mind, so completely fucked on drugs and liquor and some dream that never happened, that she might do it. She might find it easier to just end her life, and I refuse to fuck her to save it.

She sits on the ledge. Sits. Thinking.

Alien says, "No…I have a daughter."

◆ ◆ ◆

It's late morning when I wake up.

I open the bedroom doors and the place is wrecked: beer and liquor bottles, trash, random bits of food. Cigarettes are on the ground, a little wipe pattern of ash from where some chick stepped and twisted. Tables are flipped over. It stinks. Stinks like stale booze and smoke. And there's blood on the couch. A lot of blood, like somebody stabbed themselves. No body. Just a huge bloodstain on this light gray couch, the kind of stain that the maid would have to report. It seriously looks like someone died in here, and staring at the stain is making me light-headed.

I walk across the living room, knocking on Duane's door to find out what the fuck is going on. He opens up, wearing nothing but boxers and a T-shirt and I'm like, "Dude, why is there blood all over the place?"

He says, "Huh?"

We walk over to the couch and I motion to it, the blood. He looks at it, at me, searching for a response. Duane grabs his camera and starts filming it, the huge red stain streaking this fucking couch. You can see clots if you look close enough, and while Duane's filming this thing I fill him in on last night. "Alien tried to kill herself."

Duane turns away from the blood, giving me a look like, *That came from Alien?*

I say, "No, she tried to jump out the window. Where the fuck were you?"

He busts out laughing and says, "Man, that would have been awesome if she did it."

I shake my head, get my phone and call Tristan to see if he knows anything. He picks up and I ask, "What the fuck, dude? There's fucking blood all over the place."

He says, "Dude, Nik…it's cool."

"No it's not, man. What the fuck happened?" I ask. "It looks like some-one fucking stabbed themselves."

"Oh, nah man, it's fine. It's just G-Girl," he says. "She's on her period."

"Then get the fuck up here and clean this shit up, man."

"Let a maid do it."

"Tristan," I say. "You fucked this girl—you unplugged her, you O.J.'d her. Get the fuck up her and clean this shit."

Meanwhile, Duane is still taping the couch, taping me on the phone and laughing his ass off. Tristan comes up to the room, but I can already tell it's to argue his case in person rather than clean up the mess. Duane tries to hand him a wet washcloth, bitching about being recorded and that we should "just let the maid do her job." He starts working on the stain, begrudgingly, but the blood has been soaking into the fabric for so long that all Tristan is accomplishing is getting the couch wet. Nothing's coming out, and Duane keeps recording the whole ordeal and laughing.

Then I decide to give Tristan an even shittier job than cleaning period blood.

I say, "Round up the girls and get them down to the pool."

Of course, they're probably in any room but the ones they're supposed to be in. Girls like Alien and Leper don't go to bed alone, and they're never where they're supposed to be.

♦ ♦ ♦

Leper and Alien make it down to the pool at Rehab, already drunk on minibar booze and whatever pills they took. Apparently, G-Girl was too embarrassed about the period blood thing to come down, so it's the Leper and Alien show: stripping, kissing, almost fucking in this cabana that we're in. Cameras clicking away or recording. It doesn't take a lot to get them going because they're still drunk from last night, and security has to constantly watch these girls because the fucking guidos and muscle-heads are getting too aggressive. Hundreds of people are watching this play out, and if you listen closely you can hear random dudes say things like, "Those are the two chicks from last night I was telling you about."

At one point Leper comes up to me in the cabana that I'm sitting in. She plants herself down, pretty much wasted, but her body is nice and she's smiling at me like I'm the only one that matters out of all these juiceheads and tourists. She says, "I know you're the guy."

I take a drink of vodka/water. Nod.

Leper says, "You're fucking hot. But my friend likes you."

And me being an idiot, I say, "Kelli, the only reason I flew you guys out here was to meet you. You're the one I want. Not Alien." I ask her, "Can you get her the fuck away from me?"

Then Leper smiles, happy and drunk and full of something like hope, putting a hand on my knee, saying, "Okay. I'll keep her away."

Leper gets up, disappearing into the crowd, and here I'm thinking that this should take care of it. I won't have to deal with Alien's shit anymore, but all I've done is made it worse again.

♦ ♦ ♦

We reach a new low.

Most of the news comes secondhand, but what I do know is that after we partied at Body English again, the girls completely lost their shit. Alien and Leper got into some kind of weird altercation, probably because of what I said at Rehab. My staff tells me that Leper almost got raped by some guidos at the hotel and security has to be called, and none of my people can keep up with them because they're running around the Hard Rock, cracked out of their minds on a drug buffet. God knows where G-Girl is.

Leper's banging on people's doors, either looking for her room or just a place to hide out—I don't know. Randomly, one of the doors is Jenna Jameson's, who is staying with Tito Ortiz, and Jenna's saying, "I don't know you. I can't help you," because it's three or four in the morning and she's trying to sleep.

About an hour before sunrise, Alien is knocking on my door and crying hysterically, saying, "I don't feel safe. I need help."

Crying. Drunk and exhausted.

She says, "Please let me stay here. I can't find Kelli."

While I'm deliberating, Duane says to me, "Dude, if you let her stay here, at least we'll know where she is and we can get her on the plane tomorrow."

So I let Alien into the suite. She stops crying and follows me into my bedroom, trembling and wiping the mascara out of her eyes. I try not to look at her because she's such a goddamn wreck. Not even close to that girl I've seen in pictures that men obsess over, and the urine smell is even worse than before. Gag-inducing.

Alien gets into the bed and starts grabbing my cock, and I'm so burnt-out that this time I don't put up much of a resistance. She puts my cock in her mouth, sucking and jacking me off, pushing her tongue piercing into the cluster of nerves on the underside.

I relent, saying, "I'm not going to fuck you but I'll put it in your ass," because I'm thinking that if I blow my load, she'll leave me the fuck alone and go to sleep.

She says, "No, you're not doing that," pinning me to the bed, and then I push her off and pin her. Now Alien thinks I'm playing into her sexual-aggressive bullshit again, but this is just me trying to control her, the situation.

I say, "I don't have a condom."

She says, "Fine, you can put it in my ass," then Alien starts giving me head again. Spitting and slobbering all over me. She works on me until I'm hard and dripping her saliva, rolling onto all fours and sticking her ass out with that trashy butterfly tattoo on the right cheek. My cock slides in, slides in way too easily like she does this all the time, and I'm thinking, *Please don't catch a DRD[11], dude…please don't catch a DRD.*

I fuck her, breathing through my mouth as much as I can because a shit smell is comingling with urine and booze and smoke, and Alien's moaning. She's pushing her asshole against me, and my eyes turn upward to the ceiling so I don't have to see my cock or the shit coming out of her, but the smell is so intense that I can taste shit and spray-tan on my tongue. I fuck her harder. Harder. Fuck her, and when I come the orgasm is so weak I barely feel it, but now there's cum all over her back and the spray-tan looks like watercolors.

In the bathroom, I'm wiping my cock off on one of the hotel towels, and there's a brownish-orange muck coming off of it that makes me gag. I take a deep breath. Collect myself. I wash my dick off in the sink and towel off again. Get back into bed.

I ask Alien, "Can I please go to sleep now?"

Her face turns, angry perhaps, and she says, "No, that's not fair. You didn't make me come. You have to eat my pussy."

And I'm like, "That wasn't part of the deal."

I pretend to pass out, but Alien moves to sit on my face, putting her cunt on my lips. It's rotten. It's got little pieces of shit on it from when I fucked her in the ass, but she's pushing it on me, on my skin, telling me to make her come. I'm holding my breath—not breathing, twisting my face away into the pillow, but then my guts clench like a fist and my throat wants to burst. Wants an exit. The shit and fish and urine are choking the air, and I throw Alien off and run back to the bathroom where I piss and throw up at the same time. Vomit everywhere.

I wash out my mouth and wait.

Wait for Alien to go to sleep.

◆◆◆

When I wake up Alien's gone.

She's not here, but I can smell urine, and I want this to be a dream so bad that I'm actually whispering it to myself. I'm looking around the bedroom, making sure that I'm truly alone and trying to identify the piss smell. It's as strong as it was last night.

---

11 Stands for: Dennis Rodman Disease, so called because everyone in Newport says Dennis Rodman is the dirtiest guy around.

Please be a dream, please be a dream.

Urine. Shit. Vomit.

Please be a dream.

I go to the bathroom and see chunks of puke on the toilet and all over the floor. In the bedroom, the urine smell is too intense for Alien to not be here. It's like she's in the room and I just can't see her, but when I take a closer look at the bed I find the answer. Grabbing a handful of blankets, I tug everything off the mattress and see it: a large piss stain.

It's not a dream. It all happened.

I get the first flight back home and promise myself that I'll never go to Vegas again.

A Call From Justin Levine

Everyone in Vegas is still buzzing over the Leper and Alien show, going on about how psycho and crazy these girls are. The strip shows and public make-out sessions and all those rumors about drugs and fucking, most of which I believe. However, these people, the spectators, only see a fraction of what they really are. They had the luxury of remaining at a safe distance whereas I was the one responsible for getting them on airplanes and keeping them from jumping out of hotel windows. If Vegas taught me anything, it's the difference between how someone is perceived on the site and having to be around them, dealing with their bullshit. Keeping them alive.

So it's about two weeks after our premiere event at the Hard Rock; traffic is up. Everyone is commenting on the pictures we put up of Leper, Alien, and G-Girl out at Body English. The whole thing was considered a resounding success, but I'm glad to be done with it and away from those girls. Away from Vegas.

This is when Justin Levine reaches out. He introduces himself over the phone, telling me that he's one of the managing members of Opium Group, which is out of Miami and a pretty big fucking deal in nightlife. The guy is connected, so I'm really listening to what he has to say now as he talks about a club called Privé, which is out of Planet Hollywood.

I ask, "Wait, *which* Planet Hollywood?"

Please, let it be any of them but the one I'm thinking.

"The one in Vegas," he says.

My heart sinks. I just promised myself I wouldn't be going back there, so whatever this Levine dude says had better be convincing.

He explains, "Vegas is buzzing, and we want to book the next *Dirty* event…the *exact* thing you did last time but at Privé."

Already I'm thinking, *Fuck that, I just spent $25,000 on the last event.*

Then Levine tells me the one thing I don't want to hear. He says, "We want you to bring Alien and Leper back."

No, there's no fucking way I'm going to pay money to hang out with those psycho bitches.

He asks, "Does seven grand work?"

We'd still be paying, but that's considerably less than the 25K we had to shell out to the Hard Rock. I tell Levine I have to speak to our financial guy and that I'll call back. The whole deal gets pitched to my partner, and considering our shaky finances, he says that we have to do it. In his mind, he's probably thinking that if we've cut event expenses by $18,000 in only two events, maybe by the third one we'll start making money.

I get Levine back on the phone, and as much as I hate the idea of having to pay money to be around Leper and Alien again, I tell him we'll do the event. It's another opportunity for branding, to get the name out there. Just another part of paying my dues.

"Great," Levine says. "Do you want us to wire the money or send a check?"

It finally clicks that I've been misunderstanding the arrangement the entire time. *He* wants to pay *us.* This is when partying officially becomes part of our business model, the moment just before everyone finds out the truth about me.

Exposure

I had gotten busted over eight months ago for a DUI.

That was my dirt, but it had been so long that I had pretty much stopped worrying about it up until The Smoking Gun contacted me through e-mail. They want to know if Hooman Karamian and Nik Richie are the same person. There's been rumors going around that I'm the guy, but up until now, it's all been hearsay. Speculation. The arrest report The Smoking Gun has pushes it one step closer to confirming who I really am: the guy that anonymously puts people on blast, teases them, pokes fun at their lives. I've been doing this for years, and because Nik Richie has never extended beyond the confines of the Internet, Hooman Karamian has never been at risk. I never had to worry about my personal life. Until now. The Smoking Gun wants to publish this story, but they don't want to pull the trigger until they confirm everything's accurate. All it's going to take is one reply from me saying they figured it out. I'm him. I'm Nik Richie.

And I'm freaking the fuck out.

Even if I don't confirm the story for them, they might decide to run with it anyway. I talk to my advisors, explaining the situation: The Smoking Gun is ready to out me. If I'm outed, I'm fucked. All those people that said they were going to kill me can actually do it now. There's no protection. Even if I hide out in my apartment, it only takes one pissed-off psycho to track me down and put a bullet in my brain. It only takes one.

The advisors tell me to calm down.

They say, "You need to take the mug shot and put it up. You need to make fun of yourself. And you need to do it now."

"Are you serious?" I ask.

"Yes, you need to post yourself before they post you. Embrace it. Run with it. There's not a lot of choice in the matter."

The Smoking Gun emails me again saying that they're going to publish the story with or without my consent. I do exactly what I was advised to do.

I write up the post.
I expose myself to the world.

Is Hooman Karamian (nice name) the Real Nik Richie?

Posted in The Dirty | September 4th, 2008

What a tool bag... if you are going to take a mug shot with your cheese-grader face at least look sexy?

Nik Richie: If you were gay and had to be the top for this DUI Douche Bag, Would You?

Answer: No, he has $2.00 waxed eyebrows, a taliban beard, a nose that is as large as my Greg, needs Botox, was set up by Scottsdale PD for posting a picture of the Cheif of Police's daughter, has a homo skunk trail that only D-Nazi would be proud of and his chest hair is for the Gays! Dude what were you thinking? Shave that fern gully down! Also, I don't bang dudes with weird names... not my style.

I beat The Smoking Gun to the punch and they're pissed.

They even send me an e-mail calling me a coward and asking why I would out myself, which is really just another way of saying *Thanks for fucking us over on an exclusive.*

They still go live with a post of their own: the mug shot, a synopsis of the DUI, a few snarky jabs, and the full police report. All of this goes up only a moment after I out myself on my own site. Then it starts spreading: first to Deadspin, and then it's chained out over and over again down the line. Almost instantly, the world knows who I really am.

True to form, everyone has an opinion.

Everyone's been waiting for this moment.

Traffic on the site doubles, and most of it is because the comment boards are being bombarded with opinions about me. Remarks about my appearance. This time, I'm the one on blast. I finally get a taste of my own medicine.

They say: Cheetah print collar? Come on, Nik.

And: Ha! We should be asking average-looking girls "would you" for your ugly terrorist ass.

Some people commend me for coming out. Others don't.

For the most part, it's insults, teasing—all the stuff I do.

"You are a tool, and your website sucks."

"Wow, the mighty have fallen."

"You are dead to me."

◆ ◆ ◆

I'm terrified and paranoid for a good day or so. Most of the news outlets are spinning this as a karma piece. It's Matt Leinart's[12] revenge for that time I posted him with underage girls and got him benched. Or it's just karma in general. Payback that was long overdue for all the lives I fucked with.

Every time I go out I'm worried about getting jumped, spit on, or something equally not good. I'm not even talking about the clubs. Each person I walk by at the grocery store or gas station could be a person that's been up on the site, only now they know who I am. So I'm constantly in a state having my guard up, but then something very odd happens.

I'm getting emails saying that they're glad I came out. I'll go to restaurants and people are shaking my hand, smiling, telling me that they love my site. They love what I do. Nik Richie had always been popular, but now he

---

12 NFL quarterback and Heisman trophy winner.

was tangible. People could meet him, talk to him. Suddenly, I was some kind of celebrity along the lines of a Zuckerberg or Perez Hilton. I was finally real. A public figure.

I was one step closer to the American dream.

Origins (Part 1)

My parents immigrated to the United States with $1,000 to their name, and they would go on to raise myself and my two brothers in a strict Iranian fashion. We never cursed. We never talked back. Our career as American–born Iranians was to chase the American dream. That meant working hard, devoting yourself to academics, and pursuing fields that generated the maximum amount of income. According to my father, you could either be a doctor, lawyer, or engineer. The plan was simple: high school would be followed by college which would be followed by a career.

My father was an engineer.

I was going to be a doctor.

My uncle, who owned multiple medical practices, was a radiologist and my personal role model. He drove a Jaguar. Owned beachfront property. He had money and everyone's respect. People were envious, and my father never missed an opportunity to point this out to me, if only to remind me what was waiting at the end of the road.

"This is what you get when you become a doctor, Hooman," he said.

My plan to go premed, to follow in my uncle's footsteps, was more about materialism than it was pleasing my father. The quality of work didn't factor in much, either. It was all about money. If I had money, I could be like my uncle and have the things he had. This goal would be instilled in me around the age of five, and over the years, would become more of an obsession. I would graduate high school, graduate college, become a radiologist, and one day take over CIG[13], which was the name of my uncle's practice. My high school friends, especially the Caucasian ones, were not nearly as regimented when it came to their future. So I took a certain amount of pride in knowing exactly what I was doing, but more importantly, that I was going to be rich.

My brother, Brian, changed all of that.

---

13 Capital Imaging Group.

I was seventeen. Brian was seven. He was in the kitchen sawing through a baseball with a steak knife. Like most kids his age, he was curious about everything. Brian wanted to see what was under the leather and stitching. He was slicing away at this thing when his hand slipped. He screamed. Blood everywhere. The knife sliced into his wrist and he started bawling, screaming, gripping his wrist while blood crept through his fingers. My parents weren't home. I was listening to my seven-year-old brother scream as I called 911. I told them that my brother cut himself. Cut deep. I gave my address and told them to hurry, watching my brother yell, cry, bleed. I started to get light-headed watching the blood. The blood seeped through his fingers. It pooled on our kitchen floor. I watched the blood snake down his arm in deep red lines, dripping steadily from his elbow.

The last thing I remember was blood.

◆◆◆

I had a phobia.

If I saw blood I fainted.

This would happen two more times in the form of a soccer cleat injury and during the dissection of a small pig in anatomy class. I had dissected a frog before, expertly making incisions with the scalpel and pinning its stomach flaps to the rubber bottom of the operation basin. All major organs were correctly identified. This gave me a bit of confidence back after the baseball incident with my brother. The pig, however, proved to me once again that I had a legitimate problem. Unlike the frog, it started bleeding when I cut into it. Gushing, actually.

I woke up in the nurse's office a few hours later.

My plan was ruined. I couldn't be a doctor.

◆◆◆

I graduated from Mission Viejo High School, enrolling in Cal State Fullerton with little to no direction. I picked a major: psychology. I joined a frat. The plan I had for the last twelve years had been botched, so my approach to college was keeping to the things that conformed to standards. Everyone wanted to join a frat. Everyone was doing psychology. Although my father continued to preach the advantages of going premed, psychology seemed like a safe bet, even though I had no passion for it. Psychology let people know that I had a plan. The frat let people know I was a part of something.

The reality is that I was trying to find my way but I couldn't. On the sur-face, it appeared that I knew what I was doing. Hooman had it figured out, people thought. He was on the path. Years from now, I was going to have a doctorate just like my father wanted. I would find that American dream. It even got to the point where I started setting monetary goals: first million by twenty-five. I'd be a multi-millionaire by twenty-seven. Psychology wasn't going to allow me to do that, though. I wanted to get rich quick. I wanted to cut corners, and college seemed like the biggest corner of all. It was going to take at least seven years to earn my doctorate. The more I thought about it, the less I wanted to devote myself to something I had little interest in. I had the same problem that most people my age had: I wanted to work very little and get a lot of money for it. It wasn't an issue of being lazy. I was impatient, so I jumped at the first opportunity that came my way.

◆◆◆

My best friend at the time was in a band.
    The band was called Hey Stroker, and even though I didn't particularly care for their music, I couldn't deny that they were getting big in Orange County. They had a pretty decent following. Their shows usually sold out. They were going to make it; I knew that much. And I wanted to be part of this thing, but again, I didn't like the music and I didn't know how to play an instrument. What was clear to me was that being in the music industry was a hell of a lot more interesting to me than psychology. I enjoyed the scene. A lot of girls usually came out to see the band. It eventually got to a point where I was going to more shows than classes, and I had stopped checking in with the frat some time ago. The Greek system is based a lot on doing what you're told (usually ridiculous things), and I've never been very good at taking orders. I've always been the type of guy that needs to be in charge. A bunch of random dudes in a frat wasn't going to change that. When it came down to it, I'd rather go to a Hey Stroker show than a frat party any day of the fucking week. Freshman only get the leftovers of the upperclassmen. At least at the shows I had a decent selection, and the members of the band weren't nearly as pretentious.
    It finally clicked that Hey Stroker needed a manager, and since I couldn't be in the band, I figured running it would be the next best thing. I quit the frat. Dropped out of school. My father was pissed off that I wasn't follow-ing "the plan," but I knew this was the right move for me. I was going to get

these guys signed and make it in the management business. Hey Stroker was going to be the first of many, and that would put me back on the path to becoming a rich man again.

The music business, however, never works out the way you think.

◆◆◆

I managed Hey Stroker for about a year.

I was taking meetings with Elektra and Sony but it was clear that they saw me for what I was: a kid with no experience. It just so happened that I had stumbled upon the opportunity to speak on behalf of the band. I was a bullshit artist pretending to know what the hell I was doing. They knew it. The record label guys could see that within the first five minutes, and there was always talk about why the band didn't have a better manager.

Everyone kept asking why some kid was repping Hey Stroker.

People were interested, but not in working with Hooman Karamian. This was why the meetings never went well. It's also why the band never agreed to sign any contracts with me. If I found them a deal, they'd be willing to commit to me and me alone. Until then, they were going to keep their options open. So I hustled. I wanted to prove that I could make it in the business. I even responded to talent–seeking ads in the back of magazines like *Rolling Stone* and *Spin*. To me it was just a numbers game. That's all a music contract was: getting lucky. Being in the right place at the right time. I still didn't care for the music.

In hindsight, neither party was every truly committed to the other.

That made parting ways easy.

◆◆◆

The scam worked like this: Talent2K placed ads in the back of magazines essentially guaranteeing record contracts. Music magazines like *Rolling Stone* and *Vibe* and whatever else aspiring bands were reading. All you had to do was send over $400 and Talent2K would get your music out to all the major labels. That's what they said, anyway. The reality is that Carlo Oddo, the guy who ran Talent2K, was cashing the checks and trashing most of the music. I had sent him some Hey Stroker material about four months prior, so it was a little odd he called back on it. If you knew Carlo, you knew that he was never one to actually try and get someone signed. That would involve legwork and taking meetings. Carlo was more the type to sit in his bedroom all day, hitting on young girls through MySpace while the money rolled in. Or he watched mafia movies while smoking dirts. [14]

I'd learn this after he talked me into working for him.

The dream of being a doctor was over. Hey Stroker didn't work out and I really didn't feel like going back to school. At the time, joining Carlo's operation didn't seem like the worst idea in the world. He promised a commission if I could close deals over the phone.

"I'll shop and you sell," he said.

That was the arrangement.

It didn't even really bother me that Carlo was running a scam. The music business had left a bad taste in my mouth, and I was willing to fuck a few people over if it meant making money. In my mind, I had already paid my dues during the whole Hey Stroker deal. The entire industry felt dirty to me.

So I met Carlo in Chicago. He was older than me: mid-thirties. Bald. Fat. He kind of looked like a child molester, but the financial opportunity made me see past all that. He explained how everything would work: I'd try to sell these bands on our packages. Depending on the amount a band spent, that would determine what services Talent2K would provide. In the end though, it didn't matter if you spent $300 or $3,000. Carlo never actually did anything. He cashed the checks, but that was about it. My job was to help him get more checks to cash.

Carlo bought me a cell phone and I went back to California. I wasn't even listening to any of the music. All I had was a contact name and the name of the band. I'd call these guys up telling them that I was the VP of A&R at Talent2K out of Los Angeles. I'd say that we loved the material they sent and if we could get them on a bigger package (the $995 tier) we could get their music out to all the major labels. We could get them a deal. All they needed to do was provide a little bit more cash and they'd be rock gods in no time. Think of it as an investment, I said.

I sold them, scammed them. I fucked these people over the way the industry fucked me, and I was good at it. The problem was that Carlo had yet to pay me any of my commission. He was already in the hole to me for a few grand when he brought up the idea of Sun City. His grandparents lived there in Arizona, and apparently one of them had died or had a health problem. Something like that. He was going to Sun City and wanted me to come with him to set up the operation.

---

14 Cigarettes.

"We'll have an office and everything," he said. "I just need you to get on a plane."

"Dude, I don't have any fucking money. You haven't paid me yet."

"Just get here, man. Drive if you have to."

I was about to find out who Carlo really was.

◆◆◆

Carlo lived with his parents out in the snowbird[15] community of Sun City. Everyone was old. Dying. These people rode around in golf carts because they were either too scared to drive or lost their licenses. All day you'd hear the distinct whine of those carts lugging groceries or heading to the pharmacy. In Sun City, hardly anything moved faster than ten miles per hour, so Carlo and I were the minority. The outcasts. We were kids again, and he was training me to scam.

Inside the apartment, everything smelled like old people except for Carlo's room. It was filled with brimming ashtrays and junk food wrappers. Clothes were never folded. The bed was never made. The guy was a fat fucking slob, but I got over it pretty quick once he started paying me. We started making a lot of money, and in between the scamming and bogus contracts, Carlo would make me watch mafia movies. Scorsese movies like *Goodfellas* and *Casino*. Or we watched movies about salesmen like *Boiler Room* or *Glengarry Glen Ross*. We quoted them. Acted them out. In my early twenties, the most impressionable years of my life, I was hanging out with Carlo Oddo, the fat fuck scam artist. A gangster wannabe. A guy that hooked up with fourteen-year-old girls online. He had absolutely no moral compass, but I didn't seem to mind that as long as he paid me.

I bought a Porsche Boxster.

I blew $30,000 on strip clubs over the course of a year. The operation got so big that we hired a couple girls to do some of the bullshit work. Young girls. Carlo had a thing for young girls, so he scouted the tanning salons and hired mostly on appearance. They were sixteen and still in high school, but that didn't mean anything to Carlo. He just liked having young girls around that did what he told them to do. And drugs. One day Carlo asked my assistant, Morgan, if she knew any drug dealers.

As it turned out, Morgan had a guy that she led on from time to time in order to get free pot. Some kid named Anthony. He was this sketchy little drug dealer that started hanging around. He was either hitting on Morgan

---

15 Retired people that come to Arizona specifically for the warm weather.

or getting up in our Talent2K business. The kid latched on to us and it irritated the shit out of me.

I never intended to be friends with the guy.

And I never thought he'd work for me.

◆◆◆

I realized it was only a matter of time until Carlo scammed me.

In a way he had already been doing this. When he paid me the checks were always short. Money was being withheld (typically a grand or so), and he never got around to fixing it. I was also running most of the Talent2K operation by this point. Occasionally, I'd bolt. When he didn't pay me, I'd go back to Orange County and wait for Carlo to call and beg me to come back. He needed me. We both knew it. So I used that to leverage more money into my pocket—or at the very least, the money he hadn't paid me yet.

Eventually, I brought in Anthony and his best friend, Andy Conlin. I showed them the ropes, taught them how to work the phones, and delegated some of my stuff to them. Having them on freed up a lot of time. Sometimes I'd drive around in my Porsche at night and think about things: about leaving college, the Hey Stroker debacle, about Talent2K and where it was going. Online message boards were firing off about how we were a scam, how the company actually didn't do anything except cash the checks. For the most part, they weren't saying anything that wasn't true. It was starting to look like I was on a sinking ship, but the thing that made me even more nervous was Carlo's thing for young girls. Any one of these girls could be a cop running a sting operation. He was a sex predator. I was working for a fucking sex predator fat fuck, and he was going to get caught sooner or later. If Carlo got busted, I didn't put it past him to drag me down too.

That's when I decided to start my own company.

◆◆◆

I named the company CIG after my uncle's medical practice.

At the time, I had roughly $40,000 saved up because the cost of living in Sun City was cheap. It was all going to be put toward the company, and for the most part, it was established while I was still with Talent2K. Everything had to be done behind Carlo's back. He'd seen too many fucking mafia movies to just let me go and do my own thing. I was in the Talent2K "family," so starting my own company was going to piss him off. I knew that, but I actually wanted to try and go legit. No more scams. No more fucking people over.

The CIG business model was going to be different from what Carlo had been doing. Since the magazine advertisements worked, I kept that part the same. CIG was actually going to be two musical entities under one umbrella: Rap Vibe and Alternative Spin. Naturally, I placed the rap ads in *Vibe* and the alternative rock ads in *Spin*, playing off name recognition.

The main divergence was going to be how CIG approached the music industry. Carlo mailed the proposal packages out to the record labels. That's what the bands thought, at least. Even if he did mail them out, they probably would have wound up in their junk file. Or the trash.

I wanted to actually get the bands in the same room as the record label people: have them meet, have the acts perform live. It was going to be my own personal Russell Simmons hip-hop summit. In my mind it was a numbers game. If I got the record label people to come out, and if I was able to show them enough acts, one of them was bound to get signed.

So the ads were printed up. I ditched Carlo again, and this time no amount of begging was going to get me back. I even flipped Andy and Anthony. Andy came to CIG directly while Anthony stayed behind as my spy. If Carlo was going to try and fuck me, I at least wanted a little advance warning.

I had my own label, my own business model, and I even had my own team. The only thing that remained was the name. Hooman Karamian was the guy that worked with Carlo Oddo the child fucker. It also didn't sound right in the hip-hop world.

That's when I became Corbin Grimes.

♦ ♦ ♦

Corbin Grimes was actually someone I was friends with over the summer, and when he found out that I stole his name, he was more than just a little pissed off. So was Carlo. Once he put everything together—that I not only ditched him, but I set up another company behind his back—the guy flipped shit. The thing about Carlo is that he's not the kind of guy to physically confront anybody. Despite all the mafia movies, I wasn't worried about a car-bomb strapped to my Porsche or any bullets flying my way. Carlo's a fat fuck. A statutory rapist coward. He's the lowest common denominator. He did the only thing he could do in that situation: talk trash.

So while I was getting things rolling on the CIG front, Carlo hit the message boards saying that Hooman Karamian is Corbin Grimes, and that was followed by a variation of lies: that I was the guy running the Talent2K operation, that he had to fire me, that Corbin Grimes and CIG are just covers for another scam. All those people that he fucked over before Carlo and I even met—my fault. After we met: still my fault. All day and night the fat fuck trashed me online, and this would be my first official encounter with the workings of the Internet and just how much it can affect a reputation.

That part stuck with me.

◆◆◆

The first CIG event took place in Chicago in a convention hall at the Hilton. In order to get the A&R people out to the event, not only did I have to pay for all their travel and hotel, but they wanted a fee for coming out, too. Each one of these guys was costing me around $1,500, but I didn't care as long as one of my acts got signed. It was still a numbers game in my head. More record label people meant it was more likely one of them would offer a contract. The more acts I could get out, the more likely it was that one of them would be good enough to get signed.

So I got all of these people into one room—a convention hall, to be exact, and let the A&R people watch the showcase of rappers and hip-hop artists perform. It was like urban *American Idol*: act after act getting on stage and doing whatever they do. Rapping. Attempting R&B. I was paying more attention to the record label people, their faces, looking for signs of interest. Something telling me that my method worked and that Carlo's didn't. It went on for hours: record label reps watching, performers performing, and me, Corbin Grimes, waiting for something to happen. Waiting for one of these A&R people to sign someone (didn't matter who) so I could finally say that I had done something worthwhile. I wanted the money, but I also wanted to prove Carlo wrong.

He was still on his online rampage about Corbin Grimes, but I didn't fight back. All I had to do was get one of these acts a record contract and everything he said would be meaningless. Just one. The problem was the talent wasn't there. That's what the record label people were telling me. It kind of threw me off because I was still thinking of it as a numbers game, which is partially true. The other part of the equation is that I was pulling talent from the back of magazine ads (which are pretty much the want ads of the music industry).

Maybe Carlo had it right. Maybe this was the reason why he never actually tried to get any of these people signed or listened to the music. He knew it would be a waste of time. Either that or he tried and failed just like I had. He was still talking trash online, but I gave it another shot. I did the same exact thing in New York and got the same results: no one was good enough. It wasn't a numbers game. I tried to do something legitimate and lost every penny of the $40,000 that I made scamming.

The scam was where the money was at.

I had to learn that the hard way.

Dolce Vendetta

As soon as everyone finds out I'm Nik Richie is when a new club out of Dallas calls for an event, and they don't want the *Dirty* celeb thing we've been pushing in Vegas. They want me. They want the guy in charge, and they're willing to pay $15,000 to get me there, flight and hotel included.

"The club is called Dolce Vendetta—it's brand new," the booking agent says. "And we want you to be our opening celeb appearance. We're slotting you ahead of Kim Kardashian."

I'm a bit standoffish at first because my mind naturally flashes back to Scottsdale, back when random people were getting the shit kicked out of them because they were suspected of being me. Announcing publicly that Nik Richie is going to be at a certain place at a certain time could wind up being a bad move. Granted, I've never taken all the threats seriously, but you never know which ones are bullshit and which ones are real until someone is waving a gun in your face. Anyone looking to dish out a little payback could be waiting there for me. All they'd have to do is pay a cover charge.

And the booking agent asks, "So, will you do it?"

The truth is I really don't have a choice.

We need the money *that* badly.

◆ ◆ ◆

Nik Richie has never appeared at anything before, never even been to Dallas, so I decide to try and make a good impression by wearing an off-the-rack suit from Nordstrom (three-piece, gray with a white dress shirt) and black wing tips. I look like a businessman, and therefore am not feeling completely at ease because I usually avoid suits if I can. That, and the paranoia is still buzzing in the back of my head because any one of these club kids could be a guy I called a "douchetard¹⁶" or "tenderfoot¹⁷" or something they took offense to. Maybe I called one of their girlfriends a "shim¹⁸" or "slug¹⁹" or made mention of some physical feature I found disgusting. Someone in this club could be holding a grudge, so as a precaution, I've got four of the biggest, blackest security guards in Dallas. I also brought along Nick Gagliano and Ryan Jacque, who are sitting on either side of me in the booth. Drinking. Checking out the crowd, but it's difficult because this place is a fucking dungeon and the light is mostly focused on the few broke go-go dancers they have up on platforms.

Not long into the event, I get to see how people react to Nik Richie when he's live and in person. People stare. They take pictures. Some of them do this from a distance, waiting for the security guys to move out of frame before a Blackberry or iPhone fires from the dark. Girls come up to the table—first, confirming that I'm really "the guy" as they say, and this is followed by us shrugging together as a camera phone is held out at arm's length.

Flash. Thank you. Repeat.

Bottles are delivered, but not the typical Grey Goose and mixer combo. It's Cristal and Dom and top-shelf stuff that's considered too expensive for the club to comp us. These high-roller guys at the nearby tables are sending this shit over, giving a nod with a long-distance toast to acknowledge it came from them. More booze comes. Girls come. Hot Dallas girls with those Texas accents so foreign to me they're almost another language. The security guys are being paid to watch everyone be nice to me at this point. Gags and Ryan are both hitting on girls. We're drinking, having a good time. The club kind of sucks, but I'm getting paid to be here and the booze is free.

Then, completely at random, I see Leper.

◆ ◆ ◆

The last time I saw Leper was in Vegas. She and Alien were supposed to do that *Dirty* Celeb appearance at Privé—basically, repeating the Hard Rock event. True to whore form, these bitches thought that they were like *Jersey Shore* or something and started demanding money. It wasn't

---

16 Douche + retard.
17 Gay or feminine.
18 She + him.
19 Ugly slut.

enough they were getting an all-expenses-paid trip to Vegas and all the substances they could handle—they wanted cash on top of it. We bullshitted them into getting on a plane, but that's about as far as it went. They never showed up to the event and I literally only saw them once: when we crossed paths on an escalator in one of the hotels.

I was going up.

They were going down.

Neither of us said a word.

We pulled off the event anyway thanks to 8-Belles and Blonkey[20], who are a couple of my horses[21]. Levine actually didn't care about Alien and Leper flaking. Turns out he just wanted to meet me, but after that point I kind of had a *fuck you* attitude toward those two girls.

Things change though.

Dallas isn't like Vegas.

Tonight, Leper is wearing a cherry red corset, the kind that's so tight you can't even breathe normally. Little black miniskirt. An almost natural-looking tan. She's a bottle server, but word on the street is she's fucking terrible at it, so the management pays her to look hot and flirt with high rollers. So technically, when Leper comes up to my table to talk she's just doing her job. Security recognizes the uniform all the Dolce girls are wearing, pulling aside the ropes so she can pass through. I look at her, and things kind of go mute because I've got so much history with this girl but it's only the third time I've seen her in person. I think I should be a dick to her, but I'm in Dallas and she's one of the only faces I know here. And she's smiling.

She smiles and says in her little Texas accent, "See? I knew you were the guy."

◆ ◆ ◆

Leper puts it all on the table at the club. It's the first time that she's not only somewhat sober, but genuine with me. Under the loud house music, Leper says that she's sorry, that Alien led her down a dark path. One can only assume that means drinking too much, doing too much coke, too many pills, fucking too many random dudes, doing the wrong things to make money. Essentially, all the things they get posted on the site for. Rumors in Dallas have been going around that Leper and Alien will even

---

20 Blonde + donkey.
21 Girls with huge teeth and/or gums. Typically, their faces are terrible but they have incredible bodies.

do the occasional porn video when their funds get low or no one is around to spot them any cash.[22] Considering how they acted in Vegas, it's not hard to believe these things.

Leper says to me, "I loved you. I wanted you the whole time, but Lacy claimed you and there was nothing I could do about it."

Bullshit, bullshit, bullshit.

I say, "It's not a big deal. Don't worry about it."

The party is winding down. People are drunk. Hooking up. And somehow I already know that I'm going to end up with Leper tonight, even if I don't want to.

◆◆◆

After-party.

The ZaZa hotel.

It's myself, Gags and Ryan Jacque, a few girls they worked on at the club, and, of course, Leper, still wearing her Dolce Vendetta uniform. Occasionally, she'll squirm or try to adjust the corset to make it more comfortable, but you can tell she's dying to take the fucking thing off.

Our entire floor smells like weed because Lil Wayne is randomly here. We pass him and his crew in the hall, and the first thing I notice (other than the smell) is the guy is tiny. My height. About 140 pounds. He's wearing designer sunglasses (Wayfarers maybe) to avoid eye contact, but it's obvious he's scoping out every chick within ten feet, including Leper. He does this thing where he points at her and keeps walking, then some dude—which I'm assuming is his assistant, comes up and starts talking to Leper.

He says, "My friend would like to know if you'd be interested in coming up to his room," totally ignoring the possibility that maybe Leper is my girlfriend or that we're together. Celebrities can get away with that.

Leper doesn't say anything though, turning and looking at me like I should answer for her. I say, "Go, it's Lil Wayne. He's famous."

And she says, "No, I love you. I wanna be with you."

I don't respond. The group of us keep walking until we get to Gagliano's room where we order room service: chicken fingers and other stuff to soak up the liquor. Gags and Ryan are with these two chicks, drinking, flirting. They've pretty much sealed the deal. I tell everyone that I'm going to run down to my room to get out of the suit, but I'm not 100% sure I want

---

22 This is not a rumor. Alien has fucked on camera more than a few times under the alias Lacy Holliday.

to come back. It's late. Our flight leaves at six in the morning.

Right when I've decided that I'm just going to crash is when I hear something going on behind me, maybe twenty feet down the hallway. I keep walking, not bothering to turn around. Then, distinctly, it's Gags saying in his croaky voice, "Leper! Leper! Go! Nik wants to fuck you!" as he ushers her out of his room.

I'm at my door, pulling the room key out of my pocket, and footsteps are getting closer. She's standing next to me, smiling. Her tits look great in the corset, and then I see that her hands are behind her back untying the fastenings.

I say, "Kelli. No," but because Leper has got a fair amount of Crown Royal in her system, she thinks I'm playing hard to get. "I've got to be on a fucking plane in two hours."

She keeps pulling at the fastenings on her corset, saying, "No, this thing is just tight is all. I just want to talk."

I'm thinking, Great, another chick from Dallas that just wants to talk? Is that the code here?

I tell her, "I'm changing," and we both walk into my room. Leper watches me from the entryway, letting the door shut behind her as she gets back to work on the corset. It's pushing her tits up to her collarbones, and even though the nice thing to do would be to help her out of it, I don't want Leper to mistake a simple courtesy for interest. Finally, after a couple minutes, the corset loosens and she's able to push it down her body with her thumbs. Her breasts fall out, and I catch myself looking at them because she recently had another boob job and they're just now dropping. Her body is tight, and her face is skinny and well-carved. Leper's looking at me

Nik Richie with more civilian groupies in Dallas, Texas.

with those blue eyes and I have to keep telling myself I can't fuck this girl. *You can't fuck her. You can't fuck a Dirty Celeb.*

People have never understood that part of it, but it'd be like sleeping with an employee, a subordinate. Nik Richie doesn't sleep with his underlings. My legacy is that I'm extremely rigid in my standards, and Leper's jeopardizing that right now with those tits, that body, those eyes. That smile.

She asks, "Do you have a shirt I can borrow?"

There's a "Cocaine Kills" tee nearby (something *I* was actually supposed to wear) that I hand her. Leper puts it on, tugging down until the bottom of the shirt is around her mid-thigh. My phone buzzes and it's Gags saying: You better fuck her dude.

Leper asks, "Who is that?" and me, thinking I'm clever, I say something in an attempt to get her back off. I tell her that I'm currently dating a celebrity.

"Nobody knows about it," I say. "Her name is Hillary Duff."

◆◆◆

First of all, I have no idea why I say Hillary Duff because I don't find her attractive in the least. She's a little bit of a horse when you think about it. That's the name that pops out of my mouth though, and maybe it's because I saw her on *E! News* or heard one of her stupid songs by accident or subconsciously picked it up by reading a *Star Magazine.* I'm not sure. Hillary Duff isn't my type, but for the sake of keeping Leper at bay she's my serious girlfriend.

What I quickly realize is that Leper is no longer trying to fuck me, Nik Richie. The scenario has skewed in that drunken little brain of hers. Shifted. A little bit of that fame-chaser coming back. Now she's trying to fuck Hillary Duff's boyfriend, and I know the lie has truly backfired when she starts saying things like, "I promise I won't tell Hillary. It'll be our little secret," while she grabs my prick and squeezes.

I say, "Leper, no," but I'm smiling.

She smiles back and says, "Why do you call me that? I'm not like that," touching more. Her lips press gently against my neck, my face.

"I can't do this," I tell her. "Hillary's gonna kill me."

"It's okay, I'm not going to let you stick it in me[23]," she says, but I can tell it's total bullshit. She lets me grab her tits, and then my hand smoothes down to her ass where, to my extreme displeasure, is a butterfly tattoo not totally unlike what Alien has. On the nightstand is a hotel clock. I've got about thirty minutes before I'm supposed to leave, which is basically just long enough to fuck Leper and not endure any of that after-sex weirdness of cuddling or whatever. I've got a condom. No one's going to find out.

I ask, "You promise not to tell Hillary?"

Leper stops kissing me, stressing how serious she is, telling me, "It'll be our secret. I want you so bad. I want to fuck you so bad."

I get the condom. Leper fucks the shit out of me.

◆ ◆ ◆

Her cunt is a little loafy, a little lippy. Not cut quite as tight as most girls I've been with, but I'm writing that off to her having so many partners over the years, and I can't deny she's incredible in bed. Actually, too wild, like maybe she has to really show off because of who I am or who she thinks I am. She's screaming and pummeling her body on me, saying, "Daddy, daddy, daddy—fuck me good, daddy! Oh, you're fucking me so good, sweets!" in that slurred-out Texas accent, and then I feel like I have to play the game back: do something crazy. Do something that these girls, these pseudo-porn-star coke-whores are used to, so I slide an arm between us and wrap my hand around her neck. Fucking. Squeezing. Choking her. Squeezing hard so her face starts to deepen. My other hand slides under, into her ass where I jam two of my fingers inside her and she's screaming harder as I choke her, saying, "Oh sweets oh sweets oh my fucking God, daddy!" but it's obscured through the booze and accent and pressure I'm putting on her vocal cords. I fuck her, and she starts holding her breath so that she can come harder and then I come inside her, gripping my eyes shut. Tight. We come, and then I roll off of her because I need to catch a plane, grabbing the nearest articles of clothing I can find. An awkward silence has already begun to set.

Then Leper says, "I betcha Hillary Duff never fucked you like that."

I say, "You know what, Kelli—she hasn't."

---

23 This is sort of an inside joke. On the site I'm constantly being asked whether I would or would not hook up with a girl, and my response 99% of the time is some variation of, "No, I wouldn't stick it," and this is actually something I've said referring to Leper directly.

◆ ◆ ◆

From the bed, Leper is watching me pack. Nude. Relaxed. She asks me if she can use the phone sitting on the nightstand.

"Kelli, this is your room," I say, packing jeans, shirts, socks. "Sleep in. Wake up. Be safe. I don't care."

"Can I have your number?"

"Nobody has my number. I never give out my number."

"Well…how do I get a hold of you?"

I tell her, "E-mail me."

"What's your e-mail?"

"Nik@thedirty…N-I-K at the dirty," I say, packing—just throwing everything into the luggage in no particular order. I don't even have time to shower, so I'll be boarding the plane stinking like booze and Leper. Meanwhile, she's raiding the minibar, pulling out every tiny bottle of Crown Royal that's in there. Leper gets back on the bed, unscrewing one and picking up the phone out of the cradle.

She dials the front desk, maybe for more room service, but then I hear her say, "Yeah, uh, I'm looking for Dwayne Carter's[24] room."

I stop packing and shoot Leper a look like, *Are you serious right now?*

She goes, "No, it's fine. I just want to meet him…take pictures. That's all."

"Whatever, I don't care."

◆ ◆ ◆

The Monday I get back, there's a submission that comes in titled: "Leper bangs celebrity after Dolce Vendetta event," and I'm thinking, *Oh great, not even a week and the bitch has already told everyone that we hooked up.* It's not like I'm going to post it, but I'm annoyed that after all her "it's gonna be our little secret" bullshit that she can't keep her mouth shut.

So I open the submission, and in the text body it reads: "Leper bangs the shit out of Lil Wayne," and then there's a bunch of pictures attached of her and Lil Wayne holding each other and whatever while Leper is wearing the "Cocaine Kills" T-shirt. No underwear. They're making out, probably stoned out of their minds.

I'm not the least bit jealous though. Or mad.

If it ever comes back to me that Leper and I hooked up, I'll have the pictures to prove that I didn't just fuck around on my wife.

---

24 Lil Wayne's real name.

Split

After I get back from Dallas, my wife invites me out to lunch.

This is unusual for her because we're so distant from each other that she can barely stand the sight of me. She hates Nik Richie. Hates the site. It's a mixture of disapproval and professional jealousy. When my identity leaked out, there was a moment where she tried to be reassuring and supportive—perhaps because she thought it was the beginning of the end. Amanda might have been under the impression that *The Dirty* was going to have to shut down. Close shop. Now that I'm getting booked for celebrity appearances, she's back to her old self: distant, cold, and unfriendly. Ever since the incident she's been like this.

So the lunch invite is unexpected.

I meet Amanda out at Kierland Commons, and I can't help but be reminded that it's the same place where I invented the formula a couple years ago. The Nik Richie equation that got me to where I am now, but Kierland is about to take on a whole new meaning. We sit down, make a little small talk about the menu. The way we communicate is more like acquaintances now, and not long after our waters are delivered does Amanda say those magic words: "I want a divorce."

For the record, I don't want this. I'm unhappy, have been unhappy for a while, but divorce was never an option for me. In my family, or any Iranian family for that matter, when you get married, you stay married. Divorce is considered an unforgivable epic fuckup. It's shameful, and even though Amanda and I have clearly lost our connection, my intention was always to stick it out. Hope for the best. Maybe time would bring us back together, a few years from now when she got over the idea of Hooman Karamian and Nik Richie being the same guy. My plan was always to stay underground, get some investors, have them flip the site for $100M, and I'd wash my hands clean of everything. It was never my goal to be Nik Richie forever, but maybe being outed removes that as an option. That may be why Amanda is asking for a divorce, crying. She's crying in public, but I don't feel empathetic or any sense of compassion. And I sure as fuck don't feel sorry for her.

What I know is that she's lured me out to this place, a public place, and she purposely brought this up so that I couldn't do anything. I can't react. In this situation, all I can do is nod quietly and give her what she wants.

◆ ◆ ◆

I go out of town for an event.

When I get back, all my shit is packed up. My clothes are in boxes. This is Amanda's way of circumventing the awkward moving-out process. All I have to do is put this stuff in the back of my car and leave.

Amanda and I have to go to the courthouse to fill out the divorce papers, but instead of acting all cold and distant, she's actually playing up the relationship we're going to have.

"We'll be best friends," she says. "We'll still hang out and it'll be cool."

I'm a bit relieved because the last thing I wanted was to be on bad terms or anything like that. Getting a divorce is one thing, but going through one where the two people can't be amicable is another issue. The last thing I need is my ex trying to fuck up my life, especially at this stage in the game. So this makes me happy, her finally attempting to get along with me. I don't want to hate Amanda. Trashing all those years seems like a waste, so I want us to be friends. I'm optimistic that we can accomplish that much even though the marriage is about to be dissolved.

So I sign what she wants me to sign at the courthouse. The papers get filed. I tell Amanda that I'm going to be there for her. I'll send her money so she can keep up with the bills. It's not like I have to do this, but I let her have everything: the car, the house, and all the shit that comes with it. I'm left with nothing, but I'm okay with that.

Amanda is driving the white Lexus, giving me a ride back to Nik Richie headquarters, and that Pink song [25] comes on. It's such a gay fucking bull-shit song, but Amanda's singing it. She's actually singing it at me, turning in her seat and saying, "*I'm still a rock star, I've got my rock moves,*" and she's acting like she's trying to be funny but she's being serious. It's her way of saying to me, "I'm going to make it and you're not," because that's what Pink is talking about in the song. Amanda is rubbing it in my face that

---

25 "So What".

she'll come out of this on top and I'll fail. Even after signing our divorce papers, Amanda is still competing with me.

◆ ◆ ◆

The ride in the Lexus with the Pink song is the last time I see Amanda.

I'm sending her money and have called her a few times about taking Iris[26] for the week, but I get no answer. I honestly don't miss being with Amanda. The hardest part is not having my dog anymore. I'm alone now. Alone and single, and that state of being makes it so much easier to be Nik Richie. The attachment that Hooman Karamian had in marriage no longer exists. I'm free now.

I'm free to do whatever the fuck I want.

I can chase that American dream.

---

26 My pit bull at the time.

47

Lohan

Samantha Ronson and Lindsay Lohan are the "it" couple right now,
and in a stroke of genius, Justin Levine books Sam to deejay Mansion in
Miami—not necessarily because he likes her as a performer, but because
he knows that if Sam's there, Lindsay is going to be there, too. So Lindsay
ends up getting booked for $25,000 as the headliner with Sam mak-
ing an undisclosed amount (possibly less). I actually get booked too, but
because Lindsay is headlining and she's a Hollywood A-lister banging a
chick DJ, her clout overshadows Nik Richie. That's the way it works in this
business.

I have to break a celebrity scandal to get any publicity.

All Lohan has to do is sneeze wrong and *TMZ* is all over it.

So I'm looking to stir the pot tonight in Miami, telling Levine, "I'm going
to break those two up tonight."

"Get the fuck outta here," he waves me off. "Not happening. They love
each other."

"Justin," I say, "Lindsay *isn't* a lesbian. Am I the only one who sees
this?"

"Fuck off, man. You're wrong," he tells me.

At Mansion, Sam checks her equipment while Lindsay does the red
carpet. She's wearing a tank top dress (sequined, checkered black and
bronze), no bra, hair casually pulled back. People take pictures. Flashes
everywhere. These will serve as the "before" photos leading up to whatever disaster happens tonight. People expect this from her now.

So Sam, Lindsay and I all end up on the main stage inside the club, a
platform where the DJ booth is set up overlooking the lower-level dance
floor. Sam is cueing up songs in her headphones and smoking a cigarette.
Lindsay and I are drinking, watching Sam. It's dark and kind of boring. I'm
thinking that if I hit on Lindsay (who actually looks decent tonight) that

Sam will go nuts and they'll get in a fight. There's a PR chick that we're supposed to talk to if we need to use the bathroom, so I tell this girl that if Lindsay needs to go, make sure to grab me so I can go too.

A couple of drinks pass where Sam is spinning, smoking cigarettes, and Lindsay and I meander. Sometimes we'll nod our heads to the music or casually chat. People are looking on from the rope that separates the platform from the rest of the club. Taking video, pictures. Security stands around waving flashlights at people to move away from the rope. Eventually the PR girl is telling me that Lindsay is going to the bathroom, so I sidle up to them, ready to navigate the stairs and hallways. Lindsay takes my hand, leading the way through the dark.

The PR girl opens the bathroom door for us to walk through and stands guard outside. It's candlelit, but the light makes my pupils shrink. Lindsay goes straight for the toilet, pulling her dress up and sitting (no underwear), and one of her breasts is hanging out the top of the dress. I start to wash my hands and she asks me, "So, what's your story?" before doing an uneven line of coke off her wrist.

I say, "Nothing…just, y'know…partying."

Nik Richie kicks out the cast of *Jersey Shore* from Miami Beach, Florida hot spot Mansion nightclub.

I'm watching Lindsay do coke to my right, that pale tit hanging out, and it takes a couple of seconds to kick in that it's intentional. I'm supposed to see this. She wants me to. And she's doing more coke, raising her eyebrows at me like, Want some? She sniffs. Snorts. She swabs a little in her mouth and I've heard about this kind of thing on TV and in the papers, but it's different seeing it: the chick from *Mean Girls* doing blow on the toilet next to me. She's not the same girl anymore. Something's changed. She's lost her way, and seeing it is freaking me out. The PR chick is knocking on the door because she thinks we're fucking, and I take that as my cue to leave. It's too much. Too real.

I walk myself back to the DJ booth where Sam is smoking a cigarette, cueing the next track up on her laptop. Sam shrugs at me like, *Where's Lindsay?* So I get up close, up in her ear and say, "She's doing coke in the bathroom. That chick is crazy. How do you put up with it?"

And Sam says, "Ugh! I *knoooooooooooooooow,*" in a girly way I didn't think she was capable of, but other than that she's cool and down-to-earth, sort of like a dude. We're chatting in the DJ booth, laughing and giggling over Lohan drama, then Lindsay comes back and sees the two of us. She's wiping her chest off because someone spilled a drink on her during the walk back. Lindsay sees Sam and me getting along (I'm basically hitting on her) and flips shit.

Sam asks her, "Babe, are you okay?" motioning to Lindsay's wet chest.

Then Lindsay is yelling, "I can't believe you'd fucking cheat on me like that! What the fuck?!"

And I try to intervene, telling her, "Lindsay, I'm not going to fuck her. She's a lesbian. It's cool."

She doesn't even bother trying to talk to me. Lindsay turns to the nearest security guy and yells, "Get this fucking guy out of here!" before she turns back to rip into Sam some more, causing a scene. Nobody can hear exactly what's being said over the music (which, ironically, is "Womanizer" by Britney Spears), but their body language toward each other is clearly one of an argument. Everyone points. Laughs. Another camera flashes to capture the moment: the "after" photos. They feed the media another story.

Justin Levine escorts me out of the DJ booth. He's supposed to kick me out of Mansion altogether since that's what Lindsay wants, but he puts me in the back corner booth instead. I get a couple bottles of Grey Goose and chat with this half-Asian chick, Stephanie, who's gorgeous, but I can't bring myself to pull the trigger. We recap the fight and talk shit on people instead, drinking the rest of New Year's away together at Mansion. It's a little boring. New Year's is typically a letdown anyway.

When I get back to the hotel that night there's pounding and yelling. Screams. Mirrors are being broken and I don't even bother calling the front desk to report it because I'm drunk and figure someone's going to get to it soon. Come to find out that Lindsay and Sam are in the room above me. Justin Levine fills me in the next day, telling me that Lindsay absolutely shredded the room to the count of $13,000 in damages. It's on the news. *TMZ*'s all over it. Radar Online. All those guys. There's video of the argument from Mansion coming to me through my e-mail. Pictures of Lindsay and Sam at the airport are being published moments after they're taken. I'm going through my e-mail and a server at Dirty Pretty is telling me that Charles Barkley just got a DUI. He was there last night with Michael Strahan and the guy that played Urkel on *Family Matters* and wants to know if I want the receipt.

I say "yes" and the drama continues. It never stops.

Chuck

Charles Barkley's daughter is submitted to the site.

I don't need to be told it's her because the chick looks exactly like Chuck. In the pictures she's posing with a bottle of Smirnoff vodka with a friend, and then there's another one where she's doing a four-way kiss with some girls. Typical college stuff. She's underage, but it's only a big deal because of who her dad is. Thousands of girls at U of A just like her are getting away with this sort of behavior, but whatever. I do the job. I play Nik Richie. I bag on her a little and flip a Charles Barkley line, the "I am not a role model" one.

And I say: How could Charles raise his daughter to be like this?

The investors contact me a few days later saying that Chuck wants the post taken down, but he's not going the legal route. He's not sending a cease-and-desist letter or any of that shit.

My investors say, "Charles wants to know if you want to play golf with him."

I say, "I don't get it."

In this business, when someone makes you an offer, that means they want something back in return.

"Well, Charles would like the post taken down, so I guess what he wants to know is, what's it going to take? Golf? Tickets? What do you want?"

"Since when did I start taking posts down for fucking tickets?"

They say, "Yes, well, it's not your typical M.O. However, we think it would be a really good idea for you to make an exception here," they say, stressing the word "really." They're trying to strong-arm me. "Having Charles in our corner might come in handy later."

They have a point, and the post has been up a week anyway, so it's old news by now. Everyone has already seen it by this point, so I say, "Fine, I'll take it down…whatever."

"Fantastic, Nik. Would you like us to reach out to Charles for a tee time?"

I hang up.

◆ ◆ ◆

Three months later: I'm in Scottsdale with Eric Chavez[27] and Jermaine Dye[28] at the bar in the W Hotel. It's a casual night. We're catching up on stuff, talking about baseball, the site, bullshit like that. Jermaine mentions how he's afraid to hang out with me considering what he's seen on *The Dirty*.

"This is gonna be crazy, man," he says, as if it's my goal to get him into trouble tonight. Or maybe he just assumes that trouble follows me.

Randomly, Charles Barkley walks in and notices Jermaine and Eric. They start talking, Chuck orders a drink and has a seat with the group of us. Chuck doesn't know me, so he thinks I'm just a friend or brothers with Chavez. The Nik Richie thing doesn't register nor do I say anything to bring it to his attention since I'm not sure how he'll react to it. I took his daughter down, but I didn't do it in a timely fashion and I kind of snubbed the guy. He probably thinks I'm an asshole. His attention is mostly on Eric and J.D. anyway so I'm not too worried about it. I also made sure to let the guys know not to let it slip that I'm in charge of *The Dirty*.

Chuck wants to know what we're doing after this. What he actually says is, "So what are we doing next?" kind of inviting himself along and taking our quiet night up a notch in one move.

We go to Dirty Pretty.

◆ ◆ ◆

We get a table in the back corner of Dirty Pretty. The four of us are chilling in the booth, scoping out chicks dancing to hip-hop music through the beams of light, and Chuck is telling jokes. He keeps name-dropping guys like Michael Jordan and Shaq and trying to be funny, but none of us are laughing at him. The server comes up and asks us what we want. Chavez, J.D. and I all order some kind of vodka mix since we have a bottle of that on the table. Grey Goose, I think. Since Chuck has to be cool or whatever, he orders a six-pack of Heineken (which probably cost about $80). So

---

27 MLB Third Baseman/First Baseman (Oakland Athletics, New York Yankees).
28 MLB Right Fielder (Atlanta Braves, Kansas City Royals, Oakland Athletics, Chicago White Sox).

the server gets Chuck his beer, and she does this quickly because he's Charles Barkley and the rumor is that Chuck tips like a motherfucker. He's sipping on his beer, making bad jokes, and I'm like, "Chuck, you're not funny, dude," and that pisses him off a little because he's used to people laughing at whatever he says.

Regardless, Chuck and I get to a place where I think we're cool after an hour or so. We've all got a good buzz going. The scenery is nice. Chuck has stopped trying to be funny and now we're all just chilling at Dirty Pretty like we're boys. Perhaps it's the liquor that makes me do the thing I do next, or maybe my instincts are wrong, but I finally lean in to Chuck and say, "Chuck, just so you know—no hard feelings, but I'm Nik Richie. I'm the guy that runs *The Dirty*."

Chuck smirks.

He checks both ways to make sure no one is watching us, and then he leans in like he's going to say something to me. I do the same, leaning my ear toward his mouth so I can hear whatever he says over the music, then—can't breathe.

The wind is sucked out of me, and I see Chuck slowly lean back smiling at me. He just sucker-punched me in the gut, and the motion was so smooth it's like he's done it before. Hard. Effective. And no one notices. My lungs slowly unclench and take air. Hot club air, struggling into my throat, and Chuck is laughing. He's drinking his beer, leaning back into the leather couch and smiling.

That was all he wanted. One hit.

I put up his daughter and that earns me one punch. So I take it, telling Charles, "Okay, I deserve that."

Chavez is asking me, "Are you okay?"

And I'm like, "Yeah, yeah, yeah, I'm good. I'm good," trying to look like nothing happened, but this answers the question a lot of people ask.

How many times have you had the shit kicked out of you because of the site?

Just the one punch from Charles. That's it.

But I get the last laugh.

◆◆◆

While I'm in Miami with Lohan, Chuck gets popped for a DUI with a box of bear claws riding shotgun. I put it up on the site and the users start eating it up in the comment boards. They give their little two cents about racist cops and how Chuck needs to lose weight and his gambling debts. They speculate. Tease. The usual.

What happened was Chuck ran a stop sign around 1:30 in the morning, admitting to the cops that he was in a hurry to get a blowjob from some chick he had met the week before. The cop has him exit the car because of the smell of alcohol. Chuck fails his field sobriety test, and the rest is history. It's all over the news: local, national, everywhere. When you're someone like Charles Barkley, the media gets into a frenzy over stuff like this. I've been there myself. If someone's down, the first instinct most people have is to kick them.

That's how the game works: you rise to prominence, and although nobody says it, they're all betting on when you'll fall. Everybody loves a trainwreck.

Three

I'm getting appearances like crazy.

I'm single. I'm on the road. Every weekend it's somewhere different: Texas, Arizona, Nevada, California. It's a different club with a different group of people. The weekend doesn't mean the same thing it used to anymore. Every Friday and Saturday it's a different city banging a different chick in a different hotel room. It's constantly changing but a pattern is emerging.

It goes: dinner, drinks, club, flirt, fuck, fly away.

I get on a plane to do it all over again. I go to Chicago, Atlanta, and St. Louis. I fuck a bottle rat[29], a server, a socialite. And then I wake up at the Marriott, the Hilton, or the Hyatt, checking out to catch my plane on Southwest, Delta, or American Airlines.

Nik Richie is no longer just a person.

He's a brand. He blogs all week, and then he jets off to another city, another club, to have his way with another girl.

And everything is free. Everyone is offering me something.

Free booze. Free clothes. Free girls. These are the girls that normal people would have to wine and dine and break their wallets for, but not with me. They submit. Throw themselves at me. There's no challenge, so then I start pushing the envelope. In order to keep the experience alive and exciting, I start exploring the boundaries of how far I can go. How far I can take these girls before they stop saying "yes."

Another trip to Dallas. San Diego and Beverly Hills.

I'm drinking, fucking, sometimes blacking out. I spray a bottle of champagne in a server's face and tell her to clean herself off. Call her a peasant. And nothing happens. Not one person says, "No, Nik, you can't treat people like that."

---

29 A girl at a club who will find a group of guys and drink off their bottle service the entire night.

They don't tell me I'm out of control. They don't say "stop."

Then I go to Phoenix, Dallas (again), and Seattle.

There has to be more than one girl now. There has to be because one is boring. It's been done before. Nik Richie knows that he can get a girl. That's the easy part. But two...two is different. Two girls is not common, and therefore, not boring. I won't be bored if I can fuck two girls, get them to kiss each other, fuck each other. Sometimes they'll eat each other's cunts, and although that's very cool, the part that I love the most is that it's something they'd never do unless I told them to. I'm getting the girls to push the envelope with me, be reckless with me. My online persona and the effect it has manifests within these clubs, in the hotel beds where these girls do the things they never thought they would.

We're all living in the moment.

Living without consequences.

But now the bar has been raised. I go to the club, I drink the drinks, flirt with the girls. I do all that, only now I have to end up with two girls in my bed. It has to be at least a threesome or else it will be boring. Mundane and typical. If I can't have two girls it's not even worth my time or effort. I've acclimated. Adapted to having whatever I want when I want it: the life of indulgence and people loving you for what you represent, not who you really are.

I expect to be pampered and have my ass kissed.

The girls are no longer girls. They're objects.

Little things start to slip my mind, like what it's like to actually have to try with a girl or how it feels to pay a bar tab. I can't remember the last time I've been rejected, but I keep going. I stay on the road, hopping off planes, going to these dinners and clubs and hotels.

I arrive at Last Supper Club with Spencer Hawes[30], and at this point I'm limitless. I can do whatever the fuck I want to whoever I want to do it to. Spencer is tailing me through the club as we walk to our table, and there's these two girls. Two girls standing together. A blonde and a brunette. I grab the blonde and start making out with her. Grab her by the neck and stick my tongue in her mouth, and then I do the same thing to her friend.

No one stops me.

They don't say "no."

Spencer asks, "Do you know these girls or something?"

I've never seen them before in my life. Nik Richie doesn't need to be acquainted with someone to kiss them, fuck them, or make them do what

---

30 NBA player (Sacramento Kings; Philadelphia 76ers).

he wants. Nik Richie, unlike Hooman Karamian, has no boundaries. The game has changed. Nik Richie has no rules, and therefore, cannot break any of them.

So the two girls from Last Supper Club end up at my hotel. The brunette wants to fuck. "I want to fuck so bad," she says, but the blonde is weirded out. She's never known her best friend in that way. Never seen her naked. Like most people, she's never had a threesome, so it's strange and overwhelming for her. Sex still means something to her. It's not boring. The blonde doesn't want to fuck me if her friend is in the room, but I tell them that it doesn't work that way.

"I've had three threesomes in a row," I say. "I'm going to have a fourth tonight."

I say it flatly. Honestly. Nik Richie doesn't need to be coy. He doesn't need to ask nicely anymore. He makes demands, so he tells these girls that we're all going to fuck tonight.

The blonde says she wants to watch.

I'm on the bed with the brunette, and the blonde is watching. She's touching herself while I fuck her friend. I'm pumping the brunette, whispering into her ear, "Tell your friend to take her clothes off," and she does. She says it and the blonde does it. I give the orders, the brunette relays them. So I'm fucking one, just one, but it's not boring because now I'm telling the brunette what to say next. I say, "Tell your friend to touch yourself," and in between sharp breaths, she repeats it. The blonde starts rubbing her cunt, fingering herself against the wall. She grinds her fingers into herself and the brunette and I watch from the bed. Breathing sharply. The girls are moaning, and I keep fucking and giving orders. I keep pushing the envelope because that's what Nik Richie does.

The brunette and I fuck. We direct the blonde.

We're all coming at the same time. We go too far, but we do it together in our private little room where no one can see that we're losing ourselves. Losing our way. I come all over the brunette's back while her blonde friend climaxes, masturbating against cool white walls. Their eyes flutter, spent. Exhausted. We sleep together. We pass out from liquor and the exertion of too much freedom. We've pushed too hard, so we sleep.

Sleep, and the next morning reality sets in.

The girls are sober and their inhibitions have come back, more so for the blonde who is scavenging the hotel room for her clothes. She's picking up her underwear and last night's dress, balling it against her chest. Crying. Sobbing and freaked out, and the brunette is trying to calm her down, telling her, "It's okay, it's fine," but clearly it isn't. A boundary was crossed last night, and some of us weren't ready for it. We weren't prepared. I'm watching the blonde cry and fall to pieces from the bed, naked under the covers, and I go into a little bit of a shell. Ashamed. And it's the first time I ask myself if I'm losing it.

Maybe I'm taking things too far.

Perhaps I'm turning for the worse.

Nik Richie spraying civilians at Stingaree Nightclub, San Diego, California.

Pleasanton

The problem with my divorce is I never went through an alone period.

There was never a time for me to sit back and reflect on things, think about my life. I was single, but not single in the way most people are. I could have anyone I wanted. Anyone. I didn't have to try. In fact, I'd have to push girls away most nights. There was too much choice. Too many offers. I had to filter it down to the best one. Then I started pushing it, taking things further, and bringing two girls back with me.

But watching that blonde freak out in Seattle changed something. It made me reflect. Ask questions. It starts to sink in that this isn't normal newly-divorced guy behavior. I need to get stable, I think. I need to step it back before I do something that permanently fucks me up somehow. I need something real. The Nik Richie game is fun, but it's dangerous. It'll keep escalating until it hits a breaking point.

I go to Pleasanton for an event.

This is where I meet Amanda Reed.

She's young. Really young. Eighteen, blonde with light blue eyes. The kind of blue eyes that I like. She's doing this pretend red carpet interview, which is basically going to be a direct-to-YouTube upload. It's not going to be on TV, so I'm kind of fucking with Amanda when she tries to ask me questions. Any time she tries to get an answer out of me, I turn it back to her.

What are we doing tonight, Amanda?

What's your story?

The story is that she's the assistant to the club promoter and she's got a boyfriend. No one knows if it's serious or not. They just know she's not single. She doesn't fuck around on him, or at least, not that anyone has seen. And I like her. I'm drawn to her. Part of it is the way she looks, how she carries herself. The other part is that she was born in the '90s. She's young. Unspoiled. She hasn't been tarnished by the scene yet. Not yet, anyway. The liquor and late nights haven't had their chance to age her skin or break her morality. She's still got a chance to live a good life.

I love this girl.

I don't love her specifically, but I love the ideal that she represents. She could be my stability. She could bring me back from the edge. So I JanSport[31] this chick for the night. After the interview (if you can even call it that), we keep talking. I talk to her about whatever she wants to talk about. Like she's my girlfriend. I make it all about her: her interests, her life. If a girl comes to the table wanting to meet me, I either outright ignore them or make it brief so I can get back to Amanda. The entire night is devoted to Amanda, but I'm not the only one. Throughout the evening, maybe twenty or thirty times, the boyfriend texts her. He tries calling a couple times too but it's so loud in the club that they wouldn't be able to hear each other anyway. The boyfriend texts while we talk, flirt, get to know each other. Actually, it's really me getting to know Amanda. I try not to make Nik Richie a topic, thinking that she'll stop thinking of me as a brand or a persona. A blogger. I'm trying to get normal, so I keep the discussion as normal as I can.

There's no mention of *Dirty* Celebs or fame-chasers or what actress is doing which drugs in a certain club. We really don't talk about the site. During the interview we did, but we're both over it now. And the boyfriend keeps texting, wondering when Amanda is going to be home. He wants to take her from me. Steal her away. And even though I can tell that she's kind of into me and all the attention I'm giving her, another part, the responsible one knows this is leading to something wrong. She's crossed the boundary of flirting with another man, but I want to keep going. Keep pushing.

I stay on her for the rest of the night: from the club to the after-party. We drink and the hours pass. Eventually, the boyfriend stops texting. He gives up. I don't.

I tell her, "Look, it's really late. Can you please get me back to the hotel? I have no clue where I am."

It's bullshit. I'm lying. We both know it. I could call a cab and get back to the room just fine by myself, but I don't want to be alone right now. I want Amanda. And she needs to be needed if this is going to go any further. She needs the excuse of seeing another person stranded and helping them. An emotional loophole.

So she stays. We get a cab and get back to the hotel, at which point I

---

31 Also known as "pulling a Janny" or "Jannypacking." The act of picking a girl and backpacking her all night.

talk her into coming up to the room. It's six in the morning and we're both tired. Exhausted. And I'm telling her to just have a drink and relax.

She says, "I don't want a drink. I'm done drinking."

"Well, then, take a nap or something. You can't go home right now," I say. "You need to rest. I'll give you money for a cab later. Let's just rest."

She doesn't say anything. She's trying to decide.

Or she's waiting for me to make the decision for her.

"I don't want to be alone right now," I say. "Let's just talk."

As if I'm somehow channeling Leper, I use the "let's just talk" line. I use it and it works. She stays. She sits on the bed and I'm sweeping her hair back with my fingers telling her she's gorgeous. I kiss her cheek. She says "no," but it's not a real "no." It's a "yes, keep going" type of "no," and then I lock into the blue eyes and kiss her mouth. I kiss her, but not like she's a whore or a club-rat or fame-chaser. I kiss her like I love her, and I want to so badly that I trick myself into believing this is real and genuine and not at all temporary. I pretend I'm not going to be on a plane in a few hours. We're going to be together and I can get normal. I can be Hooman around this girl when being Nik becomes too much. She can be my stability.

And when we make love it's soft. I do everything soft. I'm inside of Amanda with no condom and it's slow and warm. It's safe. Innocent. She's pure and gentle and all the things that I'm not used to. Amanda is all the girls I *don't* meet at the club. She's perfect, and for about an hour we're perfect together. Unified. I look into the blue eyes and forget Nik Richie and all the things that are waiting for me tomorrow. I forget. Let go. I stop chasing.

With Amanda, making love, there's no want for the future or regret in my past. There's nothing I want other than this. So for a moment, a very brief moment, I'm content with life and there seems to be some balance. Amanda serves the exact purpose I thought she could, either fixing me, or, at the very least, repairing the wound of my divorce.

It's a temporary fix, though.

Just like Seattle, reality sets in the next day.

We exchange numbers and go our separate ways, and I try to keep this going with Amanda (whatever it is). I pursue this girl: calling her, texting her, trying to get her to come out to Scottsdale or meet me in Vegas. But she's afraid. She doesn't want the boyfriend to find out because that's her stability. Amanda is already where I'm trying to get to, so she ignores me. Over the next two months she ignores me, and there's only so much of that a person can take when there are other girls saying "yes." Girls sitting with me. Flirting with me. They want Nik. They're willing. Ready.

And I take what's offered.

I embrace the persona.

Carrie Prejean; Perez Hilton

Sometimes I get pulled into the celebrity world.

The whole Carrie Prejean thing started with Perez Hilton putting this chick on blast because he didn't like how she answered a question. At the Miss USA Pageant[32], during the Q&A portion, Perez said to Carrie: "Vermont recently became the fourth state to legalize same-sex marriage. Do you think every state should follow suit? Why or why not?"

When a flamboyant gay man asks you on national television if you support gay marriage, logic dictates that you have to agree with him.

Instead, Carrie responded: "Well, I think it's great that Americans are able to choose one way or the other. We live in a land where you can choose same-sex marriage or opposite marriage. And, you know what, in my country, in my family, I think that, I believe that marriage should be between a man and a woman, no offense to anybody out there. But that's how I was raised and I believe that it should be between a man and a woman."

Then Perez, like a fucking child, took to his video blog calling Carrie a dumb bitch for the answer that she gave to his question. It was one of those moments where she could have either answered how Perez wanted or said what she really felt. She went with the latter.

Of this moment, Carrie said: "I was being dared—in front of the entire world—to give a candid answer to a serious question. I knew if I told the truth, I would lose all that I was competing for: the crown, the luxury apartment in New York City, the large salary—everything that went with the Miss USA title. I also knew, or suspected, that I was the frontrunner, and if I gritted my teeth and gave the politically correct answer, I could be Miss USA."[33]

---

32 2009.
33 Excerpt from *Still Standing: My Fight Against Gossip, Hate, and Political Attacks* (Regnery Publishing).

So Perez and Carrie are going at it, and because I really don't give a shit about either one of them, I never directly comment on the matter. Perez's site is the celebrity gossip. I'm civilian gossip, and the only time I'll step into celebrity territory is if it lands in my lap. Well, it lands in my lap.

During this whole media frenzy, a submission from San Diego (I'm assuming from her ex-boyfriend) comes in with three semi-nude photos of Carrie attached. She was in the middle of explaining her answer to the gay question and her faith and her +2's, and then some person from San Diego sends me another tank of gasoline to throw on this fire: the pictures. Carrie posing in pink underwear, turning away from the camera, smiling, tan, young. I know they're going to be big.

I had gotten three. I post one and it's everywhere almost instantly.

Every news outlet and TV show is going nuts over this thing. People are demanding Carrie lose her crown because this is the exact kind of shit you're not supposed to do. A state pageant spokesman is saying the Prejean photos violate the contract. It's against the rules, they say. Add her whole Catholic and holier-than-thou angle and she looks like a double hypocrite.

Via *TMZ*, Carrie responds to Co-Executive Director Keith Lewis: "This was when I was 17 years old. I was a minor. It was when I was first getting into the modeling world, being naive, and young. I shouldnt [sic] have taken the photo of me in my underwear. There are no other photos of me. This was the only one I took."

The next day, I put up photo #2.

Carrie Prejean is officially caught in a lie.

Meanwhile, Perez is milking this thing because he's still pissed off about Carrie's answer to his question at the pageant. He contacts me wanting to post one of the pics on his site[34], saying that he'll link it back to *The Dirty* and send me some traffic. I decide to e-mail him one, thinking this may open the door to a professional sort of relationship between us. Perhaps in the future it could come in handy, I'm thinking, but like a true fucking scumbag, Perez fucks me over on that.

He posts my Prejean picture with no link, no watermark, and no mention of where he got it. The guy puts it up, attempting to steal my thunder because he's got a vendetta against this chick or whatever. The hilarious part is that Perez is going on about how Carrie needs to see this shit his way, calling her a dumb bitch one minute and then inviting her out to

---

34 www.perezhilton.com

coffee the next—it's confusing and about the worst way he can go about his advocacy.

During this whole debacle, he not only shows the amount of malice he'll dish out should you not agree with him, but he's also not a man of his word. Carrie Prejean, as it turns out, has a problem with lying, too.

Regarding the second photo, her excuse is that the image is Photoshopped and that she can't remember the details of the shoot because it was so long ago.

"Can't remember" is just another way of saying "I'm playing dumb until you guys dig up more facts."

Then the cease-and-desist letters start rolling my way, stating that: "Using Ms. Prejean's photograph or likeness without her prior consent, or without the prior consent of her parents when she was a minor, violates the law."

It says: "Moreover, the images of Ms. Prejean's illegally displayed on www.thedirty.com have caused her emotional distress, and harmed her professionally.'

I have my lawyer hit them back with a reminder of what the First Amendment is and that my ass is covered under it. In short, I refuse to meet their demands, and then I put up the third photo. Shit gets even worse when a video of Carrie masturbating is sold by the ex-boyfriend to *TMZ* for $10,000. Another tank of gasoline on the fire.

That was the ebb and flow of it: Prejean made herself out to be this good little Christian girl, then something would come out suggesting otherwise, then she'd lie to the media, and then more dirt would turn up, and then she'd lie again, and then more dirt would turn up. It was a complete shit show that only came about because she couldn't be honest.

That's why I stuck on the topic for as long as I did: she kept lying, and calling out liars is the bread and butter of the site. Carrie Prejean had the problem in that everything that came out of her fucking mouth was a lie, and the media took great pride in exposing every one of them.

As with most things though, no topic can stay hot forever. There's always another story, another scandal, right around the corner. Carrie got her crown taken away, wrote a book that briefly reignited the issue, but eventually moved on. It was an issue that was strung out for far too long, but was one of *The Dirty*'s few mainstream stories that resulted in a massive amount of traffic. Over 10,000,000 people.

As for Perez Hilton, I fucking hate the guy. He's a liar, but he's also extremely delusional with his whole celebrity vibe he's trying to put off.

He's a blogger. It's not a big fucking deal. There are literally thousands of people that can do what he does. Perez has even admitted that he turned over his duties to his sister.

Regardless of that, he paved the way in the market. I don't like the guy, but there never would have been a Nik Richie if there were no Perez Hilton.

Scooby Snack

I meet Kina Tavarozi in L.A.

I'm supposed to host Wonderland tonight, which is the new Lonnie Moore club, so he's taking care of everything the way that Lonnie does. Scooby drives in from Orange County and meets me at the L'Ermitage hotel in Beverly Hills. I've known Scooby since high school. He's a friend, probably the only guy who will reality-check me when I need it. Very few people are willing to do that for some reason. Scooby tries to catch a nap in the room, but I'm so amped up I find myself taking random videos on my phone, and eventually film myself smacking him in the face so I have something worthwhile to upload.

We go to this place called Geisha House on Hollywood Boulevard, which is also owned by Lonnie. Everything is red and vibrant. Orient-themed. The hostess leads us through the crowd of mostly young girls, some Asians here and there, and then we're in a room with an elongated table where Lonnie is sitting with a couple of his guys and thirty-five blondes. True L.A. girls: wannabe actresses and models, and they've all got the platinum hair with the fake tan and +2's combo. Hot blondes, but they're all so much the same that they're copies of each other. Barbie clones. Geisha grasshoppers[35], I call them.

We get acquainted, Lonnie and I, talking shop and passively flirting with these L.A. girls that the Geisha group has pretty much run through. The rumor going around is that Lonnie, JT, and Sylvain have railed out nearly every hot girl in L.A. because of their Les Deux[36] connection. Lonnie is the difference between being a fixture of nightlife and owning it. When you own the club, there are no boundaries. No rules. These little L.A. girls are candy to him. If all thirty-five of them walked out right now,

---

35 So called because they would hop on any dick in L.A. to advance their career.
36 Was owned by Lonnie Moore and prominently featured on MTV's *The Hills*. It's now defunct.

Lonnie could have them all replaced within the hour. That's what kind of pull he has. Les Deux made him like *The Dirty* made me.

After dinner the group of us move from Geisha House to Wonderland. Nearly everyone in the club is craning their neck to see what's going on because the ratio is one guy for every seven hot blondes. We're surrounded by so many girls—so deeply immersed that we're breathing their hairspray and fake tanner. Choking on their fragrances of Chanel and Clinique and DKNY, but we're all smiling slightly drunk and soaking in the attention of the crowd. Lonnie leads us over to the owner's table and the bottles start rolling out. Champagne and vodka and anything these girls want. Some are going to the bathroom to do a few bumps of coke or fix their hair. Pills are going around. The music is blaring, and we use that as an excuse to get close to these girls, pressing chest to chest as we lean in and ask if they need a drink or a tab of Molly or simply to compliment them on how good they look in whatever they're wearing.

I'm single and young and can have any of these girls—literally, any one... or two. I don't know. There seems to be limitless opportunity here in Wonderland, in L.A., where the girls don't know how to say "no," or maybe they just don't want to. My eyes finally fixate on Kina. She's nineteen. Blonde and tan. She tells me she wants to be a model. She wants to make it out in L.A. Be somebody. Kina is from Seattle. I ask if her boobs are fake and she laughs and says "no." She says everyone thinks that but they're real, and I say I don't believe her because I know what she'll say next. These girls: L.A. girls, Vegas girls, models and actresses—they're not hard to figure out. You can touch any of them. You just have to know how to ask.

Kina grabs my wrist and brings it to her chest, saying, "Here, feel them," and I squeeze, keeping my face neutral and not impressed by any of this. She says, "See? Totally real," and I nod. Smirk. I decide I'm going to fuck this girl tonight. I turn and look at Lonnie who is sitting on top of the booth fist-pumping; he's probably going to fuck five of these girls tonight. And Scooby is neck-deep in blondes. So many blondes. The drugs bring smiles to their faces and they're dancing, sometimes kissing each other so people will watch. Kissing for attention. For feeling. There's random flashes firing from the crowd catching these random moments of Kina and me flirting, blondes dancing, doing blow at the table in the hot dark of the booth. We fist-pump like assholes, enjoying the rush too much to care about appearances or consequences.

We drink. And some of us do much more than that.

Wonderland ends and I go back to Beverly Hills with Scooby and Kina, telling her that we're going to the after-party. She doesn't mention how weird an after-party with only three people is. In her mind, the night hasn't ended so she's not going to be picky. Her friend ditched her at the club, perhaps to hook up with Lonnie or one of his guys. She's not sure, but she needs a bed to sleep in because she can't drive.

At the hotel, we have a casual nightcap. Talk about bullshit. Scooby crashes in a cot that's at the foot of the bed. Kina and I finally hit that awkward moment where you're about to sleep in the same bed as a stranger, but it's mostly on her end. I assure her nothing is going to happen because that's the line you say in these situations. To ease the person. Kina starts peeling off her clothes, asking me if I can set the alarm for six in the morning.

"I've got to go to traffic school," she says.

It's past three right now so I don't even bother, and Kina doesn't notice. She slips under the covers in nothing but her underwear, talking. She talks about nothing. Rambling off while the drugs keep her alert, so it's only a matter of time. There's going to come a point where she won't have anything to say, but laying silently won't be enough. She'll need something to keep her busy, wear her out. She'll want to fill in the quiet, but she'll put up a bit of a resistance so she doesn't look easy.

Finally, one thing leads to another and we're kissing: her on top, the weight of those tits sitting heavy on my chest. Kina pulls back and says, "We're not having sex." I roll her off of me, but not in a dejected kind of way. It's slower. She knows I'm coming back. I go to the bathroom and put a condom on my Greg, and when I get back into bed we start fooling around again. I slide my hand down between her legs and finger her cunt. I'm kissing her, feeling her tits, squeezing her hard. I'm easing my cock between her legs, suggesting that she lets it in. Waiting for her to shift her legs that little bit so that we can start fucking, and she finally does. Kina is young and tight, moaning. She's fucking me, and I see Scooby move on his cot through the dark. He's up. I can tell.

I make Kina get up on top of me, facing away in reverse-cowgirl, and she starts bouncing on my cock while Scooby watches. I'm squeezing her ass and tits and letting Kina do all the work, and Scooby says, "C'mon, dude, that's gross," even though he's still watching. He does that thing where he pretends to cover his eyes, but he's still looking at Kina. Her cunt. Her tits. I flip Kina onto her back and rail her out missionary style. She's moaning, legs wrapped around my waist, and we both come hard and fall into a state of sleep.

◆◆◆

We wake up late in the morning.

Kina is freaking out because the alarm never went off, so she missed traffic school, but she's more concerned about the ten missed calls on her phone. She lays naked in the bed, checking voicemails and texts while Scooby and I brush our teeth and get cleaned up. I get back in bed and lay next to her, checking my own phone, which is mostly just bullshit texts and a couple things from Lonnie. A few fame-chasers.

Kina leans over and says, "Your friend snores a lot."

"He's just fat. It's cool."

She leans closer, asking, "What's his name again," pointing at the bathroom.

"Scooby."

"Awww, that's cute."

A few seconds later, Scooby comes out of the bathroom and I wave him over, saying, "Dude, come here and tell me if these are real."

"What?"

"Feel Kina's tits and tell me if they're real," I say, pulling the sheet down. Kina doesn't move it back. She moves her arms out of the way and gives Scooby a look like, "go ahead and check."

He squeezes one, keeps his hand there. Squeezes again.

He says, "Yes, in my professional opinion, they're real. Those are quite nice."

Kina and I exchange numbers. She puts last night's dress back on and digs a pair of large designer sunglasses out of her purse. She says to give her a call whenever we're out in L.A. or Vegas, and the three of us head toward the elevator. I joke about how Kina is on the walk of shame, turning around and taking her picture with Scooby in the frame.

"Dude, I'm going to put this up on *The Dirty*," I say with a laugh, but Kina doesn't find it funny in the least.

"You better fucking not," she says.

The thing about this random hookup between Kina and me is that the exchange was obvious. There was an implied trade. I had started to become aware of how people (especially women) would react to me when they found out I was Nik Richie, and Kina was no different in that regard. People tend to be nicer when they know you have public influence.

Hugh Hefner, for instance, gets to bang any chick he wants because all these girls want to be in Playboy or move into the mansion. They want in the inner circle. I, on the other hand, have the opposite effect. Girls like Kina sleep with me to stay off the site. They fuck Nik Richie for protection or some kind of immunity. It's about keeping their reputation intact, but I don't operate that way. I expose. I stir the pot. If you've fucked me, chances are you already drank for free all night and got a dinner out of it. It doesn't mean you're safe from being posted, and that's what Kina doesn't understand.

So I Tweet the photo to @DirtyScooby saying: "Scooby totally banged this chick last night!" and then for some reason, Kina retweets it. Now all of Twitter thinks this chick actually did fuck Scooby, and they start calling her Scooby Snack. The next morning, someone submits Kina to the site and I put it up even though I know she's going to freak the fuck out, which she does moments after I publish it.

She calls, screaming, "Take it down! Take it the fuck down! Everyone is saying that I'm a slut and that I fucked Scooby!"

"Well, this is what you get for hanging out with people like Freddy Fags," I say.

"Nik, take it the fuck down. I don't want this."

"No, you're a *Dirty* Celeb now. Embrace it."

"I don't want to be a *Dirty* Celeb," she says.

"Trust me, you'll get used to it. They all do."

Escorts & Porta–Potties

Girls like Scooby Snack die quicker than most.

Although she would become a fixture in our operation by showing up to various events in Vegas [37], the reality is the city and the lifestyle will kill you. We slowly witness this through the various posts that are put up on the site of girls spiraling downward. Girls being weathered by the scene and drugs and too many long nights out in the clubs. It's a trainwreck, but a trainwreck happening in slow motion over the course of many years.

I slept with Kina at her peak.

The problem is that Vegas ages you, wears you down quicker than most places, and Kina's no exception to that. Compare the early photos to the more recent ones and it's obvious the damage has already been done. These girls don't see the warning signs, though. Either that, or they're choosing to ignore them. They assume all these people in the comments section saying how much they've aged or how haggard they look are just "being haters." They're jealous. Liars. They're just being mean for the sake of being mean.

"Keep talking shit, you're making me famous," they think, but that's just denial washing over any possible state of introspection. It's easier to not change, to keep doing the things that feel good at the time. Girls like Kina live in the moment, and the moment can become addictive when drinking Cristal in the VIP or doing blow in some guy's suite at Caesar's Palace. These moments overtake the reality that you're dying just a little bit quicker than everyone else. Your looks will be gone just a little bit sooner. You peak at around eighteen years old and then it's all downhill from there.

---

37 Something I never minded because she'd usually bring a few of her friends from the *Blondtourage*, as they referred to themselves. They mooched off our bottles, of course, but I always liked having her around because her and Scooby together were like a power couple. It also got the rumor mill churning again that there was something between them, even though the three of us knew that couldn't be further from the truth.

These girls, the ones like Kina, most of them either work part-time as servers or make their money "going on dates." In a place like Vegas, girls can get away with this kind of thing: the trade of company, which may or may not include sex, for cash and/or drugs. Most good-looking women are satisfied with having their drinks bought or their dinner paid for. The escort business is simply one level above that.

And sometimes you'll hear me say in interviews or on the site that I'm trying to save lives. I'm giving people a wake-up call. If you're up on my site, whether you want to believe it or not, there's a reason for it. Some part of your lifestyle is being called into question, and the Vegas escort scene comes up more often than anything. Girls like Kina.

The public isn't stupid: they see a girl (an attractive girl) who doesn't work, yet they're always posting photos of Louboutin shoes or pictures of them on some guy's yacht. They're openly showing the world their new LV purse or Tiffany earrings, and meanwhile the world is asking, "Where's this stuff coming from, and more importantly, what is she having to do to get it?"

It's how the escort business works: sex for cash or jewelry or purses or shoes. Find a hot blonde on Twitter posting this shit and I guarantee you she can be yours for the right price, the right amount of coke, the right gift. In Vegas, everything's for sale, and sometimes the post that's meant to be a wake-up call serves more as an advertisement. Kina, unlike most other *Dirty* Celebs, embraced the fame just like I told her to. She used it for exposure, sometimes even hosting her own events in Vegas for cash under the Scooby Snack moniker. The problem is that by putting her in the spotlight, more of the wrong kind of people sought her out. People worse than the douchey club promoters that shell out drugs to these girls.

We're talking guys with too much money and too much imagination. No morals. These dudes wire transfer tens of thousands of dollars to girls like Kina, flying them out to someplace in the Middle East or Dubai or Miami. The location isn't constant, but the result is that they get these girls out of their element so they're basically trapped. They either do what they're being paid to do, or they're fucked. Dead. Sometimes they just have to fuck some hairy Arab dude. Other times they have to get pissed and shitted on. This is the point some men reach: so bored with themselves and their lives that they fly out random girls from Vegas to pee on them. If the girl doesn't cooperate, they either get shot or thrown off the side of a boat or smacked around.

The choice becomes, "Do I let this guy shit on me and make $25,000 or do I ask to go home and maybe get a bullet in the head?"

For these girls, it's not much of a choice. A no-brainer, really. They degrade themselves for a day and get to live off the profit for months. I try to do my part by posting it on the site, thinking that maybe these girls will think twice before they get on that plane or boat or whatever. I fool myself into believing common sense will kick in, that they'll stop selling their bodies to the highest bidder. They won't listen. They ignore it. "*The Dirty* is just talking shit again," they think.

It only takes one though. One crazy Arab or psycho rich dude, and it's over. You're done. Dead. The dream is over and you never make it back to Vegas.

The city has so many ways to kill you. Either the scene and the drugs get you, or the lifestyle takes a wrong turn. You either wind up twenty-seven years old and used up or shit on and shot in the head. It's only a matter of time. And there's always going to be a new girl. For every Kina, there's another, newer version of Kina with a fake ID. A young Scooby Snack just waiting to be discovered by the right group of people. For every hot blonde with +2's, there's ten more waiting to take her spot at the VIP table in some club. There's always another *Dirty* Celeb waiting to happen.[38] They'll die in slow motion and Nik Richie will be there to commentate. To warn. To speak the truth.

If you're fucking up, you can always count on me to say something.

---

38 The *Dirty* Celeb typically goes through three specific stages, hence, the revolving door nature:

1) Resistance: stage in which *Dirty* Celeb begs for their posts to be taken down. What they don't realize is that for every one that's taken down, about ten more come in, thus adding more fuel to the fire.

2) Acceptance: stage in which *Dirty* Celeb takes no action against the site or site moderators. They've reached a point where they're comfortable being a topic of conversation, debate, and/or ridicule. The subject will even make mention of their status in a positive light or use it for personal gain.

3) Withdrawal: stage in which *Dirty* Celeb has declined in popularity, and therefore, is no longer a topic of discussion. The subject will then act out in one way or another to encourage another post and return to their former state of notoriety.

Ginger

I fall in love with Sarah's picture.

Part of the confusion about the "Would You?"[39] section of the site is that people think I'm rejecting or bagging on these girls to appear impossible to please or a jerk, and that's not necessarily true. I actually am *this picky*, to the point where it borders on being a detriment. The flaw isn't something I go looking for. They pop out and I lack the ability to ignore them. Of course, things like caking on too much makeup or a half-inch of black roots on blonde hair stick out to me just as they would to anyone else. I'm normal in that regard. However, I also notice things like symmetry and bone structure: one breast that's bigger than the other, a jawline not cut quite right, or a nose that slopes at a curved angle rather than straight. Things like kempt teeth and body proportions matter to me. I hate tattoos. I hate body piercings and skin irregularities (scars, birthmarks, moles, etc.). Perhaps this is an actual defect or me just being superficial, but my views on women have always been this rigid. It's not an act or some personality trait of the Nik Richie persona. I'm actually wired this way.

So to say that Sarah Wood is "my type" means more coming from me than it would most people. Out of all the models and strippers and escort girls that were being sent to me on a daily basis—the kind of girls that most men would dump their entire bank accounts on—Sarah is the one I find myself saying "yes" to. Yes, I would.

◆ ◆ ◆

---

39 Refers to: "Would you hook up with this girl?" By selecting this option (category) during the submissions process you are asking Nik Richie's opinion of a particular girl. Over 99% of the time he will say no and/or suggest changes in order to improve whomever you've sent.

People start referring to Sarah as Nik's Chick on the site because they know she's my type, but that's putting it lightly. I want Sarah. I want to date her and be with her. I want a relationship, and it has to be with Sarah because nobody else has what I'm looking for. It's Amanda Reed all over again but worse. So much worse.

It comes to my attention that she works at Dolce Vendetta in Dallas and that she's actually friends with Leper of all people, but I never put two and two together that she was the bottle server at my event. Even though Dolce Vendetta kind of sucked, I actually find myself plotting a Dallas trip just to see Sarah. That's not immediate enough, though. I have this sense of urgency I don't normally have with other girls, so I send her a MySpace message which basically says: I'm going to say that you're my girlfriend because you're the only girl I find attractive these days.

It's kind of a joke, kind of not. Obviously, we aren't really going to be in a committed relationship. This is more or less my way of flirting with her, letting her know that I am, in fact, interested without completely putting myself out there.

Sarah's all about it. She changes her relationship status and I'm telling everyone that Nik's Chick is actually my chick. Even though we had never formally met, as far as the Internet world is concerned, we're an item. Then people start submitting her, saying things like, "You're always judging other girls but do you have the balls to put your own girlfriend up?"

And I was like, *Fuck, she's not my girlfriend. I'll put her up all damn day.*

Her picture goes live: she's beautiful, blonde, blue eyes, the kind of blue eyes that I like, and a shade of tan that looks natural. She's pretty much all the physical attributes I look for in a girl, so I'm proud to put her up.

Some people talk shit.

Others are impressed.

Sarah and I are kind of laughing behind the scenes about the whole thing. She likes it, likes the attention, and I like being the guy able to give it to her. It's how we connect: a very public relationship that was actually an inside joke between us. A secret. Something only she and I understood. It brought us close in a sense. Close enough that she agreed to fly out to Vegas to meet me.

◆◆◆

Officially, this weekend is an event for The Dirty.

Unofficially, I'm here for Sarah. To see if it's real.

We're in Vegas, and all the top *Dirty* Celebs are here: Leper, 8-Belles, Elvira—all the good ones. Elvira is the only brunette I've ever had any legitimate interest toward, so it's kind of between her and Sarah, in my mind.

I'm at a table with eight girls at this restaurant called Company, which is outside of LAX (in the Luxor). Sarah is sitting next to me. Elvira is across the way. She's from Boston, so I ask questions that girls like these can easily field. General ones like: *What's it like out on the East Coast?*

Dinner with me is typically a revelation for some of these girls because I'm not mean or judgmental. In fact, I'm overtly polite and aware of their immediate needs. I ask if they need another drink, if they want me to call the waiter over, if they'd like more of a particular dish—things that a good date should do. A gentleman, like James Bond. I talk about Vegas because I know a lot (perhaps too much) about the city: gambling, poker, restaurants, but the girls find it interesting. And I make them laugh. These girls are so used to one side of Nik Richie that they come into the situation with their defenses up. They're tense, and most of the time won't eat more than some salad or a few bites of bread. These girls are afraid to eat in front of me, assuming that I'm mentally criticizing them already, so I have to be funny. Be a gentleman. Be the guy that makes it okay for them to relax, eat, enjoy themselves.

So these eight girls at the table think I'm nothing like I really am, because it's all an act. A persona. They've seen Internet Nik Richie. This is date Nik Richie, the version that calls you Kelly instead of Elvira, the one that comments on your better features over the ones he finds displeasing. He is funny instead of sarcastic. He'll allow you to speak instead of speaking

Sarah Wood a.k.a. Nik's Chick (left) and Nik Richie (right)
having dinner at The Company at the Luxor in Las Vegas, Nevada.

for you. He is friendly, and by extension, a source of relief to these girls who have more than likely suffered privately to one degree or another for the sake of entertainment.

So I talk to Elvira—maybe more than I should, because I feel a hand smooth up my leg. It's Sarah, tracing the inseam of my pants with her fingers. She settles on top of my cock and starts squeezing while I'm trying to carry on a conversation. I ask some question about Boston clubs or something and Sarah pretends she's interested, squeezing, telling me with her hand: *Hey, don't hit on Elvira. You're mine.*

◆ ◆ ◆

When I like a girl, I don't fuck her right away.

I liked Sarah, and even though she moved out of Leper's room to be with me—even though she threw herself at me—I didn't give in. So Vegas basically ended up being me pampering Sarah, getting to know her, spending time with her. We did the event at Pure inside of Caesar's, but it was mostly an excuse to meet Sarah. I became obsessed with this chick. She had a boyfriend.

The boyfriend fucks everything up, and I don't mean that in the way of "oh, she's got a boyfriend so I guess I'm out." That doesn't bother me. I've hooked up with plenty of girls that had boyfriends (both to and without my knowledge), so that's not the issue. The problem with this dude, this Eduardo fucker, is that he's in the country illegally and basically mooching off of Sarah. He's an nineteen-year-old punk kid, so I'm thinking I can make short work of him.

Over the next few months I pursue Sarah: I get her Gucci shoes, LV purses, flowers. I write her love letters. I call her. It gets to the point where I'm on the phone with her three or four times a day. I buy her more stuff, more shoes and jewelry and anything else that I think she'll like. A part of me wants her to have these things because I know it'll make her happy, but another part, the competitive side, is telling this Eduardo guy: *these are the shoes you couldn't buy her…this is the bracelet you couldn't afford.* What Sarah wants, Sarah gets. She owns me. Sarah calls me all the time saying that she loves me, starts calling me Hooman instead of Nik. We're making plans. Plotting a trip to Paris. I really don't care where we go as long as I get to be with her. I'm done with the scene: the clubs and the bottle service and the empty sex. Sarah is the one. It's all about her, and I'm setting up helicopters and private jets to pick her up, sending plane tickets. Most of the time she doesn't get on. Sometimes I go out to her, out to Dallas, and I just sit in a hotel room waiting for her to call me. Waiting, watching TV in the suite for hours. If I don't hear from her after a couple days, I text her and let her know I'm going back to Scottsdale. Thousands of dollars are spent this way. It gets old. Gets to the point where she'll only meet me in Vegas, and even that has no guarantee.

Scooby and I started calling Sarah's boyfriend Lester Diamond because he was like the James Woods character in *Casino*: a piece of shit scumbag who used girls for money, did coke, cared for no one but himself, and couldn't provide. Despite all that, and despite me, Sarah always went back to him. Didn't matter what I did or said or bought her, she always went back.

If he was Lester Diamond, that meant that Sarah was Ginger.

◆◆◆

Ginger tells me she broke up with Lester.

I don't ask for a bunch of reasons why. It's not important. She's mine now. Lester is out of the picture, so we can finally be together. It's good again. We make plans, plot the future. Ginger actually lets me into her apartment in Dallas. I'm happy. I'm faithful to her. If Nik Richie has to do an event, he goes to bed alone. He sends a text to Ginger saying: *I miss you...I love you.* Ginger doesn't want Nik Richie. For her, I get to be Hooman Karamian. He's the romantic one, the thoughtful one. He's the guy that wants to take care of her.

I try to persuade her to come out to Scottsdale. Ginger's in Dallas listening to my pitch about us living together and giving this a real shot.

I tell her, "I'll even get you a job out here. You'll have work—or fuck it," I say. "Don't work. You don't have to do anything. Just come out."

So we talk about that and marriage and kids. We talk about love. I'm convinced that we're a real couple going somewhere. I finally get to be the man that I've always pretended didn't exist. For Ginger, I'm something more than a persona.

◆◆◆

Ginger and I are waiting in an airport terminal.

I'm taking her on a surprise trip to Hawaii, so I've spent the last few days setting up spa and dinner reservations, locking down a suite. It's our first official trip as a couple so I'm trying to make it good. Even though Ginger is still living in Dallas, going on a vacation together makes the relationship seem more real. It's the kind of thing that real couples do.

Then Ginger tells me she can't get on the plane.

I ask her why.

She sighs, looks at me and says, "I'm pregnant."

At first I think she's fucking with me, but her face is sincere, so I ask her, "How far along are you?"

She says, "Eight weeks."

I do the math in my head, and the last time we had sex was three months ago. "It's not mine," I say. I want it to be mine, but it isn't.

"I know," she says. "It's Eduardo's."

◆◆◆

Ginger drops off the face of the Earth for two weeks.

Actually, she cuts communication with me specifically.

I try calling her, texting her, emailing her to let her know that it's okay. I'll help raise the kid. That's how much of a fucking sucker I am. Ginger sold me so fucking hard that I'm actually trying to call her to let her know I'll raise Lester Diamond's bastard. Thing is, Lester Diamond was back in the picture, had been back for some time. Maybe he never left. I just hadn't seen him, and I trusted Ginger enough that when she said he was gone, she meant it.

I'm crushed. I'm depressed, stationed on Scooby's couch trying to make sense of everything. Ginger won't call me back or acknowledge me. I'm frustrated, and it's mostly because I don't know where I stand anymore with her. The not knowing part kills me.

Scooby is no help. He asks me why I can't just date a normal fat girl with a personality.

I say, "Because I want Sarah. I don't want anyone else...and I don't like fat girls."

The first few days of this is me feeling rejected, bumming around Scooby's place and not really doing much more than waiting by the phone. The site continues to be managed, but it's mostly just something to keep me occupied while I wait for Ginger to reach out. I drink, I post, Twitter-stalking Ginger every few minutes to see if she says anything. She knows I'm watching. When a guy texts and calls as much as I have, you know he's keeping tabs.

Ginger posts a photo of baby clothes.

Lester Diamond is Tweeting shit like: *just had the best sex of my life!* And: *thanks for the head this morning baby.*

He's saying these things about Ginger, but they're directed at me.

I'm thinking, *What kind of fucking class does this guy have?*

Lester Diamond is making shit up, saying the things that he knows will piss me off because I stole his chick for a minute. The fucked-up thing is that it's working. I am pissed off. So I sink to their level. I play the game back.

◆◆◆

Ashley Zarlin is the daughter of one of the chicks from* The Real House- *wives of Orange County. She's your classic Newport Beach girl: blonde, wealthy, tan, big tits (real ones), but just a little thick for my tastes. She wasn't fat, but my version of fat. It didn't matter though because I was intent on getting back at Ginger. Depression mode had gone out the window right when Lester Diamond starting Tweeting about getting blow- jobs and how good he just fucked Ginger. The little prick was rubbing my nose in it–that much was clear, and Ginger had yet to reach out to me or address any of what he was doing.

I had to accept that she was really going to have this baby and that Les- ter Diamond was in the picture for good. He won. That didn't change the fact that I was looking for a little payback, so I start having this very public relationship with Ashley, or Z-List[40] as she was known on the site. I'm going to parties with this girl, taking Twitpics, and she's doing @replies to me saying things like: *just hanging out with my new boyfriend!* We go out together, party together. I have no real interest in her, on either a physical or personal level. She's got too many lesbian friends, which kind of weirds me out. Ashley isn't relationship material, but she's a pseudo-celeb and someone that can potentially make Ginger jealous, and I'm constantly refreshing both her and Lester Diamond's Twitter to see if I've made any sort of impact.

It works. Ginger goes nuts.

◆◆◆

---

40 So called because she thought she was a celebrity, but the truth of the matter is that she played a very minor role in a reality show which put her way below D-List.

Ginger blows up my phone:

"How the fuck could you cheat on me like this???"

"I can't believe you betrayed me! Why would you do that?"

"That bitch is a nobody...she's only with you because she wants to be famous."

"I hope you like fucking a fatass!"

I don't respond. I'm laughing my ass off over this, not because of anything Ginger says. It's because I figured her out. I played her game better than she did. She's not the one. She's a fucking psycho, so every plane she didn't get on and all the lies about Lester Diamond make sense now. It's not my fault. It's hers.

Ginger keeps texting me, talking shit on Ashley:

"I can't believe you're fucking Z-List, Nik. She's a fucking cow."

After enough non-responses, she calls Scooby up in an attempt to get to me, see what I'm thinking, to find out if the whole Ashley thing is a joke or something. The reality is that Scooby is the last person she should be calling. He hates her. When Nik Richie goes into shutdown mode, the fun stops: no parties, no girls, no Twitpics of being out or acting like you're the king of the world at some club. No one gets laid. So when Ginger fucked me over, she inadvertently fucked Scooby over too.

Instead of being out and having bottle service, he had to come home to me being all bummed out on his couch. Scooby is a friend, but he doesn't like playing therapist.

Now Ginger is calling him, trying to dig up info and saying shit like, "What the fuck is his deal? Is he just doing this to make my pregnancy difficult?"

He says, "Sarah, it's over. Nik's moved on."

"To fucking Z-List? *Really*, Scooby?"

"He likes this girl. Get over it."

◆◆◆

Ginger texts me: You really hurt me.

She's broken. I broke her. I finally text her back and say: *Now you know how it feels.*

She says: *Nik just call me. Please call me.*

She says: *I need to hear you. I need to hear your voice.*

I shouldn't call her. I shouldn't. It should be over. Ginger fucked me over. I fucked her back. I won. I should walk away while I'm still ahead.

I don't though. I don't because I still feel for her, and Ginger makes me do things that are stupid and impulsive. So I call her, and Ginger starts going on about how I'm the one and that she loves me and she's sorry, so fucking sorry for all the bullshit and the Lester Diamond stuff. She says that she's fixed all that.

"I got an abortion," Ginger tells me. "So now we can be together."

I don't say anything.

"Eduardo's gone…I told him I miscarried."

I don't say anything.

"I did it for you…so dump Ashley and let's be together. It can be like it was before."

I'm silent.

"Hello?"

I hang up.

◆ ◆ ◆

I delete Ginger's number from my phone. I stop following her on Twitter and defriend her on Facebook. She's psychotic. I know that now. She crossed a line that I didn't believe she was capable of crossing, and I can't have that kind of blood on my hands. I can't be with someone who killed a baby for me. It's too fucked-up. Too fucked-up for even me, so I erase her. The thing with Zarlin, our public relationship cools off. She's psycho in her own way. I find myself surrounded by psychotic women, fame-chasers, instability, and I'm getting scarred in the process. There's no hope for normality, and it's getting to the point where I'm starting to think I'm the one doing something wrong. Maybe Nik Richie is the problem.

Maybe he was a bad idea.

Origins (Part 2)

In my mid-twenties, Scottsdale was like the Dubai of America. Everybody was good-looking. Plastic surgery was on the rise. It was one of those places where people went out all the time because it was so cheap to live there, so the social scene was at a pinnacle of sorts. Everybody either had money or they were pretending to have it and living off overdraft protection. The reality is that most people, myself included, made about thirty grand a year but were acting like millionaires: they'd get their bi-weekly check of $950 and spend about half of it on bottle service and drugs and whatever else they thought would help them hook up with chicks. And girls were blowing their money on Louboutin pumps and MAC makeup and eightballs of coke to keep them from eating. Or they were saving up for a boob job. Everybody was getting photographed being out, having fun, living the life. It was the point in which the city was at the height of its decadence, and the people in the scene were consumed with vanity. It was all about appearances.

Appearing rich.

Appearing successful.

Didn't matter if it was true. At that point in time, presenting a wealthy persona was almost the same thing as having one, and nobody was there to say otherwise.

Not yet anyway.

◆◆◆

I was playing the game too. Chasing money. Trying to live that life. I was out at the clubs on the weekends just like everyone else: scoping out chicks, drinking, watching guidos pop bottles from across the way. The big difference was that all of my friends, my acquaintances, weren't pretending to be wealthy. They had the Ferraris and Benzes and the eight-figure bank accounts. Unlike the office slaves and weekend warriors, they didn't celebrate every bottle of Grey Goose they bought at the club because it wasn't a big deal to them. It was normal. These guys actually had the life most people in Scottsdale pretended to have. I tried to keep up, but these guys knew I wasn't rich or even remotely in their league. Far from it.

I worked for NPMG[41], which was backed by JPMorgan/Chase at the time. People knew the name JPMorgan, so to be able to say that I worked there added to my clout by extension. I wore a suit. A tie. I shaved, did my hair, and wore the most expensive cologne. On the surface, this appeared to be a respectable existence. Again, this goes back to appearing to be more than what you are. It was a shit job. I worked in a cubicle farm as a glorified telemarketer.

Even though you'd see me at all the best clubs on the weekends, Monday through Friday I was calling up small businesses and trying to set appointments. From 8 a.m. to 6 p.m. I was hitting up the East Coast, attempting to convince these business owners to sit down with one of our SAEs[42] so they could get scammed. This place was exactly like *Boiler Room*, right down to the management saying things like, "Don't set wood[43]," and "Don't act like a fucking Canadian[44]." It was like being with Carlo Oddo the child-fucker all over again.

The first part of the process broke down like this: I would make anywhere between 200 and 300 calls a day to notify the person on the sheet that they were processing at a high enough level to cut out the middleman. Basically, every time they took a payment with a credit card or a debit card, they were hit with a fee. Over time, those fees would become substantial. "Substantial" as in thousands and thousands of dollars.

"So what we'd like to do is set you up with an appointment with one of our SAEs to cut out those fees," I'd say. "This could potentially save you around ten grand a year because we work directly with the banks."

Step two is that our SAE would go out to meet with this person, comparing what they currently paid to how much they'd save with our system. The trick, the scam, is that our SAEs were bullshit brokers. They'd convince these business owners that they needed credit card processing

---

41 National Processing Management Group.
42 Senior Account Executive.
43 Code for: an appointment in which the business owner has little to no interest.
44 Code for: nigger.

'machines' they actually didn't, and they'd never calculate our company's fees.

So when Mr. and Mrs. Small Business Owner checked their statement the next month and realized they were getting fucked, it didn't matter. They were under contract already by that point. If they wanted out, it was going to cost them $750 for the cancellation. Either way, we got them.

I was quite good at fucking people over.

Some things never change.

◆◆◆

NPMG was a chop shop, a place where college dropouts like myself could go and pretend to be businessmen, and my manager was a racist prick. This guy, Sean Mecham, would run the floor all day spouting sales bull-shit like "A–B–C [45]," and "Motion is emotion," and there was never a good day with this guy. If you set thirty appointments, you could do better. If you set forty, he'd ask why you didn't set forty-one. He had it in for me because I got hooked up with the job through Lance Moore [46], the guy who owned the place.

In front of the entire staff, he'd yell at me, "Hooman, you fucking sand Canadian, I know how you got this job! There aren't any fucking favors here!"

Then he'd take my chair away until I booked an appointment.

Sean hated me because he thought that I was coming into the place expecting special treatment. The floor hated me because they were key-ing off Sean. In this business, you listened to the guy that made the most money, and Sean made about 300K a year. He had the Breitling watch and the car and the hot wife that he cheated on with girls in the office. Sean had what I wanted. The only reason I put up with the bullshit is because Lance told me that I had to pay my dues on the phones before I could become an SAE, and SAEs at the time were making six figures easily.

The NPMG business model was a scam: we were charging hidden fees and locking these merchants into extended contracts so we could bleed them dry. I quickly became aware of that, but I was so money-hungry it didn't really affect me. There was no guilt. No liability. And I was so deter-

---

45 Always Be Closing.
46 I met Lance Moore through the club scene, we became friends, and the NPMG job was more or less his wedding present to me when I married my first wife. I'd later find out that Lance Moore wasn't even his real name.

mined to show Sean up that anytime he called me a sand Canadian it made me try harder. I was going to break him before he broke me, so I started coming into work early. I'd stay late. I'd skip lunch and not take breaks. Some saw it as a work ethic, but in reality I was just trying to prove Sean was wrong about me.

It was not a good time in my life. The job sucked. The pay was shit. My manager was a cocksucker and my marriage was on the rocks. The only real bright spot was hanging out with T.J. Feuerbach, who was sort of my partner–in–crime at NPMG. We bullshitted about sports and talked about the club scene. It was a way to kill time in between calls, and killing time was essential in a job like that. He'd point out a chick in the office that happened to come into our field of vision. She'd be going to the bathroom or walking to the appointment board, and T.J. would ask me, "Hey Hooman, would you?"

◆◆◆

When you're good at something, you can be an asshole and get away with it. Just think about all those professional athletes and Hollywood actors who treat normal people like shit. Win a Super Bowl or an Academy Award and suddenly you're above the common man. You can spit in the face of a child and the parents will thank you for it. It's a standard practice: the better you are in your particular field, the more leverage you have over people.

I was good at my job.

Really fucking good.

Between my hard–on for money and the drive to prove my racist boss wrong about me, a perfect storm happened, and from the wreckage rose a salesman. After months of Sean calling me sand Canadian and thousands of calls later, something clicked and my natural charm was being channeled into the job. The scam. I was scamming so many people. It started at around twenty per day. Then about thirty. Eventually, it got to the point where 45% of the total appointments were being set by me. One guy doing roughly half the company's work. There were some days where Sean would literally pull the chair of every employee but me. It's not that he didn't want to. He couldn't. I was too good.

The problem was that I became self–aware of the fact.

I had paid my dues on the phones and wanted the SAE job, had been asking Sean about it for quite some time. About every twenty minutes I was walking up to the appointment board and ringing the sales bell—not celebrating, but sending a message to Sean. I was telling him that I've risen to the top and I wanted out. I wanted the opportunity I had rightfully earned, yet, every time I approached him on the subject and got the same bullshit about not acting like a sand Canadian.

He told me, "You'll go out when we say you do, carpet bomber."

And then he went and took someone else's chair away from them. I had been doing the phone scam for more than a half a year by this point and Sean was going to keep me there, in my seat, calling and calling and calling for as long as he could. The calls wouldn't end. The scam had no end. I was going to be there forever if I didn't do something drastic.

I decided to take away the only thing from Sean that I could.

◆ ◆ ◆

I started tanking it.

I went from thirty or forty appointments a day to one or two. I stopped coming in early and staying late, stopped skipping my breaks. It was like being a new hire again. Me, sitting there on the phone and pretending it was my first day: flubbing my lines, screwing up my pitch. Playing with my cell phone. This was my internal strike.

I wanted something. Sean refused to give it to me.

All things considered, he should have seen it coming.

The first couple of days, he thought it was a fluke. He asked me questions about my health or if something was wrong. Sean was trying to figure out why his top producer was suddenly performing like a rookie. He was panicking because he forgot how much he had grown to rely upon me. Hooman Karamian was Mr. Dependable in his eyes, and then he became Mr. Rebel.

The flow chart of blame worked like this: the bosses saw the numbers, and the numbers were about 45% less than what they normally were. The bosses then yelled at Sean about the shitty numbers, which in turn led to Sean yelling at me in a way that only Sean could:

"You fucking sand nigger motherfucker! Do you know how much you're fucking me?! Get your terrorist ass out of that fucking chair!"

Sean's mouth in my ear, breath like stale coffee and vending machine food, he yelled, "Get your fucking ass in gear, you fuck! You hear me, you little sand-cunt? A–B–C! A–B–C! Close the fucking deal, shitbag!"

He took the chair.

I smiled. I was smiling because breaking people is fun, and the guy was cracking after only a few days. Just a few days of striking and I was going to get what I wanted, and by all means, he could have fired me. Sean could have, but he knew it would be much easier to bargain with me rather than attempting to find another golden goose.

NPMG was a shit job. It paid dick. Sean was a fucking terrible boss. The hours sucked. It wasn't meaningful work. You weren't helping people— you were actually fucking them over. It was a scam, so people either quit because of that or the pay or wanting to get away from Sean. There were plenty of places you could make 30K annually without all the stress. We all knew that. Some of us, people like me, we wanted that carrot being dangled in front of our noses: the SAE job.

He pulled me into his office and told me he knew what was going on. Sean said, "I know what you want, man."

I sat there, leaning comfortably in the chair and listened. I wanted him to pitch me. Sean was going to have to sell me.

"I know you want that SAE job, and I'll get you there," he said. "But you got to keep us going. You got to. You are the next to go out. I promise. Just keep us going and it's yours."

It's known as "turning someone out."

Typically, this is when you find a girl and get her hooked on heroin. You chain her to a bed, and then you give her a little shot every eight to twelve hours. She'll say "no" at first. Squirm. Scream. She'll resist, but a few days into it, she'll wait for that shot. And a few days after that, she'll ask for it. She'll be hooked, and then she'll do whatever you want from that point on.

That's what I did to Sean: I took his shot away.

I turned him out. Broke him.

Just like I knew I could.

◆◆◆

Three months later, one of our SAEs got popped for a DUI in Orange County. That was the sound of opportunity knocking: one of our guys getting his license suspended.

I was in my cubicle as per usual, doing my sales scam thing when Sean slapped a binder on my desk. We had become friends by that point, or something close to it, so Sean was smiling at me. This thing, a training manual, was the size of a telephone book. It contained all the information one had to learn in order to be an SAE: script, flow charts, statistics.

It was the how-to guide to making six figures out on the road as a Senior Account Executive. I had been waiting close to a year for this binder.

Sean stood over me smiling, saying, "There you go, kid," and the floor, all the people that knew how long I wanted it, how long I had lobbied for it, they stood up and clapped. Applauded. They saw hard work pay off in a place where it normally doesn't.

Training began.

I was put in a room with two good-looking college grads, people that had actually gone to school for this position. They looked at me like I was some sort of used car salesman: equal title, but a scumbag. A slick street kid. To them, my suit wasn't a suit, it was a costume. I wasn't an SAE; I just happened to be dressing like one. Yet again, I felt like I was being tested, like I had to prove myself to these two fucks and the company and whoever else. Being called a sand Canadian never really bothered me, but having my credentials questioned was another matter entirely.

There was one slight problem: I couldn't memorize the binder.

That's all they wanted from me, to get the script down in my head so I could repeat it on cue during the meetings. That was a big issue for me because I didn't like memorizing things, hated reading, and was always looking for the short cut. If you told me something took eight minutes to do, I would've been the guy trying to figure out how to get it down to seven.

I did my best.

I flew out to L.A. to train one-on-one in the field with Trey Smith, an established SAE with the company. The guy was the "rich black man" stereotype: good-looking dude driving an S-Series Benz. He wore $6,000 suits and carried a sick-ass briefcase. This motherfucker lived in a penthouse above Marina Del Rey, the kind of place that would get any pussy wet within thirty seconds because he had such good taste.

I was looking out the floor-to-ceiling windows at the skyline, soaking in the view, and Trey said, "This could all be yours."

And I thought, *Yes...yes, this is what I want. This will make me happy.*

Trey was the complete Obama package, a playboy. Educated and slick, but he was also a chameleon. I learned this much when I started going to the appointments with him. If the business owner was black, he spoke black. If they were white, he spoke white. Asian, he spoke Asian.

In sales terms, this is called "mirroring the customer."

"If they feel like they're talking to someone like themselves," Trey said, "they're more likely to pay attention."

Trey was using the same script I was, the big difference being that it sounded natural coming from him. It was like he was having a conversation that just so happened to be written. He threw in the occasional filler about going to Dodger games and vacations and stuff like that, but Trey always drew it back to that binder I couldn't memorize.

He set the bar for what I had to become.

◆ ◆ ◆

Within three months I was on pace to make 140K a year.

The shift over to SAE wasn't as bad as I thought it would be. I was so obsessed with memorizing the binder. Then I realized I could rewrite it, make it my own. So I chopped up the script, redrew the flow charts, and made the information user-friendly. It wasn't a script for any SAE. It was mine, and only I could use it the right way.

Personalization was the key to my success, and just as Trey had shown me, I became the chameleon. I learned to mirror whoever was across the table, and I even began wearing glasses to look more intelligent.

During the meetings with these business owners, I'd say things like, "I've never seen a company thrive so much in this economy. You should be proud of that."

Which set up for the line I'd later say: "God, I can't believe they're ripping you off like this," as I went over their bank statements.

Setup. Spike.

First I told them how well they were doing, then I brought it to their attention that they were getting fucked on fees and they didn't have to take that. I made it seem like I was the best option they had, but it was never really about what I said or the numbers I showed them. It was the show. The performance. These little business owners that ran mom-and-pop grocery stores or stripmall people—all they wanted was to sit at the grown-ups' table with a JPMorgan associate. They wanted to feel like they were taking the next step toward the American dream. For them, it wasn't just about starting a business, but having something they could pass along to future generations. They had an ego, and much of my sales tactics were playing off of that.

When I talked to someone, it wasn't so much a conversation as it was me breaking them down into their base parts: their motivations, their loyalty, their willpower.

I learned a lot about my capabilities by conning other people out of money. Capabilities that would soon come in handy for something bigger.

◆ ◆ ◆

My marriage was on the rocks.

There was no connection. The job had all but killed the relationship, and it had gotten to the point where the only contact I had with her was my nightly phone call to check in. I'd ask how she was, if everything was okay, and then hang up before going out to the clubs or a restaurant or whatever I was doing that night.

I was good at my job, but good in my own way.

When NPMG sent out their next batch of trainees to shadow someone in the field, I never got any of them because I was off-script. I was the pitcher throwing sidearm when everyone else was doing it overhand. Basically, the higher-ups knew I was getting the job done, but they didn't approve of the way I was doing it. Corporations don't typically embrace trailblazers.

That's when I got the call.

Lance Moore got hold of me on my cell to explain that NPMG was going to be doing some restructuring.

"What we're going to do is bring you back to Scottsdale to run the floor at NPMG," he said.

"What about Sean? I thought he was running it."

"We're going to send him back out to the field. You're replacing him."

"When's this happening?" I asked.

"Immediately. You're going to spend the next week learning his job and then we're shipping him off to Orange County," Lance said. "Based on how well you did on the phones, we thought this would be the best arrangement for the business."

This arrangement that Lance spoke of would ruin everything.

◆ ◆ ◆

Sean was pissed. Not at me so much, but he was disgruntled with the situation. He had been running the floor at NPMG for about three or four years, and now he was getting sent back out into the field. That meant having to leave his wife and kids, his home. Sean was going to have to uproot himself and live out of a suitcase like I had been doing.

For a week I learned Sean's job, but he gave me fragmented information. He went back to being a slimeball motherfucker, setting me up to fail by giving me a half-assed orientation to the job. In his mind, if I failed at doing this, the company would have no choice but to switch us back: me out in the field and Sean back on the floor.

He thought he had the company turned out.

Now he was going to take their shot away.

In my first week on the job, every meeting set is fucking wood. We were getting complaints about how the SAE didn't show up or that the business owner wasn't even interested in getting pitched. So I had to repair everything, fixing all the stuff that Sean had broke. Damage control. Back when Sean was in charge of the floor, he just ran around being racist and crude and trying to fuck girls in the office. I was hovering over the phone reps, listening for any sign of interest. If there was even a chance that they were on the way to setting an appointment, I'd take over the call and play the management card.

"You have to take this meeting," I'd say. "You're currently losing thousands of dollars, and you won't get another call like this for ten years. Five minutes with one of our SAEs is going to save you thousands."

Meanwhile, Sean was back out in the field, and he was closing everything. Literally everything. There wasn't one meeting that guy went to that he didn't close, even the small ones with a tiny commission. Even the ones where he initially got a "no" on, Sean would wait outside the business and close them on the second attempt. He was closing, but all the other SAEs were slacking. There was a mutiny underway, and Sean was the root of it, I had learned.

The phone reps were tanking on purpose.

Sean had convinced the SAEs to tank the meetings.

He had poisoned everything under the pretense of cutting me out.

And the higher-ups were calling me, yelling, "You motherfucker, you're costing us millions of dollars! You want to keep this fucking job or what?!"

Then Sean would follow up with a call of his own, saying, "I told you this kid can't do it. You want the company to fold? You want the investors to ask for their money back? Bring me back and put Hooman out in the field again."

My salary was based on performance, and my performance was shit. The bosses didn't care if Sean did or didn't influence the numbers. They only looked at the bottom line: the appointments being set were at record lows, and for the ones that did get set, they were total wood. Both quality and quantity were low.

I stopped being money-hungry and became more concerned with

the ever-increasing reality that I was going to get fired. It was a problem without a solution. I was depressed, going to Houston's most nights to have a drink by myself at the bar. No flirting with girls or polite conversation with the bartender. For hours I would sit there drinking Jack & Diets, trying to figure out the problem, to make the numbers work in my favor. Then I'd go home drunk and pass out on the couch, repeating the process the next day. And the next day.

This is when I needed the escape.

◆◆◆

Kierland Commons. A Sunday.

I was having lunch by myself at this sushi place called Ra: a Jack & Diet, California rolls (with fake crab), miso soup, and edamame. It was sunny and the patio was crowded. I was surrounded by tables of people talking about their weekend, their lives. Everyone was so happy, and there I was, eating alone and depressed about having to go back to the office the next day. I began to listen to my surroundings, the people. I eavesdropped on their stories.

At my two o'clock was a table of girls talking about Britney Spears.

At my seven o'clock was a group of guys dishing dirt on the night before.

One of the girls was saying, "Can you believe she shaved her fucking head? I can't believe it, y'know. It's crazy."

And her friend responded, "I knoooooooooow, but I still love her. Even though she's a goddamn trainwreck, I love her."

Then a guy said, "Man, I totally fucked that chick in my hot tub."

"Yeah, for $300 worth of blow I would hope that you fucked her," his friend said.

Laughter. Then, a group of women in their late thirties were talking about their tits. Specifically, breast implants. At my eleven o'clock, one of them said. "I'm thinking about going 300...maybe 450 cc's."

And her friend said, "Oh my God, you'll love them. My husband can't keep his hands off of me now."

Then, from somewhere behind me there was a table talking about douchebags that go to the clubs with holes in their jeans.

Another table was discussing some girl who might or might not have been a stripper.

All around me was gossip, and then the formula started to kick in.

I thought about all my friends that had gotten rich off the Internet. They were doing it in porn, but maybe there was another avenue I could take, I thought. Something more mainstream. Celebrities were mainstream, but it had been done to death. The last thing the world needed was more celebrity coverage. I wanted something more real. Reality TV was big at the time: *America's Next Top Model, The Real World, Joe Millionaire.* There were so many reality shows cropping up, but after the production companies were done, even those seem staged. I was drinking a Jack & Diet, listening to these people talk about clubs and breast implants and about who was hooking up with who, and the equation was starting to add up. I was putting it together: civilian reality on the Internet.

Reality Internet.

Posts

I put up a picture of some college girl doing coke in her dorm room at ASU. Another girl, a stripper actually, has sent naked pictures of herself to some guy that's not her boyfriend. In Dallas there's a doctor giving Tijuana hack jobs[47]; the "after" photos show one breast much higher than the other, nipples misaligned, incisions that will fade into deep purple scar tissue. I put up an escort girl, a shifty New York club owner, an alcoholic degenerate.

You upload. I post.

You send me a picture of some guy out in L.A. attempting to buy his status with $500 bottles of generic vodka, and then I put it up for the world to react, comment, and judge. This person, the subject, gets to see for himself if he's really as cool as he thinks he is.

You call him a douchebag, a forgy, a pretentious asshole. He's the example of how the term "VIP" doesn't mean the same thing it used to twenty years ago. At some point, VIPs went from celebrities and musicians to cubicle warriors and customer service reps. VIP used to mean that you were an actor or athlete or singer. It meant that you were rich and famous, and now we've got guys spending half their rent money trying to look the part. We live in the age where appearing important has eclipsed actually being important. Average people trying to appear exceptional. People spending $200 on designer t-shirts but can't afford $50 in groceries.

It's how the term 30K millionaire[48] was coined.

They had existed for years, but it took a Nik Richie to name them, examine them, break them down in a way that people could understand. Somewhere in your circle of friends was a guy that thought entirely too highly of himself, and rather than call him out personally, you sent him over to me.

---

47 Terminology referring to bad (usually discounted) plastic surgery.
48 A person who makes roughly $30,000 annually but spends money like they're a millionaire, typically on clothes, dinners, cars, and bottle service in an attempt to look important or rich.

That's the process: You upload. I post. The public has their say.

So you send me a picture of some *Jersey Shore* tribute with the blown-out hairdo and bad spray tan, and the world gets to react to what they see. You send me a pretend model wearing a pair of Louboutin knockoffs, and the people get to tell her what they really think. This is the wake-up call, and it's happening in every major city from coast to coast. Your night out could just as easily turn into a lifestyle review.

Guys like Anderson Cooper and Dr. Phil keep trying to differentiate between celebrity and civilian with me, but this all goes back to the original question: Does someone become a public figure when they start asking for attention or when they actually get it?

The answer is part of how *The Dirty* started.

I had seen it with my own eyes in Scottsdale: girls going out three or four nights a week, drunk out of their minds, doing coke in bathrooms, taking pills, taking anything to lose their sense of reality. These girls were going out to the clubs, shaking their shit like they were Britney Spears while dudes tried to buy their way into their pants. These guys would be posing with girls, with bottles of alcohol they really couldn't afford, taking pictures and posting them to MySpace and Facebook, and it all had the tone of: *Look at me, look at how important I am, how much money I've spent, how good I look, how much fun I'm having. Look at me wearing my sunglasses inside, my LV purse, my name-brand stuff. Look at my life. Admire it. Pay attention to me.*

All of these people, every one of them, wanted to be public figures. They wanted to be in the spotlight. The center of attention. Like so many people in the world, they wanted the good life, and they were paying hand over fist to make it appear like they were living it.

The world was changing: you could buy status now.

On the Internet, you could tell your story in pictures.

You could pick and choose the things you wanted to show the world, and so it became a competition of who could be out at the clubs the most, appearing as if they were "living the life," as they said. It became a cesspool of materialism and drugs and hooking up and photo after photo after photo of these brief brushes with glamour and luxury. It wasn't enough to simply have an experience. These people of nightlife had to archive, display, and become billboards for whatever club it was they were at. They became self-promoting socialites and local celebrities.

You send me a guy in Orlando using his daddy's credit card for bottles.

You send me a Midwestern model that sucks dick for drugs and booze.

I'm not a fact-checker or investigator. There's no contact made with the subject in order to verify if they really contracted an STD from a certain professional athlete. *The Dirty* is simply the other side of the coin.

Your Facebook photo of you holding up a bottle of Grey Goose in a club is intended for the public to think you're wealthy and important. On my site, we find out how well the façade holds up, and it usually doesn't hold up well.

The media and talk show hosts are always asking me why I'm the guy: *What gives Nik Richie the right to put these people up? What makes him qualified to judge?*

Perhaps I'm not qualified, but I've been to these places. Have seen the people. I've witnessed the worst and understand it more than most. These TV personalities like Dr. Phil and Anderson could never hope to understand girls like Leper and Alien. They can't comprehend a person that trades their body off for drugs. They're sheltered and out of touch and lack the point of view that a Nik Richie has. They understand celebrity, but they haven't witnessed the celebrity-minded, the fame-chasers, all those people trying to appear more than what they actually are.

Maybe it's a sign that we're in the middle of a vanity epidemic, but as I've said before, if there was no market for this *The Dirty* would be dead. There would be no site and no Nik Richie.

Without you there is no me.

31

I'm in Vegas again.

We're inside the Hard Rock at a club called Vanity, and it's really no different than the hundreds of other times I've done this: girls dancing or doing blow in bathrooms, girls approaching me to get their photo taken so they can post it online, either directly from their phones or days later once they've had a chance to Photoshop themselves thin and tan and whatever else they can't afford to pay a cosmetic surgeon to do. These

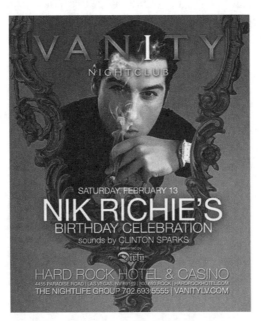

Nik Richie birthday event at Vanity Nightclub, Las Vegas, Nevada.
The never-ending drug-fueled night climaxing into a cocaine carousel.

Pepsi-heads[49] and bottle rats[50] come by in steady waves all wanting a photograph, a drink, or my suite number so we can hook up later for an after-party or "some fun," as they say. Most of the time that means sex, but occasionally (especially in Vegas and L.A.) that means doing a bunch of powder or pills, or at the very least, smoking some weed. Despite what everyone thinks, I've never been into drugs and have lately been saying "I'm too old for that shit" when they're offered, and they're offered nearly every time I'm out.

It's my birthday celebration—my 31st, actually, and Clinton Sparks is spinning some kind of hip-hop/Top 40 shit from the DJ booth as I fire off another text to this USC girl I met in the lobby earlier by the Peacock Lounge. Megan, a junior I think, she's skinny and blonde with +2's. I tried to get her to come out, playing "the birthday card," but she and these two girls from Arizona State had already made plans to go to XS, so I took her number and mentioned that I'd be doing some kind of after-party in my room later that night since I got comped the Orange Suite[51] inside The Palms.

I'm texting this chick between drinks and all the short conversations that end with a photo or someone saying "Happy birthday," asking Megan things like "how is XS?" and other bullshit to keep her on the hook. Jason Giambi (baseball player, club owner) keeps stopping by with shots of Patrón, so I'm doing those on top of Grey Goose and water, texting the USC chick that I might swing by XS even though that's a blatant lie. The reality is that all the girls at Vanity are beat except for the bottle servers, but I've already fucked them before—maybe a year ago when they didn't look so old and run-down from being out every night, drinking, doing drugs and constantly being underslept from fucking clients all night. It's made them age in reverse dog years. This city will suck the life out of you if you let it.

AC/DC's "You Shook Me All Night Long" starts to play and one of the servers (brunette, +2's) brings out a store-bought birthday cake with gold flares jammed into either side. Other servers wearing the same black corset uniform hold sparklers, cheering while a shady-looking photographer with a ponytail keeps shouting for me to look his way. Cameras flashing. Strobe lights flashing. Phones taking video. I pour Cristal on the cake, thinking that it will make it taste better, but that's still a total mystery since I never actually eat any of it.

---

49 Girls that do lots of cocaine.
50 Girls that attend clubs and mooch liquor off of people getting bottle service.
51 "Orange Suite" was how it was informally referred to due to the fact that most of the furniture was orange.

Megan and I keep texting, and eventually it gets to a point where we're supposed to meet up but because it's Vegas I'm assuming it's bullshit and not happening. They're probably already hanging out with a bunch of rich dudes at XS who are paying for all of their shit in junk bond money or whatever, and I can't really blame them. Girls like that typically have their Saturday planned a couple days before their flight even takes off. Regardless, I tell her to meet up with me later on at my suite, which is inside the Fantasy Tower and requires a special key for the elevator. I'm still not completely sold at this point that she's actually going to show, mostly because Vegas is a place to break commitments, not make them.

I text: *It's my birthday...please don't flake because I need to have birthday sex LOL.*

Make another vodka/water as I wait for a response, checking out J.T. Vegas flirting with some girls who are actually trying to get to me. Their phones are already pulled out, ready to do that thing where we awkwardly push shoulder-to-shoulder as an arm sticks out and up. Then flash. Then they say something about drugs or hooking up later. It's just a couple of cakers[52] anyway, so I let J.T. do his thing. I'm drinking, starting to regret adding the "LOL" to the end of that last text because it's so fucking forgy[53], but Megan hits me back after less than a minute with: *Yum Yum!*

Then: *My friend really wants to fuck you so we're really coming it looks like.*

Since Megan was the best-looking one out of the three, I reply back: *Well tell your friend she needs to wait in line because you're mine tonight.*

I finish my drink, telling a couple of the guys that I'm going to head back to my room even though it's only 1:40 in the morning, which is early in Vegas time. Too early for anyone to want to leave the club with me, and that's kind of the point. The girls at Vanity are starting to hit the right amount of drunkenness to make some bad decisions, dancing sluttier and flirting harder. Sweating their makeup off. Some of them are making out with random dudes already, and I text Megan again to let her know I'm leaving and to hit me up whenever.

I sneak out of my own party, alone, Yankees hat pulled low so I don't have to do another photo, and Megan says they're leaving right now. Megan, petite and blonde, a young USC girl that has probably been legal for a few months at most, asks me: *Are there any party favors at your place??*

And I'm thinking, Fuck.

---

52 A girl that wears way too much makeup.
53 Translates to: for the gays.

I say: *I don't do that stuff. If you do it that's fine I guess. I won't judge but I don't know anyone that can get you that stuff.*

She asks me: *Well is it cool if we make a few calls and then come over?*

One of the first things you learn about Vegas is you can't trust it, and I don't know if I fucked over one of these girls in the past or if this is all some kind of setup. You can't trust random hot chicks asking you for drugs, and you especially can't trust them in Vegas, so I cool off with the responses and head back to the room: an oversized suite with a skyline view that Clooney or Brad Pitt stayed in, so says one of the help who might've been trying to stroke my ego for a bigger tip.

It's about 2:30 in the morning and the buzz from Vanity is slipping; fading over to the bed is seeming like a more viable option than Megan and the ASU girls. Their little hunt for blow could take all night, and it's completely possible that if and when they find it, the guy—the dealer—he'll size these girls up for what they are and take advantage of the situation. They're young and stupid and looking for the wrong thing, so I've already written them off as no-shows right up until I get the text saying that they're downstairs. Five of them are waiting in the lobby. All girls. No dudes. Two of them are already rolling, touching each other, touching me (jokingly, flirting), on the elevator ride up. Hands smooth down each other's arms, around the ribcage and waistline, and for about a second I think about jumping on the bandwagon. Thinking: *maybe I could dabble*, but it's short-lived and I decide to stick with alcohol even though they keep pushing for me to take something, snort something.

Back in the suite I try to play host, but entertaining five girls (even if they're moderately sober) is a fucking shit show. It's almost impossible: girls running around, maybe stealing my shit, pocketing anything that's left out on a counter or a nightstand, and there's no clear line of conversation. It's mostly drug chatter and saying whatever pops into their head at that particular moment, but the constant between the five of them is that they're all young and out of control and wanting to get obliterated. We're sitting on a semi-circle orange couch in the living room, and I had just assumed that these girls had got what they needed to get (their coke or E or whatever) and did it beforehand. Then one of them reaches into her purse—a white Louis Vuitton that an ex or current boyfriend probably paid for—and pulls out a quart-sized Ziplock bag packed with blow. Two pounds of the stuff.

She drops it on the table and I ask, "Is this fucking Colombia? Where the fuck did you get that?"

These five girls edge forward on the couch, taking out credit cards and rolling up dollar bills, winding them tight. "All you girls are doing this?" I ask.

One of them shrugs, chopping up a line for herself and saying, "Well, this lasts us about a week." She says this like they've been doing this for years, and maybe they have. If it's because coke is a social drug or they're a little weirded out that all I'm going to do is watch, I'm not sure, but they keep begging, pressuring me to join them, saying, "Try it. Just try a little," as Visa Platinum cards go *chop-chop-chop* on the table. They bow their heads, a manicured finger plugging one nostril while the other sucks white lines off the table.

Chop. Snort. Repeat.

Sometimes they'll lick a finger and dab it into the pile, rubbing it like a toothbrush across their teeth and gums. Another one says, "C'mon, just do one with us," and I play the age card again, telling her I'm too fucking old for that shit but they can do whatever the hell they want. I'm not judging. But I'm not participating either.

Chop. Snort. Repeat. I'm 31.

The girls go through half the bag in about an hour, snorting five or six lines apiece, hocking up coke-spit (the drip) from the back of their throat and swallowing. Swishing vodka around in their mouth and swallowing. Snorting *seven...eight...nine* lines—I'm waiting for one of them to overdose and die inside my suite, and they're still asking me, "Won't you try just one? Try one, and if you don't like it then you can stop."

Chop. Snort. I'm older.

Repeat. I'm 31 and I'm going to get busted with an ant farm of coke.

The jets in the balcony spa are firing up, and every girl has a pair of sunburned nostrils from the drugs, and there's a lot of casual touching and flirting—especially from the ones on E who I notice keep clenching their jaws, grinding their teeth between smiles or coke chatter. There's no conversation, just words that don't add up to anything other than them being high and unaware of their own future. Then one of them asks me, "So, what do you want for your birthday?" in this timid way I didn't even think was possible when you're on the amount of drugs that they're on.

"What do you mean?"

I play the game. I'm 31.

Chop. Snort. Repeat. They giggle, laugh the way young girls laugh, telling me, "Well, this is going to be the best night of your life."

"Girls," I smile. "There's nothing you can do that I haven't done before," and they pause for a minute. No chopping or snorting. I explain that I get this kind of suite just for coming into town, that I've had fifteen supermodels at one time (*Maxim* and *FHM* girls, vodka models, Playmates, porn girls, pay-for-play girls, any girl that's ever been paid to get their photograph taken), so this, these five twenty-somethings on daddy's credit card from USC or ASU or whatever—they're rookies. Amateurs. A bunch of coke doesn't change that. This is nothing.

"It may look like Colombia in here but I'm used to Brazil," I say, and this either makes them feel like they're competing with every other girl I've ever partied with, or triggers some kind of unadulterated freedom. Either way, when I advise Megan to tell her friends to take their clothes off and jump in the hot tub on the balcony, she says "okay" with zero resistance.

Within ten minutes we are, all of us, naked and wet, kissing each other. Me kissing them, girls kissing girls and then I go down on Megan underwater, sucking on hot chlorine and cunt. Fingernails dig into either side of my skull, her palms pushing me down and in between her legs—she screams, kissing one of her friends between breaths, and then I start to see white lights. Sucking. Carving her out with my tongue. The lights get brighter as my air runs out, and when I try to surface Megan pushes all of her weight on my head and clamps me in with her legs. I'm suffocating. I'm 31.

I tap the side of Megan's ass, but not in a sexual way because I'm a few seconds from drowning in a pool of coke-whores. She finally lets me up and I'm gasping, smiling, breathing deep and bringing my lips to hers. Then I kiss one of her friends, and even though we're all naked I'm not fucking any of them. Kissing and touching is enough. It's enough to not feel alone on a night like this, but the girls don't understand that concept. They are young and fearless and living for the moment, the one in which they're high and ready to be fucked by someone famous. They're ready to make a story, a Vegas memory, and so the game has to keep escalating into something bigger.

It's later now, closer to five or six in the morning and I'm taking a shower while Audrey or Amber sucks me off, jacking my cock, saying, "You can't go to bed. I'm high. You have to fuck me," and even though I'm not really into her, I'm hard and in a position to make whatever demands I want.

I tell her, "If you want me to fuck you, you need to get all of your friends into the bed so they can watch."

We escalate again. I'm 31.

I finish my shower, dry off and walk into the bedroom, a circular bed covered with young, wet girls. Laughing girls, high and warm and unable to say "no" to anything that pops into my head, so I hold up a finger and tell them I'll be right back. Turning, walking to the living room where a pound of coke is on the table next to curled dollars and designer clutches. My prick and balls are still a little wet from the shower so I put them in the coke, dipping, using a credit card to shovel cocaine on my prick until Greg is a ghost.

I return to the bedroom and flip a switch on the wall. The bed starts to slowly rotate and I step onto the mattress so that I'm standing with the five girls around me, saying, "You can either snort or suck. Doesn't matter to me."

They lick. Inhale. Mouths go numb. They snort. Repeat. I'm 31, spinning like a cocaine carousel. They're giggling, getting high. Acting playful. Being young and reckless: the very thing you're supposed to do in Vegas and now there's natural light entering the room. I'm fried. Exhausted because I've been drinking all night but in a casual way that leaves a person feeling sleepy, not drunk. Then one girl, God bless her fucking heart, she mentions something about taking an Ambien and we all grab one. We lie on the bed, all of us touching and waiting for the comedown. Slivers of sunlight invade further, and somehow we manage to sleep through it.

I'm 31 but I've done this before. It's just another night.

As I said, there's nothing Nik Richie hasn't done.

But it's starting to take its toll.

Jason Giambi (left), Nik Richie (center),
Richard Wilk (right) celebrating in Las Vegas, Nevada.

Colors

Jason Strauss invites me out to Tao to meet Jay-Z, but I'm too busy picking myself apart in front of the bathroom vanity in my hotel room.

You're getting fatter.

You're balding.

Nik Richie should show up and sit next to Jay-Z and party and get
photographed and look really important by association. Nik Richie should
fuck a hot blonde that was in *Playboy* or *Maxim*, a platinum blonde with
+2's, no refund gap, weighs no more than 102 pounds, and has extremely
blue eyes. Deep water blue. The kind I can drown in. The kind that makes
me forget.

Your nose is too big.

Your skin is terrible.

Nik Richie should meet up with Strauss, then go have bottle service
with Jay-Z, and the three of us will drink Cristal and maybe talk about
Beyoncé or the new album. We'll do it like gentlemen. So I need to pick
out something cool to wear in front of Jay-Z, but nothing that would make
it look like I'm trying too hard. Then I need to look Jay-Z up online so I have
some idea of what he's been up to recently before I meet him. Nik Richie
is a fan of no one, but he's aware of what's going on. I'm still in front of the
mirror though. Shaking. Seeing colors.

You're disgusting.

You're a joke, Nik.

We live in Pleasantville[54]. Everything is black-and-white, happy, and
simple. Our world lacks drama. It's when things get too real, too overwhelming, involve too many emotions—that's when the colors kick in.
Skin prickles, and spiders crawl up your arms and chest and neck. In the
bathroom vanity everything looks completely normal, but you can still feel

---

54 Refer to the 1998 comedy-drama *Pleasantville,* starring Tobey Maguire and Reese Witherspoon.

them. The spiders. Crawling. Biting. It's like you've been drugged, and then you start to ask yourself fucked-up questions and think things that are very un-Nik Richie.

What is my life becoming?

What am I doing?

I'm dating girls and fucking their best friends. I'm running around, cheating, partying, fucking, drinking too much, not sleeping enough. I affect the lives of people I'll never meet, change the way they look at themselves without guilt or consequence. I'm doing everything that normal people don't do. Now it's backfiring, and all the flaws that I routinely point out are my own. For some reason, tonight, Nik Richie decides to bag on Nik Richie. I try to outthink it, to rationalize it in a way that's logical.

This is simply a moment of self-doubt. It'll pass.

No, you're just a delusional fuck realizing the truth.

Seeing colors. Feeling spiders. Spiders crawling up my bare legs and the back of my skull. Spiders crawling under my skin, prickling like little needles. Cold. Painful. My arms and neck shake uncontrollably. My guts twist.

I take a Xanax and try to relax, looking online for either a rental car or a flight home. Not my apartment in Scottsdale. *Home* home—like, to my parents' house where things are normal and we don't talk about Nik Richie or what the papers are saying or celebrities. They probably don't even know who the fuck Jay-Z is, and that's okay. I want boring. Something real. Quiet and simple. I want my old life back, if only for a little while. Just long enough for the colors to go away and the spiders to die off. It's late though. Midnight. Nothing's flying out. I'm stuck here alone in a Vegas hotel room with myself and a bottle of Xanax. Dr. Segal told me to take these "as needed" so I take another one, then eight more. Nothing happens. After five or ten minutes, the spiders are still there chewing on my skin. Marching. Biting. I take the rest of the bottle. Twenty-three Xanax are in my system now, and it actually makes perfect sense that I would die here when you think about it. Vegas made me. It should unmake me. I'm lying down in the bed, and all of those little blue pills that did nothing before are turning on at once. The spiders die and my blood stops moving. Skin goes numb. And everything is quiet now. Quiet and peaceful, and I'm thinking how wonderful this is to go out like this. Everyone will remember me and my name. Dying has always been the best way to insert yourself into a conversation.

♦ ♦ ♦

Half an hour later. Wake up. Vomit. Vomit my stomach into the toilet. Stick my finger into my throat and retch. Vomit blood. Torrents of blood. The toilet water is a deep, dark red and there's blood all over my gag-hand and face. Chunks of stomach matter pollute the water, coat the rim of the toilet, and my body is shaking but not from cold. My body is fighting, resisting all the pills I fed it. Pushing, ridding itself of drugs and blood and liquids. I throw up blood. More blood, and I'm too fucked-up to be afraid of it. I flush and the water is still pink and holding parts of my stomach. Every limb is dead. Can't feel my chest, my face. No heartbeat or breathing. Just burning vomit. Sour bloody vomit. I should call someone. A hospital. Can't move. I pass out again. Sleep in the toilet. Sleep, and the world keeps going. It's totally unaware of me.

♦ ♦ ♦

The next day, Scooby is lecturing me. He doesn't talk down to me or yell at me. It's not a one-man intervention. He's simply asking the questions I should be asking myself.

"How is this fun anymore?"

I don't answer. I don't have an answer. What Scooby knows is that I'm in bad shape. I don't have to explain the part where I overdosed in my hotel room or woke up naked and covered in vomit. Telling him I saw "colors to the max" is enough to get the point across.

"You're going to Vegas and what—partying out of spite?"

I couldn't go to my parents. They don't support the Nik Richie thing, and I've got too much pride to admit that he's broken. My father is tradi-tional Persian, so having one of your identities blow up in your face doesn't exactly earn sympathy. I had to go to somebody that gets it.

Scooby asks, "You're so concerned about leaving a name for yourself? What name are you leaving?"

No answer. Again, he's not yelling at me or trying to make me feel bad.

These are the questions that I should be asking.

That's all.

◆◆◆

For twenty days, I'm depressed.

I stay at Scooby's place, literally on the couch all day unless it's to use the bathroom or get food. Most of the time I'll text Scooby to bring me something from Jack in the Box or Carl's Jr., and he's too nice to tell me to fuck off and get it myself. He's either coming home with greasy comfort food or booze. We eat in his living room, and sometimes he'll try to bullshit with me about sports or make small talk but I'm not feeling it. His heart is in the right place, but at this point I'm a fucking wall. I'm not acting like me. I don't feel like me—Nik Richie or otherwise. Something about that overdose in Vegas has stuck and I haven't shaken the numb feeling. I'm defective, and even though I can technically be a sad fuck on a couch and hide from the world, *The Dirty* has to appear business as usual.

For twenty days, I blog.

Submissions come in the same as they always do, asking me if I'd fuck this or that chick. They want my opinion on some stranger's social life based off of one photograph, and the photograph is them drinking or partying or making out with some girl that's not their girlfriend. It's all the stuff that I do, but I'm exempt from my own rules. I can be the double standard. I can say this chick is too fat or she needs a nose job. Nik Richie demands improvement of everyone but himself, and he's doing this from his best friend's couch after an almost-suicide. He can't answer basic questions about where his life is going and who he wants to be, but he can eat a cheeseburger in his underwear and tell people they need to change. You're the one with the problem. Not me.

For twenty days, I act like I'm fine.

Running the website helps sell it. If you can work, people assume you're perfectly healthy and happy. That's the beauty of what I do. I can work from anywhere without anyone having to see me. I can work from a couch and not shower for two or three days. As long as I say my little remark regarding some chick's hopeless modeling career or whatever, people continue to think Nik Richie is fully operational. So I blog all day. Scooby brings me food, brings me the occasional bottle. Not to get drunk, but to stay calm and keep the spiders away. Sometimes I'll put the laptop aside and stare at my phone. People call. Text. I'm trying to figure out who my friends are. Who cares or who's just saying "hey." It's a string of non-personal stuff: if I can get a table for someone at a certain club or a girl who wants to hook up or it's business-related. Everybody wants something.

Everybody has an agenda. I don't return any calls or texts, and everybody is okay with that because they just assume I'm too busy.

So for twenty days I hide in Scooby's apartment on his couch, not talking to anyone, essentially hiding from the world, but I'm doing just enough so everything appears normal. I'm on an island that only one other person can see, and he's the guy bringing me food and booze and the occasional sympathetic glance. Then, close to three weeks after I set up camp in Scooby's apartment, he brings me news. Fucking terrible news. A death sentence.

He tells me, "We have to go back to Vegas. You're hosting again."

Nik Richie hosting LAX nightclub at the Luxor in Las Vegas, Nevada with the sixteen hottest girls in America.

Vegas; Lavo

I'm in Vegas again. How many times have I been to Vegas?

Scooby says I have to be here even though I'm not feeling it. We've already been paid up front to host, and giving the money back now would look really shady. People will start asking what's wrong with Nik Richie, if he's having personal problems, and we can't have that. Also, I believe Scooby secretly thinks that if I get back out there, back in the scene, I'll get over whatever my issue is.

So we're sitting at the table at Lavo with all the usual stuff happening: bottle service, house music blaring, photos firing off, people yelling, screaming for my attention, and I've got my hood up with my hat pulled down. Ignoring it. Hiding. Not talking to anyone. I'm being paid five figures to look bored right now. Scooby tries to get me to perk up, suggesting I have a drink or talk to a girl.

"Chill, man. Try to have fun," he says. "It'll be okay."

"It's not fun. What part of this is fun?" but it's a stupid question.

Scooby can't see what I'm seeing. He didn't watch me almost die, so he won't understand what I'm about to do.

◆◆◆

We're at Lavo: myself, Scooby, and twenty–five girls from ASU.

I'm drinking. More than usual. I've never drank so much before. I'm standing on a small ottoman-type thing, drinking, college girls are chugging to keep up while the club lights cut through the dark and hip-hop music plays. I don't even like hip-hop music, but I'm above the crowd, drunk out of my mind and pretending like I do. Our bottle server approaches and I yell at her to bring me a bottle of Jack. An entire bottle. I want to bury myself. A blackout. Bring it now. And there's twenty-five girls around me, laughing, dancing, smiling. Careless. Just living in the moment–hoping that they somehow end up with me. Any one of them could be mine, but none of them love me. They don't know me. It's the story they're after: the night they partied with Nik Richie, so I give them what they want and keep drinking. Keep going because I want to show them the worst.

My fingers start to unbutton my shirt, and now my bare chest is out and soaked in liquor. Girls from ASU are rubbing their palms on me, touching and groping, and then I lose my footing and fall off the box onto the floor. Sal Wise, another Vegas promoter, is asking if I'm okay. He's yelling this over the PA as he props me back up onto the box.

Asking, "You good, man?"

I say, "Fuck you!"

"Are you okay?" he tries again.

"Sal, I know what the fuck I'm doing–I fucking run this place," I yell. "Watch this," and then I grab the nearest ASU girl in my vicinity–not caring what she looks like or her name or if she's even into me. I grab one and shove my tongue into her mouth, squeezing her with liquor-soaked hands until I've gotten the point across. Order another bottle. Grey Goose. I pound it like it's water. Then I order a bottle of Patrón, screaming at the help that it better have fifty flares attached to it, and the servers are looking at me like I'm not okay. After seeing me do this for two years, they can sense something's not right. It's not going well anymore. They start to see the cracks, the damage, but they bring me the bottle anyway and I pound half of it. Scooby finally asks me if I'm okay, and maybe I'm mad at him for showing his concern too late or I'm just *that* drunk, but I plant my hand on his face and push him. Maybe I'm hoping he punches me–hits me so god-damn hard that I go unconscious, but he doesn't. He gives me my space, backing away as I try to give the bottle of Patrón to an ASU girl. She makes a face and refuses to drink it. I call her a cunt, take the bottle back and drink it myself. A different girl, a blonde, comes over to kiss me, and I'm too drunk to say no so I do it. My tongue slides over hers, and we're grabbing each other under the club lights and music, and she's clawing my chest and probably saying something about wanting to get fucked, but then I fall over again. My skull claps against the ground, but there's too much liquor in my body for me to realize I have a slight concussion. It doesn't even hurt. Arms are hooking under my armpits, lifting my body off the ground so I can get back onto the box. People are asking, "You all right?" and I'm like, "I'm good, I'm good, I'm good. It's her fuckin' fault. Get her out," and all these ASU girls are looking at me like I'm some kind of rock star.

A god. Not someone who's obviously falling apart right in front of them. So I take more liquor. I put so much fucking liquor into my little 140-pound body that I'm sweating it. Can't focus. Or think. I'm incoherent as I fall off the box again, but this time there's a glass table behind me. A corner pens its signature from my lower back down to one of my calf muscles, cutting through my jeans and underwear. Blood is seeping out of my leg and I have a concussion, but I'm back on the ottoman again, drinking, yelling at these ASU girls who are going to grow up and have careers. No one is taking me out. We're going hard, I tell them, and then I shake the bottle of champagne and spray it on the crowd.

That's the last thing I remember.

◆◆◆

I wake up in a hotel room, a bed—which I'm assuming is my bed, and everything hurts so bad I could vomit. Liquor clings to the inside of my mouth. My skin. I stink like vodka and tequila and the smallest traces of girl, although I'm waking up alone. Can't remember the last time I woke up with just me. And there's blood. So much blood. My leg has been bleeding all night—enough to soak through the bedding into the mattress. Everything's fuzzy and unclear, and I think I might have tried to kill myself with alcohol. The back of my leg needs stitches and my skull feels bruised. It's the first time I consider that I might have a legitimate problem with alcohol. I need help.

◆◆◆

Five hours later, Scooby comes by my room.

He asks, "Dude, are you okay? You were fucking crazy last night."

I tell him, "I honestly don't remember."

I just tried killing myself with pills, and then I tried it again last night with alcohol. Scooby still can't see the problem. I'm too proud to tell him, so he's going to keep pushing. He tells me it's time to go again. Flip the switch. Be Nik Richie again.

"Let's get you a Gatorade…get you back on the horse," he's saying. "You gotta host Tao, man. You've got to host the beach."

He's saying this, looking at me in a bed covered in my own blood, and it's obvious this is the last thing I want to do. So he keeps pushing me.

"You can't pull a no-show, man," he says. "You can't. Nik Richie has never *not* shown up to an event."

I break. Openly.

"I can't do it. I can't," I tell him. "I need to get on a flight home. I need to go home. I need to go to rehab."

He keeps pushing.

He gets closer, saying, "One more time. You can do it one more time."

◆◆◆

I'm wearing board shorts, flip–flops, sunglasses, a fedora, and a white Venetian robe that I stole from the hotel room. My head hurts. I'm still drunk. The gash on my leg has a soft scab but still bleeding, and Sal Wise is telling me about last night, some bullshit about how he's seen a lot of celebrities come through Vegas and he's never seen someone get as crazy as I did. He's saying this, but he doesn't sound impressed. He's worried, so this is Sal's indirect way of asking me if I'm truly okay.

Maybe I'm an alcoholic.

Maybe this isn't that cool.

I'm in a cabana at Tao Beach with Scooby and those twenty-five girls from ASU, drinking the hangover away, and some of them are coming up to me in their swimsuits, telling me I'm such a great kisser and whatnot. Some overweight, not-very-attractive chick is saying I kissed her, made out with her. Denial kicks in and I snap at her, saying, "I didn't fucking kiss you. Get the fuck out of my face."

Tao Beach is doing some kind of bullshit where they're going to baptize me in the pool to "wash away my sins," as they put it. I don't find it particularly clever, but Scooby says that I'm contractually obligated to play along and get my picture taken. He keeps pushing, but unlike last night, I don't try to kill myself with alcohol again. I turn on the Nik Richie persona for the next ten minutes, walking into the Tao Beach pool. A bolt of white-hot pain shoots up my leg from the chlorine licking the gash, but I force a smile, wading out toward the middle of the water where Reverend Marklin is waiting to dunk me. To save me.

◆◆◆

I do the baptism.

Take the pictures.

I tell Scooby I'm leaving, that I'm going to check into Promises or something. He gives me this weird look like, *Oh...you were serious about that?*

Everyone keeps drinking. The party continues. Even when I leave, it'll keep going. I'm right in the middle of sneaking out of Tao Beach in my wet bathrobe when I get the call from Lonnie Moore. He's also in Vegas for the weekend, asking me if I'm okay and if everything's cool.

"I heard about Lavo," he says over the background noise. It sounds like he's at one of the casinos or Sports Book. Maybe a restaurant.

"Dude, Lonnie, I need help, man."

He says, "Come over and meet me at the bar. I'm down 50K at the tables—*I* need help."

Lonnie makes light of the situation, but that's more or less his way. He's the devil. That doesn't mean he's a bad person. He's a friend. We're close, and that's largely to do with the fact that we're so similar. We're both in "the scene," as they say. Lonnie still runs Geisha House in L.A. He's a good businessman. Charismatic as fuck. Gets people to do bad things, but they're the bad things that are fun. Others have said the same thing about Nik Richie, but Lonnie is on another level. He can wake up hungover with five chicks in his bed and be cavalier about it. Lonnie doesn't play by the same rules I do, and now he's wanting me to meet him at a bar in The Palazo.

He says, "Dude, you gotta meet my blonde friend."

I tell him I'm not in the mood to meet anybody. *Anybody.* If you say no to Lonnie, you might as well say it twice. "I'm going back to my room. I'm going to bed," I tell him. "I'm shutting the whole thing down. I'm never doing another event ever again in my life," and people are walking by. Staring.

Lonnie says, "That's fine, but I'm still down 50K. Be a fucking gentleman and have a drink—or don't drink. Just come by."

So I figure, *what the hell?* I'll stop by, have a quick chat, and then go back to the room and start getting my shit together. Lonnie's down 50K and my life is falling apart. Maybe we can get each other's minds off of things...shoot the shit...whatever. I ditch Tao Beach and walk over to The Palazo, which is only about a five-minute walk through the hotel. A few people give me weird looks because of the wet bathrobe.

Lonnie is posted up at the bar having a drink, something mixed. I walk over and he's sizing me up, making sure that I'm okay. Functional. Of course, Lonnie is surrounded by chicks. He always is, and normally I'd be down to talk to every one of them, but I'm set on making this quick and easy so I can get back to the room. In my head I'm making a mental list of shit I need to do: pack, book plane tickets, contact the rehab place, etc. Lonnie can tell I'm not feeling social, so he has to give me a reason to stay. It's the thing he's good at: giving people reasons to keep going.

He says, "Nik, I want to introduce you to a friend of mine."

It's the blonde he mentioned. She's small. Beautiful.

Lonnie says, "This is Shayne Lamas."

Nik Richie hosting LAX nightclub at the Luxor in Las Vegas, Nevada with staff and random groupies.

Shayne

Shayne Lamas is about to save my life.

Neither of us know that yet. In fact, by the look on her face, this little sneer she's giving me (probably due to the wet bathrobe), I can tell she's not into it. Into me.

Lonnie bolts, saying that he's going to use the bathroom real quick, but that's total bullshit. He knows I'm in a bad way. Something's off, and he's thinking Shayne will get me back on point. She'll bring out the classic Nik Richie and everything will be okay again. I'll stop talking about shutting it all down and rehab and changing my ways, and for a second it almost works. Old instincts kick in and I almost start to flirt, to turn on the old charm, but then I remember two almost-suicides and pull back. Shayne's beautiful, but she's not what I need right now. I need to go home. I need help. Not another distraction.

"Your fingernails are painted black," she says. Out of all the things she could point out, she notices that. "So…what? Are you a DJ or something?"

"No, I run *The Dirty.*"

She sips her drink, shrugs cluelessly. "What's that?"

"I'm a blogger…Nik Richie," I tell her, pausing to see if the name rings a bell, but none of this is registering and it's pissing me off a little. I ask, "How do you know Lonnie?"

"How *everybody* knows him," she rolls her eyes. "Through Geisha House."

"Well, I've never heard of you."

"I'm Shayne Lamas—I'm on a show called *Leave It to Lamas*[55]," and she says this much in the same way I did when I rattled off my credentials: like I should know this already. "My father is Lorenzo Lamas," she tacks on.

---

55 Aired in 2009 for one season on the E! network. The show documents the lives of Lorenzo Lamas, his ex-wife Michele Smith, their two children, Shayne and AJ Lamas, and Michele's daughter with ex-husband Craig Pike, Dakota.

"Okay, name-dropper…relax for a second."

"I'm totally relaxed, buddy," she says half-mockingly. "So what are you doing here? In Vegas," she flutters her empty hand in the air. It's like she doesn't really care what my answer is but she'll talk to me just until Lonnie gets back, so I get a little smug.

"Well, I'm actually hosting Tao this weekend," but I say this flatly—not like I'm bragging or anything. Shayne takes a sip of her drink, thinking about what I've just said to her.

"So…you're a blogger, and you're out here in Vegas…hosting events?" she recaps. Her face sours a little, and she says, "I don't know. Sounds like kind of a loser thing to be doing if you ask me."

She calls me a loser. Not teasing or poking fun. She genuinely means it. For the first time in two years, someone is calling me a loser to my face and treating me like I'm just some random dude. Then, to top things off, Shayne loses control of her drink and spills it on me. Jack and Diet soak into the Venetian robe and Shayne blushes, apologizing profusely, so I take advantage of the situation and offer to buy her another drink.

Like a goddamn gentleman, I say, "Let me get you another one."

"But *I* spilled it on *you*. I don't need your money."

"Look, it's not about money. I was trying to be nice is all."

I'm thinking, *What a fucking bitch!*

And Shayne, it's obvious something along the lines of *This guy's an arrogant prick* is going through her head.

It's the worst ten minutes of conversation I've ever had with someone in a very long time. We have no connection, no chemistry. In fact, the whole first impression is a bust—a pissing match of who's more famous, who has more notoriety. You'd never look at the two of us and think we'd be married in the next 24 hours.

◆ ◆ ◆

I'm walking Shayne over to a cheerleading competition that's going on inside the hotel, limping a little bit because the gash on my leg is still on fire. Bum leg or not, there's no way I'm letting this girl call me a loser and walk away scot-free. Nobody does that. *Nobody.* Certainly not some chick who thinks she can name-drop me into submission, so in a way, Lonnie's plan worked. He got my mind off things. *Shayne* got my mind off things, I should say, and that puts me in a hard situation: making the choice between going home and getting better…or chasing. Chasing this girl.

"My sister—she's thirteen," Shayne says, "and we're all here to see her cheer but my stepmom was annoying the hell out of me, so I left."

"What was she doing?"

"Drinking," she says, giving me a look to see if I'm passing any sort of judgment. I don't bother mentioning that I almost got alcohol poisoning last night or how I got the gash on my leg. Shayne says she's thinking about going back to L.A. in a tired voice. We walk through the hotel, but now I'm not thinking about how to one-up her or anything like that.

I'm trying to figure out how to get her to stay.

◆◆◆

Back in my hotel room, I'm putting the plan into action: book a flight, pack up, and check into rehab. I've texted Scooby to let him know I'm taking off, and am currently looking into Promises to see what their guidelines are on Internet usage. Ultimately, that will determine whether or not the site goes on hiatus or if I continue to run things from the clinic. Of course, posting about drunks and cokeheads might be frowned upon. There's also the issue of what kind of program I actually need. Intensive Outpatient Treatment doesn't require any sort of check-in, but since I'm surrounded by all the wrong people, the kind of people who expect me to lead the party, perhaps that kind of freedom would be a bad thing.

It's all a bit disconcerting but I have to do this. I almost died twice. If I keep this up, if I continue to play this Nik Richie role of partying and fucking and doing whatever I want, it'll go too far and my luck will run out. Next time my friends throw me into bed after a wild bender, I might not wake up.

I'm in the middle of my whole research process when I get a text from a random number: What time is dinner?

Actually, maybe it's not that random at all.

A couple of hours ago I met Shayne's stepmom, Shauna Sand[56], and her sister, Victoria. We were introduced. Both of them kind of gave me the *who's this guy* look because I was wearing a stained bathrobe and (unbeknownst to me) a backwards fedora. They were standoffish, and Shauna, as Shayne has mentioned earlier, was drunk and acting a bit belligerent. Slurring. Off-balance. Occasionally, Shayne would have this look on her face like she couldn't have been more embarrassed. I felt bad for her, but it wasn't my place to say anything so I kept quiet.

We left the competition together shortly after, and Shayne asked what

---

56 Playmate of the Month, May 1996.

I was doing in an offhanded sort of way. She was making conversation, not trying to see more of me or anything like that.

I told her, "I'm doing that celebrity appearance at Tao tonight. You should come out," tacking this on like an afterthought. Not how I meant it. Honestly, I really wanted her to go.

"I don't think I'm doing anything," she said. "I might go home."

"No, come out," I press a little bit harder, but still keeping it casual. "How about you come out, you can be my dinner date, and then you can check out Tao with me? It'll be fun."

Shayne wasn't into it, though, so in a last-ditch effort, I gave her my number and said that if she changes her mind, to shoot me a text. In no way did I actually expect her to do it.

So her getting hold of me to find out what time dinner is—it's not so much random as it is completely unexpected. I'm a little confused because it's clear that Shayne doesn't like me, but here she is texting me, wanting to know what time she should be ready for dinner. Then another text comes in that reads: *My step-mom and I aren't getting along…really don't want to be around her right now.*

Out of all the people in Vegas, this girl, this apparent celebrity, contacts the guy she's known for a total of a few bad hours. Right in the middle of a personal crisis, Shayne is fucking with my plans. My recovery. The little angel on my shoulder is telling me to leave Vegas, get well, get my life back together. The devil reminds me that this is a girl that Lonnie Moore hooked me up with, and Lonnie Moore doesn't hook you up with good girls. Lonnie gives you girls to fuck and throw away, so this Shayne Lamas chick is a red flag. She should be, but before I even know I'm doing it I reply back to her. Meet me in front of Tao at nine, I tell her.

No way is she fucking going to show, I'm thinking.

Why would she? It's been a disaster so far. Her wanting to see me again doesn't make any sense, but I want to be prepared anyway. On the off chance that's she not fucking with me, I need to have all my ducks in a row.

I text Strauss: *I got a girl that I want to bring to dinner. I LIKE HER.*

No bullshit. I fire it off in all caps and everything like I'm fifteen years old. Strauss says: *No problem.*

Immediately, I text Shayne again: *You gotta come now because we're having dinner with the owner.*

I'm being Nik Richie again: showing off, acting like a big shot, but it's different this time. I don't want to impress her for those same temporary reasons I do with other girls. I'm showing her that I've got resources, things worth sharing. I can be a provider.

Scooby and JV are hitting me up about dinner, too. Those twenty-five girls from ASU got some sort of package deal where they spend the weekend with us, so now my guys are trying to get the details on where their table is and all that. I cut them off. No replies. They can figure shit out for themselves for once. I'm going on a date. A real date. Haven't gone out with a girl like this since high school. These bottle rats and fame-chasers—I ask the ones that I like to come out to dinner with me but they never do it. They're all about the photo op and sitting in the best section at some nightclub. They avoid genuine connection, and now that I have a chance at one with Shayne, I'm protecting it.

I don't want her to see that part of my life yet.

For the first time in years, I don't want to be Nik Richie.

◆ ◆ ◆

Outside of Tao, around nine, I'm waiting for Shayne to meet me when Scooby comes up asking me what's going on.

"You need to leave me alone right now," I say. It's about the nicest way I can snub him. Then I see Shayne approaching—totally fucking gorgeous: Gucci scarf and top, YSL shoes, a model, a perfect ten. Every guy in the lobby is craning their neck to check her out, but she's looking straight ahead. At me. Only me. Scooby can tell we're zeroing in on each other, trying to figure out what the fuck is going on here, but he can't know yet. It's important that I keep Shayne as far away from certain parts of my world until the time is right.

We meet in the middle.

I say, "Thank you so much for coming. I honestly didn't think you were going to show."

She smiles, reassures me, "Of course I came. Why wouldn't I?"

"Well, we didn't exactly have the best conversation."

"Oh, don't worry about that. The past is the past."

And in a moment when I'm trying to fix myself, my life, those words click:

The past is the past.

The past is the past.

The past is the past.

I take her hand, folding it into mine, and we walk as a couple into the restaurant.

◆ ◆ ◆

It's Strauss, his date, myself and Shayne, and we're sitting at "the owner's table" which is located in the corner of the restaurant. Private. Away from the crowds.

Strauss leans in slightly, toward Shayne, and says, "You look really familiar. Are you Shayne Lamas?"

"Yes," she says, and then Shayne gives me this look like, *See? People know me.*

I let her have the win. I'm happy. I'm on a date with a bombshell, having dinner with the owner of the restaurant. Finally, I get to do little things like pulling out a chair and making sure a person is comfortable, not getting wasted. We're talking like adults, not yelling over some DJ's house set. It's civilized. Grown-up. It's the thing Nik Richie has been missing out on.

Then I see JV walking toward our table: skater shoes, ball cap, probably stoned out of his mind. It's embarrassing on more than a few levels.

"Hey boss, where are we sitting?" he asks.

"I have no idea, JV," and then I shoot him this look that I'm hoping, praying he's got enough sense to interpret: *go...get the fuck away...don't talk to me—don't even look at me.*

He turns and goes back the way he came.

"Who was that?" Shayne asks.

"Oh, he works for me. He's a good kid."

What I don't say is that JV is a friend of mine, that he's one of the few people that I trust, but I can always revisit that later. As far as I'm concerned, it's probably best that Shayne knows as little about what I do and whom I associate myself with for the time being. I'm being selfish with this moment, and Scooby and JV are just going to have to deal with that.

Shayne excuses herself to use the restroom, and as soon as she's out of earshot is when I ask Strauss, "Okay man, who is she?"

"She's a celebrity, man," he says. "Seriously, how do you *not* know who you're dating?"

"What has she done?"

"*The Bachelor*[57]...she won it."

"Must have missed it." Adding, "She doesn't really know much about me either."

Strauss smirks, "And I get the feeling you're okay with that for some reason." He motions to what's going on across the restaurant: JV,

---

57 Season 12: *London Calling.*

Scooby, and twenty-five ASU girls being seated at a long banquet table. Scooby and I make eye contact, but I turn quickly turn away from him and my old life.

◆ ◆ ◆

Dinner was nothing short of wonderful, although a bit stressful as I essentially had to hide the fact that I was supposed to be at that table of twenty-five college girls. I'm also noticing that as Shayne and I spend more time together, the personal questions regarding who I am and what I do are on a steep incline. We're past the point of trying to outdo the other person. Shayne wants to know me. She wants to get acquainted, but I'm resistant for fear that she might not like what I tell her.

So when Shayne asks me, "What's *The Dirty*?" I say, "It's just a website." No frills. Short and to the point.

For the first time, I'm downplaying the thing I was once so proud to be associated with. I'm afraid that unlike every other girl, Shayne might be turned off to the whole idea of it.

She says, "Well, I'll have to check it out."

I say, "Nah, it's no big deal. Really."

For the entire night, I run from Nik Richie for the sake of Shayne. I ditch JV and Scooby and all those girls, running off to Tao. Just Shayne and myself. At the club, I get a different table from the one I was scheduled to be at. Something private. I introduce Shayne to the management and a few other people. Affluent people like Brandon Rocque and Mathew Glazier. She doesn't know the connection, only that they're all happy to see me and they're important, apparently. DJ Vice is spinning, and I leave Shayne briefly under the premise that I'm just saying a quick hello. Vice shakes my hand, and I tell him I really need his help tonight.

"I'm with Shayne Lamas tonight," I say, and Vice nods like he knows the name. "I need you to shout her out like a hundred times tonight."

Vice smiles, nods, says, "No prob, man. I got ya."

Rush back over to Shayne who's having a drink, smoking a Marlboro Light. Normally, I hate smokers, but I'm okay with her doing it for some reason. DJ Vice gives Shayne a shout-out and her ears perk up.

"Was that my name he said?"

"Hmm, maybe," I smirk, playing cool.

We drink, hips touching in our little private booth, and I'm sort of glad it's loud in here because we have to get mouth-to-ear in order to talk. It's those little things like feeling her breath in my ear or her smell that get me, the way she smiles. DJ Vice gives Shayne another shout-out, and this time she knows she just heard her own name.

"Nik! Are you doing that?" she laughs.

"Hey, you're famous. I can't help it if you're getting recognized."

We sit there in the club, drinking casually and talking in what looks like whispers to the crowd. It's a date. We're a couple. Tonight, Nik Richie is here for one woman, not the twenty-five ASU girls across the club. Not the bottle rats or the fame-chasers. From time to time, I'll get a text from Scooby or JV as to whether or not I'm going to come over and hang out, but I don't even bother answering. They can have it all: the girls, the booze, and the special treatment. I don't care anymore. DJ Vice gives Shayne another shout-out, maybe the thirteenth or fourteenth of the night, and she's blushing hard enough to see in the almost-dark. She leans in, and I think it's to say something in my ear but then she kisses me. A little one.

I say, "That's not a kiss."

She smiles and comes back at me, harder this time, lips sliding over mine. A real kiss. A meaningful one. I can feel it throughout my entire body, in my heart, like I'm a kid that's doing it for the first time.

"We should get married," she says, smiling like it's a joke but not completely. She laughs, takes a sip of her drink and curls into me.

I say, "I know. We're kind of perfect for each other," but she has no idea how much I'm downplaying it.

In reality, I'm thinking, *I'm done, I'm yours, I want to have babies…get me the fuck off this* Dirty *train.*

"There's something I don't get," Shayne says. "You're hosting, but you don't have any friends here…I mean, is this really your table?"

I feel like I can be open with her now.

I say, "I'll be honest with you—that table with the twenty-five chicks," and I point so I know Shayne's looking at the same spectacle I am. "That one's mine."

"*That one?*" she points too.

"Yeah, don't judge me."

It's our little moment of truth, but instead of getting all weirded out or turned off to the idea that I'm some kind of player, she smiles. Shayne kisses me again, because what she sees is that I could be over there with the girls, all those young stupid girls, and yet, I choose to be here with her. I want Shayne, and I'd give it all up to be with her.

◆◆◆

We tried to get married last night.

One of the big misconceptions about Vegas is that people think it's so easy to get married, as if you can just drive through some chapel and it's a done deal. It's not. We found that out the hard way. We tried, but everything was closed down for the night and getting married is a process with documents and paperwork. It's not like the movies where you can make a snap decision and it's over before you know it.

Regardless, I wake up feeling good—better than I've ever felt.

Shayne is in my arms, curling hard into me like we're on our honeymoon. We're in bed. Nude. Warm and comfortable. We made love last night. I took my time with her because I never wanted it to end, still don't want it to end. Even now. I'd love to just lie here with her body pressed into me, breathing, kissing. Last night I told Lonnie I'd see him before he went back to L.A.

In the bathroom vanity, I'm looking at myself smiling, smiling like a goddamn happy idiot who's doing the wrong thing that feels right. I'm thinking, *You're doing it again...you're chasing...you're gonna chase this girl and she's going to hurt you.*

Brush my teeth. Clean up a little.

I go back out to Shayne who's laying in bed, wrapped in blankets, and I say, "I've got to see Lonnie before he goes, so I have to leave soon, but...I'd *really* like to hang out in L.A."

I stress that last part. I'm so used to fucking girls and throwing them away that it's important Shayne knows that I want to see her again, that this wasn't a one-night thing for me.

"I would love to, Nik," she smiles at me from the bed.

I'm not ready to say good-bye.

She was almost my wife.

◆◆◆

At Rehab, Lonnie name-drops me and we get all of our drinks comped.
He's trying to chase down some *American Idol* girl, and I'm trying to talk to him about Shayne.

I say, "Lonnie, I like this girl."

He says, "Forget about it, dude. It's not going to happen."

"We had a great time together last night."

"Did you fuck her?" he asks.

"No, nothing happened," I lie. I don't know why I lie. I've never done that to Lonnie before, but I don't want to cheapen what Shayne and I did.

"That chick is impossible, man. Forget her. Move on."

"Why? Why should I move on?" I ask.

"Because every one of my friends that has tried to hook up with that chick has never been able to do it, so forget it. Enjoy your weekend."

"Lonnie, we tried to get married last night."

"You're lying. Why do you lie? Just relax, Nik."

We're in a cabana. Scooby is there along with all these girls. Hot girls. They're drinking, flirting. I've seen it before. I'm bored by it. Scooby asks what the hell happened last night, and I give him the short version. I like Shayne. I tried to marry her.

"Well, thank God that didn't happen!" he says.

I'm having to come to terms with my friends and inner circle not understanding this. They don't get it, and maybe there's a good reason for that. I've been with a lot of girls, and the few I've gotten close to have fucked things up. Last night with Shayne was real though. She and I know that. If it wasn't, I wouldn't miss her as much as I do right now. I wouldn't be so happy. It's got nothing to do with the girls or the attention or the booze—it's none of that. It's Shayne. Only Shayne.

I'm sitting in the cabana with Scooby and these girls, thinking about Shayne and when I can make it out to L.A. My iPhone buzzes, and the text reads: *Still want to get married?*

Shayne says: *I've researched it. I know what we have to do.*

I say: *Yes.*

◆ ◆ ◆

It moves fast.

We get married at The Little White Wedding Chapel. Shayne wears a loose-fitting cream top, a tissue-white veil. I'm in a black T-shirt. Jeans. There's maybe eight or nine people attending. Lonnie is MIA because he's passed out somewhere, I'd find out later. Scooby is our "flower girl." People are pointing Flip cameras and taking photos with their cell phones. It's the first time I actually want people documenting me. Us. Shayne and I, we're happy, embracing. She says, "I'm a bride today," to the cameras, smiling. Glowing. We say our vows. Sign the papers. It's a done deal. We're married. The group of us go out to Lavo to celebrate.

Meanwhile, the sharks are moving in.
Now that I have Shayne, I have something to lose.

Media

CBS gives us 48 hours.

Most of the other news outlets are making snide little comments about how we got married at the same place Britney Spears did the first time, the same one that was over 55 hours later. Everybody is placing bets on this thing like we're a fucking craps table.

Two days. One week. Not even a month.

In the articles reporting the marriage, there's usually a couple of pictures to coincide with the text. Just in case you have no idea who Shayne Lamas or Nik Richie is—sort of like how we weren't aware of each other. The press usually snags a pic of Shayne from her *Bachelor* days, or some modeling shoot she did. Full hair and makeup with the occasional Photoshop touch-up.

As for me, the villain, the "Internet scumbag," the media has taken the liberty of posting my DUI photo all over again. That grainy little piece of shit is cropping up everywhere, and the comment boards are eating it up.

"You mean she married him? *Is she on stupid pills?"*

So there's the issue of how we "don't go together" along with the ever-growing speculation that the whole thing's a sham. "A hoax," they call it. One attention whore deserves another. That sort of thing. Even my friends are asking me if this is some kind of publicity stunt. Texts are rolling in from people I haven't talked to in months, pretty much asking the same thing in one way or another: if this is for real?

I might as well send out a mass text:

Yes, I'm really married.

No, it's not a hoax.

I'm back in Scottsdale watching Shayne on *TMZ*. She's coming out of the LAX terminal carrying a few small bags, clutching a Blackberry and not at all surprised that there's a camera waiting for her. If she's caught off-guard, she's certainly hiding it well. Her fingers keep coming up to her forehead to brush the hair out of her eyes and the cameraman is asking her about the "wild Las Vegas weekend" she had.

"I found a husband!" Shayne says, and quite happily.

"You did!" the camera guy says, "And it's actually Nik Richie of all people."

"Of all people" is tabloid code for: *you could have done better.*

I watch my wife get on her phone while this guy tries to get the story from her. She's looking around the terminal for her ride, and this guy asks her, "Is that his real name?"

This is actually a trick question. *TMZ*'s bread and butter is catching celebrities either looking stupid, getting into trouble, or humanizing them in some way. Most of the show concentrates on the third thing, so even though Paris Hilton getting a coffee or Lindsay Lohan picking up dry cleaning may *sound* boring, for some reason people are watching it. In Shayne's case, however, this camera guy is trying to make her look stupid. The *TMZ* crew knows that certain people are going to come through LAX at certain times, so they prepare lines of questioning to see if they can get a wrong answer on film.

When the camera guy asks Shayne about my real name, he's hoping that she doesn't know it because it'll make for better TV. She knows I'm Hooman Karamian, though. It was right there on the marriage certificate. No matter what the world thinks about me, I'd never marry a woman without being up front on a few things, and that includes my name.

Then the camera guy says, "You seem like a pretty honest person, Shayne," which is just more tabloid speak for: *I'll fuck you over if you lie to me.*

He asks, "Will you tell me the honest truth? What happened? Is this like a publicity stunt?"

I'm in Scottsdale, watching my wife on TV when I should be with her. She's miles away while this jerkoff is asking her the same stupid question every other news outlet has. Shayne isn't camera-shy though. She laughs at this guy and his tired-ass question. Laughs convincingly.

"I wouldn't get married to a man for a publicity stunt[58]," she says. "I actually met Nik and I fell in love and we got married, so why not?"

"Love at first sight, actually," camera guy says. Not genuine. Sarcastic. People forget that you can still be sarcastic without sounding it out ver-

---

58 Refer to: Matt Grant.

bally, and that's why Shayne is speaking to him instead of telling the guy to fuck off.

"It was—well, we're not *in love*. We're in love with being, y'know, in like with each other…and we're doing it backwards," She says. "We're getting married *and then* we're dating."

I'm watching this play out, thinking, *Fuck, babe, why did you say that*?

"Doing it backwards" is a term Shayne came up with in Vegas. It was time to leave, and I needed to know what she wanted to do next. For my own peace of mind, there needed to be some kind of a plan. She told me to fly home, and that she was going to fly home, too. Let's be married and then be in love, she said. We were doing it backwards. Of course, saying that to a TV camera out of context is made us look like idiots.

That's how *TMZ* came about using *I'm Not "In Love' With My Hubby* for the title. Up go the ratings.

I'm watching my wife on TV, and a blue compact pulls up in the terminal to pick her up. Shayne is putting her bags in the backseat, and now the camera guy knows she's about to leave so he pulls out the big guns.

He says, "Are you kind of worried that Nik is so critical of girls? He always says that every girl is ugly."

The *TMZ* dude is referring to the site, the "Would You?" section, and all those times I bagged on girls for being too fat, too tan, too hairy, too unattractive. He's trying to bring it to Shayne's attention that her husband is too judgmental, but she has no idea what he's talking about. Shayne hasn't seen what I do yet.

I get on the phone to tell her I'm coming out to L.A.

◆◆◆

The next day I'm in Los Angeles with Shayne, driving around in her Lexus convertible while she wears big designer sunglasses and smokes in the passenger seat. We're holding hands, cruising along in no particular direction because right now just being together is the most important thing. We talked about the news reports and what people are saying about us, coming to the same conclusion that there's always going to be talk, but that doesn't mean they know anything. It's just noise. Spectacle.

"It'll die down," she says. "It always does."

Then my phone rings, and it's Harvey Levin from *TMZ*. *The* Harvey Levin. I've never spoken to the guy, but I recognize the voice from the show. So at first I'm excited because Harvey-fucking-Levin is calling me, and this is a guy that I respect and look up to. Then I remember yesterday's clip of Shayne at the airport, thinking that what *TMZ* ran and Harvey calling now might be related, and possibly not good.

Harvey says to me, "I just wanted to let you know—and this is no disrespect to you, but I'm going to say that your marriage is going to last three days." He tells me, "I wanted to give you a heads-up so you don't hate me forever."

It's a professional courtesy. There's an entire world devoted to talking about celebrities, spreading gossip, taking cheap shots. Marrying Shayne meant becoming both the gunman and the target, and I'm okay with that. It's business. She's worth it.

I say, "Harvey, thank you, man. That means a lot to me."

Shayne squeezes my leg, smiles at me. Wind blows through her hair.

"Do what you gotta do, man," I tell him.

We say good-bye and hang up. Shayne grabs my hand again and I notice something's missing. Not missing, really, but not right, and I decide that there's an easier way to get the point across about how serious I am about Shayne. Something these people will understand. We didn't have what the press calls "a real wedding," and that's part of why we're taking so much flak. We're "moving too fast." We're "doing it backwards." No one is supposed to understand it but us, however, it's important to me that Shayne knows how serious I am. Even if the world questions what we have, the last thing I want is for her to question me.

So I have a plan now.

The first thing I do is get Shayne a $135,000 wedding ring. Not in spite of the media or as a defense mechanism. She deserves it and I'm devoted. Maybe we didn't have "a real wedding" but she's damn sure going to have a real ring.

The second part is more important. Even though Shayne is fine with her "doing it backwards" plan, I'm not. I need her. I need my wife.

I ask Shayne, "Will you come back to Scottsdale with me?"

◆ ◆ ◆

We get to a point where we ignore everything.

It's us. We're in love. Shayne said "yes."

She's agreed to come to Scottsdale and live with me, so we're packing up all the stuff from her Malibu pad. You can learn a lot about a person by what kind of stuff they have. Shayne owns a lot of leopard print, I notice.

Lots of designer sunglasses and watches, a ton of makeup, but that's nothing compared to the shoes. There's hundreds of them. Hundreds. And they're not cheap either. Every pair is Louboutin or YSL or Jimmy Choo or some French designer I can't pronounce. Gucci...Chanel...LV. It's easily over a hundred grand just in shoes, but Shayne's a girly girl. She loves fashion. It makes her Hollywood legacy more real to me, now that I'm actually sorting through her belongings.

Packing gives me a lot of opportunity to think: about this new direction in life, how we're going to work as a couple, and family. I dwell on that last one for a bit.

Shayne had no family at the wedding, no friends. Obviously, she didn't want to invite Shauna Sand because they don't get along. Her father, though—he was sort of robbed of that "walk your daughter down the aisle" moment. We've been so busy getting to know each other that the topic of family hasn't come up that much. My own mother found out through the news.

She was yet another person asking, "Is this real?"

Yes, I'm really married.

No, it's not a hoax.

Shayne hasn't said anything about her parents" reaction. Come to find out it's because she never told them. They found out the way the rest of the country did.: through the news.

On *TMZ*, Shayne's father, Lorenzo, is being filmed by these guys. They're asking him what he thinks about his daughter getting married, and reacts the way any father would who was left out of the loop: he's fucking pissed. He's angry, telling the camera, "Shayne, call me!" like she just got caught sneaking out on a school night. We look stupid again. *TMZ* succeeded in that regard.

So we finish packing and I tell Shayne we need to make this right.

We need to see Lorenzo and explain things, and hopefully, I won't get the shit kicked out of me in the process.

Optima

Shayne paints her nails, sometimes six or seven times a day. Pink or turquoise or black. Whatever "feels right" at the time. I think it's more about the ritual than the actual color. She'll penguin-walk over to the shaded patio, toes separated and spread apart by foam dividers, and smoke a cigarette (usually a Marlboro Light) while she checks her Blackberry. Shayne never checks her Blackberry until 2 p.m. It's one of the few rules that she has, possibly to deter becoming a slave to e-mail and texts like so many people have. I actually admire this about her.

She enjoys fitness and fashion.

Shayne does not enjoy movies.

We've yet to make it through one where she doesn't leave the living room. Madison usually follows her. Her dog is a Westie-Bichon mix, and like most of Shayne's possessions, is very girly-looking. I don't mind Madison but am not particularly attached to her, either. Shayne will baby-talk Madison sometimes, or they'll curl up on the couch while she reads *US Weekly* and *People*. It hits me that Shayne probably knows most of the people in the magazines on one level or another, so for her it's like reading the school newspaper. She could call some of these people if she wanted to. Shayne lives in her own little bubble though, which I refer to as Shayne's World. It's a place where the concept of time and money barely exist, and she does the things that she enjoys. She shops. She goes to Starbucks. She gets dessert at a café. Sometimes she'll try on outfits just to see how they look. Or she'll cut a couple of dresses up and make a new one. Shayne spends her day doing whatever she wants. This approach to life has resulted in her being an especially calm individual. Carefree. This I also admire about her. Being Nik Richie is a stressful existence, but Shayne brings a certain level of tranquility to this place.

We live in Scottsdale, in an area called Optima.

We love each other. We say this and believe it, but we're still very much in the process of getting acquainted and Shayne's just settling into the apartment. I've never been one to own things. Nik Richie doesn't have a nesting instinct, so the apartment is minimalist: a couch is a couch and nothing more. A bed is just something to sleep in. If I buy a piece of furniture, it's for function, not fashion. I'm not trying to impress anyone with a bath mat or toilet seat cover. I don't need designer throw pillows from Pottery Barn. This place is a source of shelter, not a home. So when Shayne walked into the apartment for the first time, this look crossed her face like, *Oh, I've got some work to do.* She had a project.

So Shayne brought in her framed photographs. She brought leopard-print rugs and blankets. Jar candles. Art. Music. I've literally never bought a CD in my life, and now we had stacks of them. My dishes were "too boring." We had to get some with designs. And she brought in more photos: her smiling, modeling, us on our wedding day. Us in Vegas. Another photo of us kissing. If someone robbed us, they'd at least know who lived here now. She brought in shoes, dresses, bras and underwear with little bows on them. She brought in fragrances, the smell of girl. Bottle upon bottle of nail polish. Cosmetics. Lotions. Tampons. Even Madison has a little wardrobe of dresses and shirts.

While Shayne delivers her woman's touch to the apartment, I blog.

I blog just like I normally do, commenting on some chick's +2's and Shayne walks by and says, "That's hot." Shayne has still never been on the site. The closest she's come to it are the passing glances she steals while she puts the apartment in order. Making this place livable.

My plain couch now has pillows, blankets, and a dog on it. My perfectly functional coffee table has coasters, a candle, and a centerpiece that wasn't there before. I keep blogging, but every time I get up to go to the bathroom or get a snack in the kitchen, something's different. A girl lives here now. The medicine cabinet is now packed with facial and hair care products. My once blank refrigerator is covered in magnets and photographs. Slowly but surely, Shayne shifts this place into a home. It's culture shock, but a welcomed one. I would have done anything to get her to move in. Allowing Shayne to take over my empty apartment and do whatever she wants isn't a big deal in the grand scheme of things.

The actual marriage, on the other hand, is another issue entirely. We're fine, Shayne and I. Happy. I've never been this happy. We took that initial beating in the press, and even though that's died down, it's been replaced by more personal assaults. Girls from my past: Sarah Wood, Ashley Zarlin, even a few that I don't remember–they've all reached out.

Sarah goes fucking crazy, texting Scooby: *How the fuck could he do this? I loved him. That was supposed to be me.*

To me, she says: *Out of all the times we were in Vegas, you never once tried to marry me. Why? I want to know why.*

Ashley Zarlin talks all sorts of random trash. Her friends are all calling me every name they can think of. I kind of expected this. Wood and Zarlin are both crazy. This kind of behavior is right up their alley. It's the randoms that get me: girls that I haven't seen in forever, girls that somehow got my number that I don't remember giving it to.

The twins in Scottsdale that I fucked text me to ask why I got married and why I'm trying to upset them. What's creepy is that the texts come from one number but they refer to themselves as "we" and "us," as if I was dating both of them.

While Shayne gets the apartment in order, randoms call and leave upset messages. They text how they had been waiting for me, that they loved me the entire time. "I always wanted to be with you," they say. So many calls come in that my voicemail box fills up. Pictures of tits flood my e-mail. Vaginas pried apart by manicured fingers are SMS-messaged. Fingers knuckle-deep in soft cunt that I may or may not have had at one point. I delete them. All of them. Sometimes they come in as early (or late, depending on how you look at it) as four in the morning.

All day and night it's: "I love you"…"I need you"…pictures of tits…ass… cunt…"It's not too late for us to be together"…a masturbation video… video of tits…" You'll regret this, Nik."

Delete. Delete. Delete.

I turn my phone off so I can concentrate on the site, but the attacks are there, too. Traffic on *The Dirty* is up, but I attributed most of that to the fact that I got married so quickly. There was no warning and none of my fans saw it coming. What I didn't consider was Shayne's following: *Bachelor* fans, fans of *Leave it to Lamas*, fans of her father. All these people who have never heard of me before are asking why she'd pick an Internet scum-bag over Matt Grant. They think I'm abusive, that I'm going to hit her or hurt her somehow. These bored housewives scour the site and surmise that I'm hyper-judgmental and "not right" for her. Or they think it's a publicity stunt that Shayne and I concocted together.

A part of me wants to ask Shayne if she's getting this kind of backlash, if ex-boyfriends are reaching out to criticize her, to tell her I'm not right or it's not going to work. I wonder how many random shots of abdominal muscles and cock she's gotten on her phone, but Shayne's World is different from that of Nik Richie. She is elegant and composed. When Shayne sees something she disagrees with or doesn't care for, she discards it from her mind. She's somehow able to do this quite easily: picking and choosing the things she wishes to retain.

Shayne is able to let things go and carry on with her life, which may or may not be a by-product of her Hollywood upbringing. In a world where scrutiny is constant, Shayne has been trained in the delicate art of tuning people out. While I was flipping shit about *TMZ* and all the other news outlets bashing us, Shayne was painting her nails and telling me to relax. Chill out. It's no big deal, she said.

"I love you, Hooman," Shayne tells me. "That's literally all that matters. And I know you love me, too."

In public Shayne calls me Nik. When we're alone she calls me Hooman.

Nik Richie invented *The Dirty*. He hosts events in clubs like Marquee and Pure and LIV, usually sleeping with one or two girls a night. He gets drunk and out of control, and on a couple occasions, has almost died because of it. He is, in fact, hyper-judgmental and lacking sensitivity. Nik Richie will tell you what he doesn't like about you. He will treat you like shit if he feels like it. Nik Richie, however, is not the name on the marriage certificate. He's not the guy Shayne met in Vegas. Nik is a facet of Hooman Karamian, a small fraction of the overall persona that is showcased online. He's a blogger, not the guy that Shayne fell in love with.

That's why this works: we don't have any preconceived notions of each other based on websites or reality shows, and because of that, can be our true selves. Shayne can lounge on the couch with Madison in her pajamas. I can be the romantic that enjoys holding her hand and taking her on dates. We don't have to be "on" or "in character." We don't have to put on a show. We can be normal, and considering our individual backgrounds, normal is something we don't get to be very often.

I've been Nik Richie for so long that I forgot how good it felt to be Hooman Karamian. One of the reasons I love Shayne so much, maybe even the main one, is that she lets me remember. That is our life in Optima: two normal people living in a modest yet comfortable apartment. We go on dates. We laugh. We love.

We get to be ourselves for a change.

Meeting the Family

Oddly enough, I meet Lorenzo on Father's Day. He's out in Scottsdale directing some movie, so there's no avoiding this now that we're in the same city. My hope is that he's cooled off since the *TMZ* thing that happened a couple months ago, but from the pictures I've seen of him online, I can't count on it. He's like this all-American biker dude with the leather pants and shit, and I'm this Persian Internet guy that puts people on blast. It wouldn't surprise me if he hated my guts, not just for what I do, but for marrying his daughter behind his back.

What I learn is that Lorenzo is the most normal one of the Lamas family. He's got this very chill vibe about him, mostly just wanting to get to know the guy his daughter married. Specifically, he's trying to find out if the Nik Richie in front of him is the same Nik Richie from the site.

He asks questions like "Is this real?" and "Are you really that guy?"

No, this is not a hoax.

Yes, I'm that guy, but that's not the guy Shayne married.

There's a public Nik Richie and the husband Nik Richie. The person you are at work is not the person you are at home. Doesn't matter if you're a congressman, a plumber, or yes, even a website owner.

His fiancée doesn't see it that way, though.

"All my friends are on that site," she says, sneering.

Lorenzo was born in 1958. His fiancée is younger than Shayne. Like I said, he's the most normal one, but in the Lamas family, that doesn't mean much.

Lorenzo and I get along. He's a good guy, but he's the center of a highly dysfunctional family. I can see that already. At this point in time, I know that Lorenzo is Shayne's biological father, and I know that Lorenzo used to be married to Shauna Sand, whom I've already met in Vegas. What I don't know is why Lorenzo and Shauna split.

This is where Lorenzo's son comes in: A.J.

◆◆◆

I've spoken with A.J. a couple times.

Shortly after the news broke on the wedding, this kid called me up all pissed off, saying, "I don't fucking know you, man. You just married my sister without running it by anyone."

I thought, *Oh shit, this is like a structured family.*

He's just looking out for his sister.

A.J. said, "You know Shayne owes me money, right?" but he didn't wait for an answer. Instead, he just started demanding I send him cash.

So the first time I actually go to meet A.J., Shayne drives us up to this mansion in Beverly Hills. The place is enormous. There's a $300K Mercedes parked outside. If A.J. is living here then I don't know why he'd be so stressed over a measly half a grand.

I say to Shayne, "Your brother must be doing well for himself."

She shakes her head and says, "No, he's just crashing here," and then she starts walking toward the side of the house, toward the maid's quarters. "This place belongs to a producer or something like that," she says.

We walk through a door and down a flight of stairs. It's dark, and there's a smell that's getting stronger: cigarettes and booze and body odor. Shayne doesn't seem to be concerned that we're walking into a basement where the only source of light is a TV. A few steps in and my eyes adjust. A.J. is sitting on the couch with a bottle of Jack in his hand. There's coke all over the table in front of him, and A.J. barely acknowledges us because he's fixated on the TV, watching *The Dark Knight*.

Shayne raises her voice over the movie, saying, "A.J., this is Nik."

There's shades of Lorenzo in him, the movie star looks, but he's in bad shape. He clearly hasn't showered in days. He's got long greasy hair, and this nasty fucking beard on him like he's *Dirty* Jesus. If I didn't know any better, I'd say he's been on a three-month binge, and then it clicks that this is the reason he's been calling and asking me for money.

"A.J.," Shayne tries again. "I want you to meet my husband."

He looks my way, and I give him a little nod. A.J. sets the bottle of Jack on the table and says in this creepy voice, "Let me give you a hug," as he wraps his arms around me. He smells like shit. A.J. sits back down on the couch, picking up the remote to rewind the movie.

Shayne tries to engage A.J. in a discussion, asking him what he's been up to, but then A.J. starts repeating lines from the movie like he's auditioning.

"Let me show you a magic trick," he says in the Joker voice. He leans forward to grab the bottle, pounding it like it's fucking tap water. Meanwhile, Shayne is sweeping coke off the coffee table into a small wastebasket, beyond embarrassed. And A.J. says again, "Let…let me show you a magic trick."

"A.J., what are you doing?" Shayne asks, but it's clear to me that he's been up to the same thing for quite a while: drinking, doing coke, watching Batman.

He rewinds the movie. Hits play.

"Let me show you a magic trick," A.J. says, attempting to sync his voice up with Heath this time.

I lean over to Shayne, placing my mouth to her ear, and whisper, "He's not okay. He needs help."

She says, "No, it's fine. It's L.A. This is how it is."

A.J. is rewinding the movie again, mumbling to himself, "Great actor. You don't even know how great of an actor Heath is." He hits play again, saying in his Joker voice, "And I thought *my* jokes were bad."

"A.J." Shayne says. "A.J., seriously, can we like talk…or whatever."

"Let me show you a magic trick."

◆ ◆ ◆

We end up leaving A.J. minutes later.

Shayne is embarrassed. I'm creeped out.

I tell her, "Shayne, your brother needs help."

She waves me off, saying, "I know, I know, I know," like she's heard this too many times already. This is when we get into the discussion about *Leave it to Lamas.* I've never seen the show, so Shayne has to explain why Lorenzo and Shauna Sand split. What happened was that Shauna came on to A.J. because she's got a thing for young dudes. A.J. fucked her because she was hot and he was too stupid to say no. Of course, when Lorenzo found out he cut ties with both of them. The TV show reunited Lorenzo and A.J. after a long silence of many years. They're cool now, but it's still a little weird. The kid fucked Lorenzo's wife, so of course it's weird.

"Oh, and Shauna has some porn tape[59] out," Shayne says. "Like, she leaked it on purpose for publicity or whatever."

---

59 *Shauna Sand Exposed.*

Leave it to Lamas, I find out, was pretty much a fucking disaster. Unlike the Kardashians, this family couldn't deal with the cameras and all the bullshit. They got sick of each other, and by the end of filming, they unanimously agreed they needed a break from it.

"The only good thing to come out of it," Shayne says, "is that it finally got Dad and A.J. to talk again."

I nod. It's hitting me just how much I still have to learn about Shayne.

"Okay, let's go meet my mom," Shayne says, driving through Beverly Hills with her big designer sunglasses, a cigarette pinched between her fingers. Shayne looks at me with a small grin, and tells me, "She's crazy too."

◆◆◆

Michele Smith is Shayne's mom, Lorenzo's first wife.

We meet her at this tanning salon in the Valley that she works at—my first thought upon seeing her is that she looks a lot like Crocodile Dundee. She looks fine for her age, but her skin is pretty much what you'd expect when you work at a tanning salon and have been partying hard for most of your life. Michele Smith was one of the top publicists at PMK in New York, and was a bottle rat before bottle rats existed during the Studio 54 days. That's how she met Lorenzo. She was his publicist.

"Y'know, Shayne and I were twins in another life, Nik," Michele says, laughing in this kind of actor-y way, like she's on TV.

"See? Crazy?" Shayne says. "Don't listen to her."

"I mean, hell, we could be twins *now* for all I know, right?" Michele says, and this is when I'm supposed to be polite and agree but I don't.

"Mom—ugh! You're crazy!" Shayne says. "Nik, don't listen to her. We're not twins."

"Yeah...I know."

"Nik, do you like animals?" Michele asks. "You look like an animal lover."

"They're...okay," but it comes out sounding like a question.

Michele starts ranting about cats and dogs and shelters and whatnot. She's an animal kook, and she talks to me like she's known me my entire life, which makes me uneasy. The entire family makes me uneasy.

Then we meet Dakota.

◆◆◆

Dakota Pike is Shayne's sister from a different father.

She was also on *Leave it to Lamas*, although Shayne was featured more prominently due to her actually being a Lamas and her *Bachelor* stint. Regardless of them having different parents, Shayne and Dakota still look at each other like real sisters since they grew up together.

Dakota has roughly the same issues that A.J. does (drinking, pills, coke, etc.), but to a lesser degree. She hasn't yet hit that stage where she's doing blow in a dark basement quoting the Joker. Her problems aren't the in-your-face kind. She hides them, or tries to at least.

Dakota is in a fucked-up relationship with this dude named Benry, who was on *Survivor*[60], I would later find out. For the most part, Dakota and Benry do drugs and fuck, but it's not like they love each other. Celebrities or people with a name gravitate toward each other like junkies. When you're cut from the same cloth it only seems natural that you date some-one on your level, and that feeling is intensified when you add drugs into the mix.

So Dakota and Benry have both been on TV, they've both have had their fifteen minutes, and now that it's over, they both want to do drugs and party. In a place like L.A., these kinds of relationships are more common than you'd think. On the outside, Dakota and Benry look like a perfectly happy and normal couple, but behind closed doors it's about as dysfunc-tional as you can imagine.

Shayne and I will see Dakota, and she'll be strung out on pills and liquor and possibly coke, and she'll say, "Benry beat the shit out of me last night. Look at these bruises." Dakota models her arm, and it's spotted with welts and plum blotches. She's crying hysterically, telling Shayne, "I'm fucking done with him! I'm done!" and Shayne will put her arm around her sister, patting her on the back like she's seen this a million times. Calm. Collected.

The next day, Dakota will act like everything's fine again. Her and Benry will rekindle things, party together, or do whatever it is they do to make things good again. Maybe get high and fuck. I don't know. It's unstable and not normal. I know I don't want to be around it.

After meeting Dakota and seeing her drama play out—that's right around the time I conclude how I want things to work with Shayne and me.

---

60 *Redemption Island* season.

◆ ◆ ◆

If meeting Shayne's family did anything of positive note, it's that it made me realize what a good job my own parents did. Granted, I'm not the most well-liked person on the planet, but I've never touched a drug in my life, I've never been in an abusive relationship, and I've never had a kid I didn't take responsibility for. I set rules for myself that most people in my position wouldn't bother doing. I'm good to my wife, and I want to start a family with her, but not with these people around us.

That's the conclusion I make.

I tell her, "I would like to start a family and have kids, but I'm not going to have people like A.J. and Dakota in their life. Lorenzo—fine, but I'm not having this dysfunctional shit around my kid."

Shayne nods. She gets it.

If we're starting a family, we have to give the kid a fair shot at being normal. Even though Shayne and I have long forgotten what normal is or feels like, we have to try.

Origins (Part 3)

Because the concept of reality Internet had never been done before, I wondered if it was even legal. I was going to put it all out there: the drugs and the girls with plastic surgery and all those guys going out every weekend pretending to be something they weren't. Unmitigated exposure. What had once been confined to the clubs and celebrated, I was going to question on an open platform. I was going to break the façade. Satire it. Whether or not that would be something I could get in trouble for remained to be seen.

Beyond legality, the other issue was that I knew nothing about the Internet, outside of checking my e-mail and playing fantasy football. I had no clue how to build, maintain, and manage a site on my own. It was all uncharted territory, but the allure of the idea and my dissatisfaction with my personal life combined to be a great motivator. I needed the escape, an outlet. And no one could know. It was going to be my secret vacation away from the world, and I didn't want anyone along for the ride. Didn't want to share it because I had something—I knew that much, but wasn't sure as to the scope of how it would affect the world.

So I began the process of building this thing with the little information that I had, oftentimes Googling basic questions regarding hosting and templates and stuff like that. GoDaddy.com was sponsoring Danica Patrick, and since my wife was friends with her, I was familiar with what it was beyond the name and Danica posing in a bikini. At that point in time, the commercials didn't give you much more than tits and a web address, but Danica brought up what the business actually did during a previous conversation.

The first thing required was the selection of a domain name, and *Dirty Scottsdale* was the one I had in mind going into it. Jim Schaffer, a friend of mine, used to joke about how we should start a clothing line called *Dirty*

Scottsdale for the club kids to wear. Maybe lingerie, too. He even bought the domain name for it, but that's about as far as it went. I got busy with the NPMG scam and Jim got busted for some Internet porn scandal, and the last I heard about the site was that he let the domain expire.

So I bought *Dirty Scottsdale* for $19.95 with this package deal called "website tonight." It was a basic three-page layout. A starter kit, really. There was never any intention to have millions of visitors, so the whole thing started out small and janky: basic fonts, crappy layout, a gay-ass Lamborghini at the top of the page. At the time I thought it was cool, though, because I was building a voice. A persona. This was going to be the place where I could say the things that were on my mind and people could respond. Right at the top, I wrote, "First ever reality blogger."

I researched sites like *TMZ* and *Perez Hilton* and noticed that they had this kind of funny, snarky tone to them. Perhaps if I'm funny and sarcastic and just say what's on my mind, I thought, maybe it'll work. I was going to be the *TMZ* for civilians and non-celebs. Fame-chasers. The name was missing though. My name. My Internet handle. *The Simple Life*[61] was big at the time, and Perez had already ripped his name from one of the girls. Paris was that hot chick that just wanted to be loved and fucked. Nicole was darker. So maybe I could be the cool and edgy Nicole Richie, I thought. A Yin to Perez Hilton's Yang. He could do the celebrity bullshit; I would be underground.

And that's how Nik Richie was born.

◆◆◆

I found pictures of Alexa Carlson.

She was at the clubs every night: Pussycat Lounge, Suede, and 6. They were the same clubs I was going to, but we were there for different reasons. She went to be seen, to be photographed and adored. Alexa was one of the "it girls" of Scottsdale. Everybody knew her, or at the very least, knew of her. So I made her an example. On the site, I put up her picture and said, "She looks like a gorilla. We should call her G-Girl."

I said what was on my mind. No filter.

No regard for how she'd react or feel.

Meanwhile, at NPMG, I was officially checked out. Sean was trying to weasel his way back in from the field and I had lost all motivation to stop

---

61 Reality series starring Nicole Richie and Paris Hilton that aired from Dec. 2003 through Aug. 2007. The first three seasons aired on the Fox network with the final two airing on E!

him. At any given point of the day, I was either job-hunting on the company's computer or working on my blog: posting another club promoter, another socialite. I was posting these people and I noticed the comments field was steadily growing in numbers. It was going viral right before my eyes. Not even a few days later, I woke up and had over two hundred comments, saying things like:

"I'm going to kill this Nik Richie guy."

And: "Who the fuck is he?"

People were talking, and not just online. I would go out to the clubs and the tone had changed. Guys were pissed off; girls were worried they'd be next. It was the first time in my memory that photographers were being turned away for fear that the picture would end up on my site. There was speculation and paranoia. There was laughter. Bartenders were asking me, "Dude, have you been to *Dirty Scottsdale* yet? It's fucking hilarious."

To which I'd say, "Nah man, haven't seen it. I'll have to check it out."

The intrigue around Nik Richie and who I was going to post next took over the nightlife scene. People either loved me or hated me, but no matter what, I was the center of conversation. A point of distraction. A voice people listened to. There was finally someone calling out the guidos and tool-tards [62], all those guys trying to buy popularity with overpriced liquor and Ed Hardy shirts. People had always had unfavorable opinions, but it took a Nik Richie to actually come out and say them. Nik was the ego-check that Hooman Karamian couldn't be, and the reactions varied from mild amusement to violence.

People were getting jumped in bathrooms. There was a $10,000 bounty being offered to the person who discovered my identity. I was still going out at night to interact with these people, to study them, but the air had clearly changed. The state of decadence that had once defined the city was slipping, and it was all Nik Richie's fault.

◆ ◆ ◆

At NPMG, I set the meetings up for the next two weeks. Good meetings, the kind that our SAEs could close half-assed and hungover. I even hired on Anthony and Andy from my CIG days, telling them it's just like the music scam but with credit card processing. It was sort of my last-ditch effort to do the job right, even though it was about to be taken away from me. While I was building my name as Nik Richie, Sean was doing everything in

---

62 A combination of "tool" and "retard."

his power to ruin Hooman Karamian, and after enough lies and gossip, he got his way. The call came in that I was to go back out in the field and that Sean would resume his position as the floor manager. By that point, I didn't care. Being Nik Richie was proving to be more satisfying than any career ambitions I had. Even though my wife hated it and the site made no money, it became the only thing I looked forward to during the day. So I went back into the field, closing one or two meetings a day to keep afloat—basically, doing the bare minimum not to get fired.

Shortly after Sean got his job back I'd learn that we had made the most money in company history, and it had nothing to do with him. It was me. My meetings. That didn't stop Sean from taking the credit, though. All the bosses were convinced that this guy just saved the company when all he really did was vulture my numbers, but I was sick of fighting with him. Sick of trying to prove myself to these people. *Dirty Scottsdale* made NPMG feel like a job, not a career. It was temporary, a way to make money for the time being instead of for the rest of my life.

My hour a day as Nik Richie far exceeded anything I had ever done as Hooman Karamian. It was a high. A release. I spoke and the people, the city, they hung on every word. At the time, I thought you couldn't put a price on that kind of power. That's right when the bill came.

◆◆◆

Server fees. *Go Daddy* wanted $6,000 for something called "server fees." At first I thought it was some kind of bullshit charge in the vein of an NPMG scam, but my wife explained that they were legitimate. Traffic kept pushing the server past the maximum bandwidth level so the bill and the charges were real. She finally had the ammunition she needed against me.

"It's done," she said. "It doesn't make any money. All you're doing is staring at half-naked girls all day and talking shit on people. Shut it down."

My wife was jealous, but it had nothing to do with the half-naked women or what I said on the site. The bill for $6,000 wasn't an issue, either. It was the fact that I made something that was more successful than any-thing she had done. My wife was a businesswoman, and a cutthroat one at that. Although her ambition was one of the things that drew me to her, the drawback was she never stopped competing. Even with me, her husband, she couldn't help but think of me as an opponent. An enemy. And I could have dropped Nik Richie at that point, but I loved it too much. More than

I loved her. In my mind, Nik Richie was bigger than our marriage, so I was going to do everything in my power to keep him alive.

I invested more into him. More time. More money. I bought the domains for *Dirty Newport* and *Vegas*. I made a *MySpace* account, friending chick after chick. Networking. Spreading the message. The Scottsdale market was getting so big that it caught the attention of Bob Parsons, the owner of *Go Daddy*. He wanted to interview me for his radio show, and I said, "I'll do it under two conditions: no one can know who I am, and we need to take care of these server fees."

That would be the first time I used the Nik Richie persona for personal gain. Bob and I cut a deal: I'd do the interview and he'd drop the fees and put me on a more affordable plan. That wasn't a normal practice for Bob, but he was a fan of the site and wanted to meet Nik Richie so badly that I could have asked for anything. He just so happened to catch me at a time where I wasn't aware of my own power. I knew I had influence, but I had never been one to make demands or flaunt myself.

Self-awareness slowly crept in as time went on. There was a correlation between how much traffic the site got and the amount of times I heard my own name out at the clubs. Nik Richie was a celebrity, but he was also a ghost. No one knew where he was or what he looked like, so he could be everywhere or nowhere. He transcended the limitation of being a person, and the site played off that anonymity with its users. People could say what they wanted without guilt or consequences. Without fear. Free speech had always existed; I just happened to invent a new version of it, and people couldn't get enough.

Once it got to the point where people were refusing to take pictures, I could no longer go to the nightlife websites like I had been doing. The well had run dry. If the site was going to continue, the users were going to have to step up and help, so I opened the floodgates. At the top of the site, I made my intentions known, typing, "I'm looking for civilian paparazzi. If you have photos or intel, please submit by clicking the link."

At a casual glance, it looked like I was asking for help.

In actuality, I was forming my own army.

◆ ◆ ◆

Traffic was up. Submissions were rolling in so fast and frequent that I could barely keep up with them—most of which were people I had seen already at Suede or 6 or one of the other clubs in Scottsdale. The diversity of douchebags and cokeheads and pretend models went through the roof, familiar faces that finally had names and backstories to go with them. Popularity grew as did adversity to the site. Those on the receiving end, the people being submitted, were pissed. They either wanted to kill me, sue me, or both. Death threats were being made in the comments, and there were rumors going around that I was the guy, but I was more concerned with losing my site. Losing my voice.

I became convinced that the lawyers were going to swoop in at any moment and shut me down, so I called the only guy I could trust with my secret for legal advice. His name was Ben Quayle: future congressman and son of former vice president Dan Quayle.

On the surface, that sounded prestigious, but the reality was that Ben was a fun guy to hang out with. He was a drinking buddy. Someone to chase chicks with. Never did we get into his political background or any-thing he did over at Snell & Wilmer, which was the law firm he practiced at. I never talked about NPMG or the site. If we were out, it wasn't to talk about work. Not extensively, anyway. So when I called him about the potential legal issues I had, it was more or less out of the blue.

I told Ben I was Nik Richie, asking him to check out the site and see if there was anything that could land me in a courtroom. Claims were being made that the site was libelous and invaded people's privacy, so I asked Ben to find out if those claims were valid. He agreed to do it, intrigued by the idea that I was living a sort of double life. Up until that point, I think Ben had only heard about *Dirty Scottsdale* in passing.

I never thought he'd want to write for it.

◆ ◆ ◆

Ben got back with me to let me know I was legally in the clear, and he also referred me over to a different lawyer to help me incorporate the site into an LLC. What I didn't expect was for him to want in, to want to work with me.

He said, "Hooman, this site is awesome. I want to write for it."

"Well, I'm kind of the only guy writing as Nik Richie. I don't know how it'd go over with someone else doing it."

"No, you keep doing that," he said. "I'll do funny little articles about Scottsdale and the scene and everything, and I'll go by a different name. I'll go by Brock Landers."

"Okay, but if we do this, no one can know," I told him.

"Deal—okay, so what do you want me to do first?"

"Okay...well, you're Brock Landers," I said, "and your job is to find the hottest chick in Scottsdale."

◆◆◆

The Legend of Brock's Chick (and the reason that is her name):

As I wrote in my first post, every once in awhile I will post a picture of a foxy lady who resides in Scottsdale. I requested submissions from the DS readers, and thanks to all of your emails, I received a whopping zero pictures. Jesus...I almost feel like the kid who eats paste in elementary school...almost.

Fortunately, after spending a night sitting on my couch, in the dark, with a bottle of whiskey, rhythmically flicking the switch on my table side lamp on and off, I remembered that I had the entire DS picture vault at my disposal. Flush with this realization, and coupled with the fact that I have a king-sized ego that can overcome any emotional setbacks, I pored through the numerous pictures on file at the DS headquarters and found the first lady worthy of some recognition.

This girl seems awfully popular since DS has received tons of pictures of her and she's all over the worldwide Internets. Obviously this girl friggin loves to be photographed—it's like crack to her. In fact, I'm fairly certain that she purposefully runs red lights so she can get her picture taken by the red light cameras.

Because of this, I was a little hesitant to choose her as my first foxy lady of Scottsdale. And, truth be told, I'm more of a brunette guy, so blonds have to be all the more stunning to gain my attention and admiration. That being said, this lady definitely passed the rigorous requirements that this site sets forth, and she is definitely foxy. See for yourself: (photos were embedded in the post of Brock's Chick, most of them in her blonde phase)

I think she looks smart. I imagine us sitting around debating the modern implications of Sun Tzu's teachings in "The Art of War," except replace the first part of this sentence with "tickle fighting while listening to Kelli Clarkson" and you get a gist of the message I'm trying to convey.

Unfortunately, such dreams will never happen because we will never be able to date. The Arizona legislature recently passed a bill that forbids me and this young lady from being an item because we're too good-looking. The debate surrounding this bill was very heated because our classic good looks are polarizing, but I understand their line of thinking. If we were to be seen together, our level of attractiveness would be a combined 142–and that's on a scale of 1-to-5. There is a distinct possibility that persons in the general public would keel over and die from being inundated with such a high level of concentrated beauty. So, for the good of the public health, it is probably better if this lovely lady and I stay apart. I think we both deserve some sort of medal.

Latro,

Brock

◆◆◆

We were like Batman and Robin.

Office drones by day, bloggers at night.

Nik Richie continued to produce snappy one-liners and Brock Landers came out with a new article every couple of weeks that usually got the comment boards in a frenzy. We had always been those guys at the clubs who enjoyed the people-watching aspect, but now it had a purpose. If we saw a chick with stripper streaks[63] or a guy all tatted up, chances were Brock Landers was formulating another article. Another breakdown of the Scottsdale scene. We weren't just hanging out anymore as drinking buddies. We were casing the place, gathering material. There was something about having Ben in on the joke that made it all the more funny to me.

Being outed was still an issue, but I thought it was cool that people were on a wild goose chase to find out our identities. Every time we waited in line at the club to get in or at the bar to get a drink, the names Nik Richie or Brock Landers were rolling off someone's tongue. *Dirty Scottsdale* was on everybody's mind, even if they didn't say it. We were the reason people waved away photographers and declined bottle service. If I said people were fake-tanning too much, the next weekend all the girls in the club were pale. If a post went up saying Ed Hardy or Burberry sucked, everyone would stop wearing it.

We were cleaning up Scottsdale, Ben and I, and we were doing nothing more than giving our honest opinions. The site was popular, so much so that the mainstream news stations were doing stories about us. That's when Ben said he couldn't do it anymore.

---

63 Multi-colored hair extensions typically worn by strippers.

"It's getting too big," he told me. "I'll never out you, but I've got to distance myself from this and focus on my career."

I didn't like it, but I understood. He had explained to me more than once
how if anyone found out it about Brock Landers it could kill his family's
political name, so I didn't fight him on it. Nik Richie continued on, and Ben
Quayle broke ties with both him and Hooman Karamian.

It would be the first of many occasions I'd lose a friend over the site.

Ben's secret, however, would not stay hidden for long.

It'd come out at the worst possible time.

Ben Quayle

Ben Quayle is running for Congress in Arizona, and he's pretty much an automatic shoe-in because of his name, but I don't really take an interest until *Politico* reaches out to me. They call me up wanting dirt, saying, "There's speculation that you and Mr. Quayle used to go out together a lot."

It's the "guilty by association" angle. Take a seemingly stand-up guy, pair him up with someone like a Nik Richie who is viewed unfavorably by the mainstream media, and the first person is no longer as likeable. I can see from a mile away that they're trying to make Ben look bad by his former association with me, but I'm not going to lie. So I tell the reporter that it's true.

"Ben and I were friends," I say.

"*Were* friends? You mean you're not friends anymore?"

"We were drinking buddies, but I haven't talked to him since we started *Dirty Scottsdale* together."

The reporter asks, "What do you mean you started it together? You're saying Ben Quayle was a part of that website?"

"Yeah, he used to go by Brock Landers."

"We heard that he drank and did drugs," the reporter says.

"To my knowledge, he never did drugs," I say. "Not that I've seen."

"Mr. Richie, I'm going to check a few things and give you a call back."

I wasn't trying to out Ben. I didn't think I was providing any new information about his past, but the next thing I know the media was all over it.

◆◆◆

It's everywhere: Politico, *Associated Press*, Vanity Fair.

Every major news outlet is talking about how Ben Quayle used to write for *Dirty Scottsdale*, linking all of his articles and quoting him, saying he has no moral compass. The media is bum-rushing him, and his political opponents are using Brock Landers against Ben in their commercials and interviews. They paint him as this depraved individual who's not ready for office, and for every time Ben tries to do damage control, the media tosses another Brock Landers quote in his face.

In true political fashion, Ben lies about the issue, telling people that he was never Brock Landers and had no affiliation with the site. He pretends like I never existed and I can't help but wonder why he would lie since he's going to win anyway.

Just own up to it, I'm thinking. *Just be honest.*

All Ben has to do is say that he did it for a while, but when it got too hot, he backed out to focus on his political career. We were kids. It was only for a little while. People will understand. Ben keeps denying it, though. So the media gets into an even bigger frenzy because they've got a politician caught in a lie, not to mention me calling him out on the site.

I post:

Wow, if he is denying that he is Brock or any association then he better be ready for a sh*t storm. Ben this better not be true. I was just trying to help you get votes by outing you…there is no need to lie to the American people. I miss those days three years ago in my kitchen hanging out hungover thinking about what club douche bags in Scottsdale to target next.
—nik

Traffic goes up.

Ben changes his story.

It goes from him having nothing to do with the site to him admitting to the media he posted a few comments here and there to boost traffic (which is still a lie, just a different one). He maintains that he was never Brock Landers, and he plays dumb regarding me coming to him for legal advice at Snell & Wilmer. Ben says he had no hand in helping me incorporate the company. He does what all *Dirty* politicians do: deny and lie. Ben bullshits the media and I keep calling him out on it.

Vanity Fair quotes me saying: *"I am not attacking you, I am just being honest. Stop listening to your bullsh*t advisors because they are making you look stupid. If you don't remember me or Brock Landers that is cool. I guess I don't remember the time you banged [redacted] (a chick) in* *my spare bedroom. I just let randoms spend the night and have sex with strangers...should I continue?"*

I reiterate my side of the story, the truth. I explain that I even made him an e-mail[64] where chicks would send him dirty pictures all day. Half of me is waiting for Ben to fess up, the other half is expecting another lie to come out of his mouth. The more he and I jab back and forth at each other, the more the media feeds on it. They find the worst image they can off the site—typically a naked chick, legs spread wide and covered with hearts, and say, "This is what Ben Quayle was a part of."

It's a complete shitstorm, a couple of guys publicly fighting that used to be best friends. We used to be the Batman and Robin of Scottsdale, but politics had clearly changed Ben for the worst. He was one of them now, and as much as I used to get along with the guy, the situation proved that I didn't know him anymore.

◆ ◆ ◆

Ben ends up winning the election.

Despite the Brock Landers clusterfuck, he manages to pull it off. Even though he lied to the media and snubbed me, I still posted on the site that any registered voters in Arizona should vote for Brock Landers. I did my part in pushing the polls back his way, and I figured that's the least I could do for an old friend.

After Ben resigned from *Dirty Scottsdale*, there were a few times that I had run into him out and about at the clubs. He was still up to his usual shit: drinking, having a good time, chasing girls. We'd talk about the site and he was happy to see how big it had gotten. It was easy to slip back into old conversations: who's the hottest chick in Scottsdale and the current tool-tards of the scene. That's the Ben I miss talking to.

So I decide to give it one more try and give Ben a call, not really knowing what to say beyond "congratulations." His voicemail kicks on and I leave a generic message wishing him well on everything. It's probably one of hundreds he's gotten, and I have no expectations of him actually calling me back. Too much has changed. The both of us, we're too different now. He's no longer the guy I met in Lake Tahoe that chased chicks with me, and I've all but killed off Hooman Karamian. Ben's the politician. I'm Nik Richie. Public perception won't allow two guys like that to have a friendship without it causing a bunch of drama.

Sometimes to move up in the world, you have to sacrifice your friends.

---

64 brocklanders@dirtyscottsdale.com

$11M

During the whole Ben Quayle drama I find out I lost $11,000,000.

Associated Press puts it out on the wire that Sarah Jones got awarded a default judgment when I didn't show up to court. The problem is that I don't know Sarah Jones. I don't know her lawyer, Eric Deters, either. Both the names are new to me, and I don't even recall getting served papers about this. When someone is suing you, usually you get papers about it, and that didn't happen.

The story about how this Bengals cheerleader went up on *The Dirty* are only vaguely familiar. The first one alleges she hooked up with the placekicker. There's another one saying that her husband cheated on her and she's got STDs. I don't deny something went up. The first thing I do after reading the AP report is check that there is, indeed, a post about Sarah Jones. And there is. Two of them. That much I can confirm. The rest of this shit: the lawsuit, the $11M payout, this Eric Deters fucker celebrating a win over me—it's coming out of nowhere. Meanwhile, everyone's calling me about it. My friends are all getting hold of me to see if I really just lost $11M. ABC and NBC both want to get my reaction on losing that much money. At this point, I'm not even sure if I did or didn't. In my mind, Associated Press are the journalists of the journalists. Maybe they know something I don't.

◆ ◆ ◆

David clears everything up.

He does what he does best.

My lawyer looks into the situation and finds out that this fucking moron, Eric Deters, sued the wrong site. He sued thedirt.com. Not thedirty.com. They're Dirty World Recordings. I'm Dirty World. You could say that's a small mistake, but not when $11M is on the line. And AP spreading this bullshit is only making it worse. Everyone is still calling me to find out if I'm shutting down the site or what I plan on doing, if I'm broke now. The comment boards are lighting up on the Jones post. Teasing me. Gloating. Saying I got what I deserved. There's relief in knowing that I'm in the clear, but in this business, even the appearance of vulnerability can hurt you.

So I put up the post about how Eric Deters fucked up and that I actually haven't lost any money. I'm fine. They're the ones who fucked up. Of course, AP doesn't give an apology or issue any sort of retraction. The rest of the media outlets do, often citing how incompetent one would have to be to sue the wrong site. I agree. You have to be pretty fucking dumb to sue the wrong site.

We look into this Eric Deters guy a little bit more. He calls himself The Bulldog. He has a radio show in Kentucky. He fights in cage matches. David surmises that this guy is trying to ride in on the coattails of the Ben Quayle scandal. Just like in Hollywood, sometimes you do things for money, and sometimes you do them for publicity. Recently, Ben and I have been in the media quite a bit. David thinks Deters is going after the hot target for the sake of itself, to draw attention his way. He wants to put his name out there.

In other words, Deters is a fame-chaser.

He's using Nik Richie as the platform to chase it.

Dr. Phil

The producers of Dr. Phil contact me wanting logos and shit like that because they're doing an Internet-related show. They say it's going to cover *The Dirty*, Facebook, and this movie called *Catfish*, which I guess is about an online relationship that goes sour. Collectively, this is all going to add up to an anti-cyber-bullying type of episode in which Dr. Phil gives his take on things with no one present to contest him. Since I don't like the sound of that, I tell the producers that I want to come on. I'd like to be there to give my side of the story, and if that means me having to fly out to do the show then I will.

Now, they don't have to agree to this. Dr. Phil and his producers can do and say whatever they want because the show is their turf. They don't *have* to invite me, but it makes for better TV if they do. Controversy equates to ratings. We both know that, and we've both been applying that rule in our own way. So this episode of Dr. Phil ranting about cyber-bullying quickly turns into Dr. Phil vs. Nik Richie.

I fly out to Los Angeles, right into the lion's den.

◆◆◆

In the green room at Paramount Studios, I'm sitting with Shayne and my lawyer, David Gingras, as he goes over what I should and shouldn't say. It's like he's preparing me for trial, and in a way, he kind of is. *Dr. Phil* is a nationally televised show. People are going to judge, and we're all well aware that Dr. Phil has already made his decision about what kind of guy I am. The trick is proving otherwise, or at the very least, giving the audience a few reasons to *think* otherwise.

"Don't be a heartless asshole," David says. "It could really help us out down the line if you at least try to be pleasant."

"Okay…I will *try* to be pleasant," I say, but it comes out sounding fake.

"I'm serious, Nik. You don't need any more bad PR."

Of course, Zuckerberg doesn't show. He's in charge of the biggest social networking site on the planet. When you're the most popular kid at the table, you don't need to do little bullshit appearances for good PR. He's already got all the good PR he can handle. The only ass Zuckerberg will kiss is Oprah's.

I, on the other hand, don't have that luxury.

It must look like I'm nervous because Shayne squeezes my hand and says, "Hey, it's going to be okay. It's just TV."

I'm thinking, *Well, I've never been on TV before.*

◆ ◆ ◆

Production comes to the green room to escort the three of us out to the set. After a few hallways, we emerge from the backstage and I see a crowd of mostly middle-aged women talking amongst themselves. The place is packed, cameras and crew members everywhere. Freddy Fags [65] and Scooby Snack are in the audience, and them being here is just too damn convenient to be a coincidence. They're both dressed up like they're about to go clubbing, and Freddy is still sporting that spiked haircut that makes it look like he made out with an electrical socket. I'm not really worried about anything they could say, though.

David, Shayne, and I are seated in the center section of the audience, front row, and the production assistant is speaking low to me, saying, "Dr. Phil is going to come out. He'll do an introductory bit, and then when he's ready for you to come up, he'll introduce you by name." She says, "You'll sit in the chair nearest him. Got it?"

I nod like I understand and she takes off.

The theme music kicks in and I start shaking, feeling cold. Freezing actually. Music is playing and the lights are frigid and bright the way you'd think of death, and then the audience starts applauding when they see Dr. Phil come out. My breath shortens and I can't stop my hands from shaking, and suddenly I'm doubting myself and everything I've done with my life. It's cold and Dr. Phil is up on stage, a giant. He's wearing a dark suit with a purple paisley tie. A crisp white shirt. Women are cheering as Dr. Phil reads off a teleprompter.

---

65 *Dirty* Celeb best known for his association with Scooby Snack in the Vegas club scene. It's rumored that he is her pimp, although this has never been substantiated.

He showcases screenshots of the site.

He reads user comments word for word, opting to keep in the curses because they can always bleep them out in post. Not even three minutes into the show and already there's a disapproving energy mounting in the audience. I can feel it. Through the cold lights, it's thickening.

Dr. Phil says, "Nik, come on up."

◆ ◆ ◆

Everything seems to go away when I step onto the stage: the noise, the people, the cold. Even the lights seem to dim down. Muted, more like a soft glow that's focused solely on Dr. Phil and myself. Our conversation begins:

Dr. Phil asks, "You created this website, correct?"

I say, "Yeah."

He requests, "Define the website for me in your view."

I flash back years ago, to that lunch at Ra Sushi where I'm miserable and the pieces finally come together: reality TV + Internet. I briefly explain the concept of what I've termed as "Reality Internet."

We arrive at the first point of conflict when Dr. Phil points out that these people on the site aren't public figures. He says, "These are regular people just going about their own business."

Well, we could disagree there. I could bring up girls like Alien and Leper, the cokehead, alcoholic, stripper/porn star/prostitutes. I could say what they did at those clubs in the Hard Rock, and how Alien threatened to jump out the window if I didn't fuck her, and I could mention how Leper fucked me and then immediately went to Lil Wayne to fuck him. I could share this information, and I wonder if Dr. Phil would recant his previous statement of how "these are regular people just going about their own business." Alien and Leper clearly aren't normal in any capacity. And their business, as he refers to it…well, I've seen that first-hand. I've watched them go about their business, and it's a complete shit show.

I don't say any of that, though, nodding my head slightly because Dr. Phil is still talking. He explains the process of the website as he understands it, saying, "Somebody takes their picture that doesn't like them, or…for whatever reason, and then they just write terrible, insulting things about them on the website."

But if the picture doesn't lie…if the subject is truly what everyone accuses them to be, is what they say still terrible? Is it slanderous to call a cokehead a cokehead? If I think someone isn't pretty, does it become an insult by voicing it? Since when did it become criminal to have an opinion? Or is the crime the act of documenting it?

These are the questions I should be asking. I should elaborate on the very small amount of information he's been given about me and the site, but instead, I respond, "It goes both ways, but yeah...there's a market-place for it, and what I'm doing is a business."

That's my way of saying: It's not personal. It's a job.

Dr. Phil comes back with, "Well, there's a marketplace for heroin too but that doesn't justify being a heroin dealer."

Fucker got me.

Now I toss out my big numbers, saying, "Yeah, but if fifteen million people weren't coming to my site, then obviously it's something that's demanded and needed, and I'm—"

"—Whoa, whoa, whoa, whoa," he cuts in. "You just said it's *"demanded and needed"*."

"Correct. Yes. I believe it is."

"You think it's needed? You think it's a necessary element in today's society?"

But now I'm not even listening anymore. I'm waiting my turn to speak.

"It's a form of holding people accountable for their actions, Dr. Phil," I say, almost yelling it because he's trying to cut me off again.

"Holding them accountable?" he asks, clearly offended by the idea. "You actually think you're holding people accountable? Who are *you* to hold people accountable?"

And now Dr. Phil and I are overlapping because he keeps asking questions while I'm still attempting to answer the first one. The interesting part about this, the part I don't think about because I'm so caught up in the moment, is that I could just as easily turn the tables on Dr. Phil. I could ask him, "Who are *you* to hold *me* accountable?"

We both do the same thing: we're shown a particular issue, and then we react or advise based on what we see. We're not the source of the issue. Neither of us go on the hunt for these cases. Dr. Phil doesn't tell people to be bad parents or cheat on their spouses the same way I don't force people to do drugs or sleep around. Yet, here we are, a TV person-ality and an Internet personality, doing approximately the same thing but in an apparent argument.

Dr. Phil tells me that what I do is "reprehensible" and "destructive to people."

He berates me, cyber-bullies me—except it's on national television. He television-bullies me. I can't complain because I knew this would happen. It's not like I came on here thinking Dr. Phil would be kind and cordial and understanding, but then the cameras cut, and something very odd happens.

Nik Richie's debut on Dr. Phil.

◆ ◆ ◆

When the show goes to break, the lights on the cameras that indicate they're recording blink out and the pieces start moving around. Beyond the stage, there are lines of tape stuck to the floor, and the cameras get shifted over on wheel carts to align with the next "mark." Angles change. The lighting adjusts. A production assistant yells how much time they've got to do this, which is about thirty seconds. During that period, a makeup girl comes onto the stage with a white foam triangle and foundation kit.

This girl is touching up Dr. Phil's face as he says to me, "Nik, thank you so much for coming out, I really appreciate it."

I nod like, *Yeah...whatever, man.*

"Hey, don't you live in Scottsdale?" he asks, but he's asking in this genuinely friendly way like the last ten minutes never happened.

I say, "Yeah, I'm in Scottsdale."

"It's beautiful out there," he says, and the makeup girl gives him one final touch-up and bolts off the stage. "Hey, we should go golfing some-time."

I never get a chance to say yes or no.

The cameras are back on, and so is Dr. Phil.

◆◆◆

We talk about suicide.

One of the things not very many people realize about *The Dirty* is that we actively avoid high school stuff. Technically and legally, I *could* post it, but that's not our demographic. The site was founded on the twenty-one-and-over club scene, so anything high school-related I want nothing to do with. If I get a picture and the person even *looks* like they could be in high school, I pass on it. Although it's unofficial, that's always been my policy. Of course, no one tells Dr. Phil this beforehand.

He's listing names off: Ryan Haligan[66]…Jeffrey Johnson[67]…Rachael Neblett[68]…Megan Meier[69]…Jessica Logan[70]…Phoebe Prince[71]…Alexis Pilkington[72]…Tyler Clemente[73].

These kids, he tells me, killed themselves all due to bullying/cyber-bullying-related instances.

"In my opinion," Dr. Phil says, "it's not a matter of "if,' but "when' that's gonna happen based on what's being posted on Dirty.com [sic]."

I'm thinking, *Is Dr. Phil trying to mindfuck me?*

Five minutes ago he asked me if I wanted to go golfing.

Now he's saying I'm about to have blood on my hands.

I have difficulty evoking empathy because I grew up in a time when bullying meant getting the shit kicked out of you and having your money taken. It meant coming home with bruises because you were physically overtaken. You were helpless. Fast-forward to the present, and we've got kids offing themselves because of a rumor or some mean thing so-and-so said. Gossip can kill now. We officially live in the generation where hurting someone's feelings is just as powerful as a loaded gun.

My viewpoint of suicide is black-and-white in that I blame the trigger-man, not the guy who sold you the bullets. You don't commit suicide because of something done to you; you commit suicide because you're done with yourself. Dr. Phil and I won't agree there because he's one of

---

66 Age 13; bullied in person and through Instant Messenger.
67 Age 12; bullied in person and through Instant Messenger.
68 Age 17; bullied in person and through MySpace.
69 Age 13; tormented through a fake MySpace account.
70 Age 18; ex-boyfriend circulated nude photo.
71 Age 15; bullied in person.
72 Age 17; cyber-bullied through Facebook.
73 Age 18; was filmed without his consent by roommate performing homosexual acts.

the many who believe suicide is like murder: it takes at least two people to do it. One provides motive and the other executes.

Currently, my site has no suicides, so that fact that he's associating what I do with these dead kids pisses me off. He's speculating, but the audience is eating it up like he's telling the truth.

Dr. Phil says, "I think it's a real danger, don't you?"

I shake my head, saying, "No…no."

He's trying to get me to bend. Trying to break me, make me turn on myself. Incriminate myself. Get me to admit fault. But I just keep shaking my head, saying "no" or "wrong" or "that's not right."

We go to break.

It happens again.

◆◆◆

Cameras and lights are shifting.

A production assistant is yelling out to the crew.

Now Dr. Phil is saying to me, "Y'know, you could do your site a little differently. There's a few things you could take down, but overall, it's pretty entertaining."

I'm like, "Great, could you please say that on-air now?"

Filming resumes, and it's like the conversation never happened.

◆◆◆

The next segment is with a girl that was posted on the site, and already she's playing up the victim card. Crying. Wiping her eyes with Kleenex. Dr. Phil asks leading questions to make this girl seem as normal as possible, which is sort of an interview trick to get the jury on his side. This is his star witness, so to speak. The intent here is that when the episode finally airs, everyone is going to think that every post on the site is exactly like this girl: a poor little nobody who took a few modeling pictures. She's just like you. Nothing special. They won't think about girls like Leper or Alien because they won't know any better.

This girl on the big screen behind us is attempting to look sexy or whatever in these modeling pictures. Spray-tanned orange and confident. Live and in person, she's on the verge of losing her shit again, saying, "That's my first photo shoot I ever did. That was my very first one. *Obviously*, I don't have practice," she explains. "But because of that, I don't do anything. Because of you, in a way...and you pretty much ruined my life because of that," but the last part of that sentence comes out sounding jumbled from the crying.

I tell her, "It's not because of me; it's because of your friend or the person that actually submitted it."

"Who's the creator of the website?" she asks.

"I am," I say.

"Exactly! You're the one accepting all these pictures."

It's a faulty argument to begin with. If someone is harassed on Facebook, you can't really blame Mark Zuckerberg. Fake accounts became extremely popular on MySpace back in the day, but you couldn't get upset with Tom Anderson. What it boils down to is that 99.9% of any problem is going to be user-related, and it's not specific to just my site. Pick any YouTube video or Yahoo! News article and you'll find it: racism, sexism, bigotry, foul language, threats of rape and murder. Just check the comments section. It's all right there. People are horrible now. Give them the cloak of anonymity and it's even worse.

Dr. Phil brings us up to speed, quoting what people said about her on the site: "She looks like a tranny...alcoholic...druggie...not up to par... stop giving Washington a bad name...she gave her stepfather a blowjob in exchange for a boob job...she's got herpes...she could use a nose job."

People saying whatever they feel like saying with no accountability: this is what the 1st Amendment has become. I'm the one that has to defend it on national television.

So we fight:

I explain that the comments are all third-party. I didn't make them. The girl reminds me that I did, in fact, make a comment of my own. That's true. For every post that goes up, I make a comment. It's not always bad, but I imagine for her it was.

She asks me if I remember the comment I made.

I say it was probably two years ago.

She says that I said she looked like a man, but that doesn't sound like Nik Richie.

"Shim," I say. Based on her masculine facial features, specifically, the jawline, I probably called her a shim. I'm not afraid to say it to her face. I'm giving my honest opinion of her looks. Dr. Phil asks me why. Why would I say that?

"When I say something, it's what I'm thinking. I'm truthful," I say. "That's just how I am."

Lots of people do this. The difference between those people and myself is that I'll attach my name to it. You'll know the source. I'll even say it to your face.

Dr. Phil keeps asking leading questions to make me look like a monster. The girl calls me a joke, says it right to my face.

And the audience applauds.

◆ ◆ ◆

There's no small talk during the next break.

A production assistant is getting my wife and my lawyer into their respective seats. Dr. Phil is going over his note cards. The model is silently fuming.

I'm slowly learning that even though Dr. Phil and I are in the same venue of entertainment, the methods are vastly different. It's not just that he's a TV guy and I'm an Internet guy. Dr. Phil is a surgeon. He's crafty. He can carve a conversation into whatever he wants, change the mood of the audience with one comment and turn your own words around. Whereas I'm more blunt with my comments, Dr. Phil always manages to ask just the right questions to make you look bad.

He does this with Shayne and me.

Dr. Phil asks Shayne how long we've been married.

She says six months, so we're still considered newlyweds.

Dr. Phil asks if Shayne knew about the site when she married me.

She says no, so now the audience thinks she's an idiot. You can practically hear them thinking it: *What kind of woman marries a man not knowing what he does?*

Shayne tries to explain *why* she didn't know about the site, but Dr. Phil cuts her off and drills her with the next question.

"How long did y'all know each other when you got married?" he asks.

It's just like *TMZ*. He already knows the answer; he just wants everyone to hear her say it.

"Twenty-four hours," Shayne tells him, and the audience scoffs.

The audience judges our marriage. Like a reflex.

Dr. Phil asks, "Where did you meet?"

Shayne says, "We met in Vegas."

Now the audience is laughing, openly laughing at us and our joke of a marriage: because it's not long enough, we barely knew each other, we did it too quick and met in the wrong place. That's what they think about us, and they're laughing and judging and doing the thing I'm being crucified for on national TV. All people judge. It's just a matter of showing them something they disagree with. This is why we'll never settle on one religion or one brand of politics, because it's human nature to dismiss the thing we don't automatically agree with.

Right now, the audience is dismissing us. Shayne and I.

"I married my husband, who you all *don't* know…and I do," Shayne says, motioning to the audience. "And we married and it's been amazing."

This is Shayne's eloquent way of saying: *Sitting in a studio audience doesn't mean you know anything about us.*

Eventually, Dr. Phil gets to the part where he throws what my site does in my wife's face. He flips through his note cards and says, "You grew up in an entertainment family, then you got into the entertainment world, and they've written about you in the tabloids."

Shayne nods. "Yes," she says.

"I wrote some of those down," Dr. Phil says. "Reality TV star, Shayne Lamas, shows off big new boobs…Reality star, Shayne Lamas, busted for DUI…Lorenzo Lamas' ex, Shauna Sand, had an affair with his son… Shayne Lamas caught cheating on bachelor, Matt Grant. So they take shots at you," he says.

"And those don't feel good," Shayne says. "Absolutely…but I know who I am and I know the truth."

Then, like the class act that Shayne is, she tells this model not to let me or anybody else stop her from pursuing her career. She tells her to be confident, to own her image. Shayne tells her she's beautiful, and she says this genuinely and with the utmost sincerity.

It's true what they say: for every man there's a better woman standing behind him.

◆◆◆

Next segment: My lawyer, David, finally gets to speak.

The interaction literally lasts less than three minutes, and there's a good reason for that. It's a matter of control. In a conversation which has mostly been dominated by Dr. Phil, David is the one guy that could turn the tide. That's what lawyers do. They're fixers. They take an issue and present it in a simple and convincing way that an audience or jury can understand, and now he's going to do that with *The Dirty*.

He explains that there's a difference between what the law is and what's right. David admits that some of the comments made against the model fell into the "not right" category, and he offers his own personal apology for that. It's sincere. He means it. David is the guy that's always told to me to be nicer, to have a heart.

David explains, "The law allows Nik to do what he does because he's not the one writing those nasty comments."

Dr. Phil counters with, "What do you think of the fact that he just said he took responsibility for it by the fact that he evaluates and edits all the comments before they go up on the site?"

"Legally," David starts, "I know that doesn't make any sense, but that is irrelevant. If I—"

"—It's not irrelevant," Dr. Phil cuts in.

"It is absolutely."

Dr. Phil points at David like he's talking to one of his kids, telling him, "It's not irrelevant and you know it."

Never mind the fact that Dr. Phil isn't a lawyer and is, at most, making a wild guess how the law on this works. Because he's saying it with conviction, the audience begins to clap. David waits for the storm to pass. He breaks this down so any idiot could understand it, explaining that if he went onto Dr. Phil's website and made a comment—doesn't matter if the comment was offensive—the subject can't sue the owner (in this case, Dr. Phil) because it came from a third party. Just because a comment is allowed on Dr. Phil's website doesn't mean that Dr. Phil made the comment himself. Same thing applies to *The Dirty*.

When a user comments on a picture claiming that the subject is a nasty cunt that needs to stop going out in public, no one is liable for that but the user. If the law viewed this otherwise, there would be no YouTube. No Facebook or Google. Anything with third-party content would be extinct.

"And it does not matter if he edits it," David says. "The law actually encourages him to do that kind of editing."

Dr. Phil concedes that although he'd like to see more editing on my part, he's glad I at least do some.

David goes on to explain, "You have to keep in mind the law draws a distinction between the user's comments and the website's comments. They're not legally the same. And in this case, most of the nasty comments that you quoted about this woman here are user-generated comments. Nik is not legally responsible for those, even if he can edit them, even if he doesn't edit them. They're not legally his responsibility."

It's just like David said: what is legal is not always what is right. And now the world knows the difference.

◆◆◆

In the next segment, Scooby Snack has a back–and–forth with Dr. Phil about what it means to be a *Dirty* Celeb and how she got her name. There's two versions of that story.

The first, the one that Scooby Snack refers to, is how there was a picture of herself and Scooby that was put up on the site: her in the forefront wearing big sunglasses, Scooby in the background, walking behind her. They were getting off an elevator, and naturally people thought she was on the walk of shame. I claimed that Scooby only fucked her once, hence the "Snack" portion of the name.

She goes on to explain to Dr. Phil, "It was a fabricated name based on a situation that never happened."

That's absolutely true.

What she doesn't talk about is the other version of the story, the part about how she and I fucked, and then Scooby took credit for it. Or got blamed, rather. He "took one for the team" as they say.

Scooby Snack doesn't out me on the show. It would be a good opportunity to do it. Here on national TV with my wife and lawyer and Dr. Phil and this studio audience. The cameras and crew. She could say, "Nik and I fucked, and because he was so ashamed of it, he made it look like I did it with his friend."

She could say that, and it would be true…but she doesn't.

Eventually, Freddy Fags gets his turn, but Dr. Phil only asks him one question about what his name means and moves on. I almost get the feeling that despite our disagreement for the past hour on these issues, Dr. Phil can see why some people end up on the site based on Freddy's appearance alone.

◆◆◆

For the final segment, everyone but Dr. Phil is relegated back to the audience. Shayne is holding my hand, telling me I did fine up there. "Don't worry. You got to say what you wanted to say." Dr. Phil gives his little spiel on how the Internet is both a wonderful and terrible place, and then he opens things up for comments from the audience.

"He doesn't care. I think he knows he hurts people."

Then some guy says: "I like to call these kinds of people "bottom-feeders' of our society."

Then applause.

Everything kind of goes back to square one. I try to explain that the site is far more than one failed model. We expose politicians, scandal, drug dealers, crooked club owners. We break national news stories and celebrity dirt. We've been doing this for some time now, but because this particular show is all about the model, the audience can't comprehend that. In their minds, she represents every post on the site. When I point that out, Dr. Phil says it's because the language on the model's post was one of the few that was clean enough to be read on basic cable.

I continue to urge people to go to the site and judge for themselves.

It's not all about this one particular girl. Not even close.

◆ ◆ ◆

After taping, Shayne, David, and myself are all back in the green room. Personally, I think it went horribly, but David and Shayne are saying otherwise, that it could have been a lot worse had I *not* shown. At least the people know how the site operates legally speaking, David says.

Dr. Phil comes into the green room and thanks all of us for coming on. To me, he says, "I hope I didn't go too hard on you. If you could help us on other shows that would be great. The last thing I want is for you to have more lawsuits, Nik," and he gives a quick look over to David who nods in agreement. "I wish you the best of luck. Keep on keepin' on," and then Dr. Phil shakes my hand with a smile.

He's got the whole world fooled. He's an actor.

Although Dr. Phil would never admit it, he and I are more alike than people realize. He spent the last hour hating on me and my work, but I know if I called him up for that golf game, he'd say yes in a heartbeat.

Origins (Part 4)

When Ben Quayle resigned from *Dirty Scottsdale*, it meant more than losing the contributions of Brock Landers. My legal connection over at Snell & Wilmer was also cut. It couldn't have come at a worse time because I had actually just received my first cease-and-desist letter, and back then those seemed much more threatening than they actually were. I freaked out about them, so I was looking for legal representation the very next day.

There was a really popular site called *Ripoff Report* that was always in legal trouble. The reason they were on my radar is because my company, NPMG, was always on there, so I made a habit of checking it out to see what people were saying about us, the scam, and all that. Most of the claims were fairly accurate. It was a chop shop. The word had gotten out, but I continued working there because it was a steady paycheck that allowed me plenty of Nik Richie time while I was on the road as an SAE.

My thinking was, whoever *Ripoff Report* was getting representation through had to be good, so I did some poking around and found out who their lawyers were.

This is how I came to meet David Gingras.

Nik Richie was the sword; David became the shield.

♦♦♦

I met with David and another lawyer named Maria over at the offices of Jaburg & Wilk. Maria was a cunt. Abrasive. Anytime David tried to answer one of my questions she'd cut him off mid-response. We were sitting in one of the offices, and I asked if I was doing anything legally wrong on the site, anything that might be considered harassment, invasion of privacy, libelous, etc.

David said, "No—"

"—What you're doing is 100% legal," Maria cut in.

"So what's with the cease–and–desist letter?" I asked. "How do I deal with this?"

David said, "Yeah, you're probably going to get a lot of those, however—"

"—however," Maria cut in again, "you're protected by something called the C.D.A.[74] So, for example, this person is saying that you're the author of the post, correct?"

"Right."

"But all you did was publish it. The content came from a third party, and the legal system recognizes that difference," she explained. "Anything said in the comment board, you're not liable for. Anything that comes in from another person, you're also not liable for. That's how the C.D.A. works."

"Well, I'm pretty sure that I'm going to need you guys," I said. "The problem is the site doesn't make any money."

"That's definitely a problem," David said.

"Even if you're legally in the right," Maria told me, "you're going to drown in legal fees trying to defend yourself."

The meeting made one thing explicitly clear: if the site was going to continue, I needed to turn it into a profitable business. Otherwise, it was going to sink.

◆◆◆

I needed money.

I needed investors.

The site was so popular that even the people at NPMG were talking about it in their cubicles. That's when it hit me that I was doing something positive: stealing time from the man and giving it to the poor. I was making people laugh, providing a distraction from their shitty jobs. It was the first time I considered turning the site into more of a business and less of a recreation.

I sat down with my wife to tell her that I was going to take $25,000 to invest in the site, that I was going to turn it into a business and start cashing in on its popularity. We currently had about a $50,000 nest egg,

---

74 Communications Decency Act (Section 230): No provider or user of an interactive computer service shall be treated as the publisher or speaker of any information provided by another information content provider.

and my wife had drawn from it before for her own business endeavors. I wanted to do the same with *Dirty Scottsdale*.

"But I need your blessing," I said. "Can I have your blessing?"

Without even thinking about it, she answered, "No fucking way."

◆ ◆ ◆

I loved the site more than I loved my wife, so I went ahead and took the money. I quit my job at NPMG and didn't tell her. We were so distant from each other at that point that I wasn't worried about the consequences: divorce or anything else she could throw at me. Nik Richie made me happier than the marriage, so I risked it.

Everything escalated.

The site was in five markets: Chicago, Newport, Dallas, Vegas, and Scottsdale. I went hard. Before I was making two or three posts a day. Suddenly, I was putting up eight or nine in each market. I made MySpace pages for each of them, friending more girls, seeing more douchebags and fame–chasers. All these club kids were checking it out. It was going viral again. More and more people from around the country were becoming aware of me, the site, the message. Nik Richie was spreading just like he had done in Scottsdale.

If you were in Vegas about to get your photo taken, you thought twice about it.

All those buxom Dallas girls doing coke in the bathrooms got a little bit paranoid.

Once again, people were asking, "Who the fuck is Nik Richie?"

And: "I'm going to fucking kill this motherfucker!"

Just as I thought, the method worked, but I still needed money. It wasn't a business yet, just something people went to and commented on between Facebook and MySpace. I needed someone with some real business sense, and as much as I didn't want to, that meant telling another person who I really was.

◆ ◆ ◆

I ended up going with a guy named Saroosh.

We had become friends because he was the only other Persian dude that I saw out, and we had been traveling in close circles for a while out at the clubs in Scottsdale. I was in the calm circle of married guys and his people did drugs and fucked all the bottle rats. They were out of control and I wanted no part of it. Saroosh was a cool dude, though, the guy that wanted to take care of people: get them deals on bottles or tables or getting them into the VIP. He was always hanging with rich people and getting the highest-priced shit on the menu, but what I liked about the guy was that he was never flamboyant or in your face about it. Saroosh was low-key, and that's a big part of why I thought I could trust him with my Nik Richie secret.

So I let Saroosh in, told him who I was and how well the sites were doing on traffic. I asked him straight up, "You know rich people. Do you think any of them would be willing to invest in this?"

Saroosh knew nightlife—he had been living in it for quite some time, and *Dirty Scottsdale's* core demographic was the people in the scene. He simply added two and two together and pitched the idea of doing a party, explaining, "We'll call it a pull wool party and charge $20 a head."

I said, "Saroosh, no one is going to fucking come to this thing."

"Yeah, they will. You're doing this as a business, so just out yourself."

"No fucking way," I said, "but I got an even better idea. How about we get an actor to play Nik Richie at the party?"

◆◆◆

The buzz was out.

Nik Richie was going to host an event at Axis Radius. I put it up on *Dirty Scottsdale* that this was going to be my coming out/pull wool party and you could buy tickets off the site. At the time, I was making fun of Southwest Airlines (referring to them as Southworst) so I had these tickets with the letter "C" on them. Southwest had that A–B–C seating policy, and I always used to say that it was better to get the C group because no one likes to sit in the middle and you could get next to the hot chicks on the flight.

The party sold out.

So many tickets were bought that it went over Axis Radius' 1,200 occupancy limit and they had to open up Suede across the street to handle the overflow. Everyone wanted to see Nik Richie, but anyone who came out that night and thought they were speaking with me or taking a picture with me really wasn't. It was my buddy John Carlo from Orange County.

He was one of the few people I told that I was Nik Richie, and I basically tricked him into doing it under the premise that it'd be cool to see how many chicks tried to get with him.

"It's no big deal. Go take some pics on the red carpet and hang out," I said. "We'll be up in the balcony watching."

So I waited in line and paid the $20 cover. Meanwhile, John Carlo was exiting a limo to news cameras and photographers in his face. He was walking the red carpet with two black security guards and the hottest chicks in Scottsdale. There was twenty of these chicks (all blondes) just hanging on the guy. All the douchebags I made fun of were there. G–Girl was there. John Carlo was popping bottles and getting photo–bombed while the real Nik Richie watched silently from above.

◆ ◆ ◆

We had invested $25,000 into the event.

We made back $25,000, but we did a little better than just breaking even because now *The Dirty* had another, more tangible element to it. Even though the real Nik Richie was hiding up in the balcony, the party added another dimension to the persona. He was a less of a ghost now. There was a face to go with the name, and quite honestly, John Carlo is a good–looking dude. It dispelled all the rumors that Nik Richie was some fat fuck hiding behind a computer. There was a lot of chatter that I was a guy that talked shit because I had no money and couldn't hook up with girls like Alexa Carlson or Brock's Chick, and John Carlo put an end to all that. Not only did Nik Richie understand what the scene was really about, but he could bang any of these chicks. He was the real deal.

In the wake of the party's success, I told Saroosh that if he wanted to stick around and try selling ads that I'd give him a commission. Honestly, we thought that it would be like shooting fish in a barrel because Nik Richie had just sold out two clubs, and on a Thursday night (which was usually dead). What we found out was that the site wasn't so much popular as it was infamous.

Saroosh went after clubs to run promo ads on the site, but the clubs didn't want anything to do with me because Nik Richie made fun of their clientele, and sometimes the clubs themselves. The last thing they were going to do was pay a guy that may or may not speak badly about them or their customers, so everyone passed. Even the guys Saroosh had connections with said they wanted nothing to do with it, that it would be bad for business. People loved Nik Richie, but only to an extent. Even though I was popular at the time, no one believed that Nik Richie would last or become a functioning business. The media also discovered our little actor trick when they interviewed John Carlo and he knew nothing about the site.

I had to let Saroosh go. There were no hard feelings; it was just business. He promised to keep Nik Richie a secret and we went our separate ways.

I was back to the drawing board.

◆◆◆

I got an e-mail from Harry Morton.

Harry was famous for a couple of reasons. The first is that he was the son of Peter Morton, who owned all the Morton's Steakhouse restaurants. That meant that the guy had money to burn. The other reason people knew Harry is because he was banging Lindsay Lohan during that period in her life where she wasn't too crazy and getting arrested all the time. She was still big from doing *Mean Girls*, not from all the DUIs and bad press.

So Harry emailed me, introduced himself (even though I knew who he was), and told me that he was a big fan of the site and wanted to meet with me. About business. He wanted to meet in Scottsdale, in person, which meant that one more person was going to know that Hooman Karamian was Nik Richie. And the threats hadn't died down. They had actually increased now that all five markets were booming. Everyone kept saying that if they saw Nik Richie out they were going to kick the shit out of him, in Scottsdale or otherwise. The cease-and-desist letters were coming in, too, so I started making all these weird demands.

I told Harry that I'd meet with him, but only if the meeting was completely private and there was a partition at the table that kept us from being viewed by everyone but the waiter. David Gingras from Jaburg & Wilk came with me so I could look like I knew what the hell I was talking about. I liked David. I liked him a hell of a lot more than that cunt Maria, and it mostly had to do with why he became a lawyer in the first place. He told me that when he was younger, a cop punched him in the face for absolutely no reason. David said that when that happened he felt so violated, so absolutely helpless, that he never wanted anyone to have to go through that again. As a lawyer, David had to keep my confidentiality, but as a person, he was completely trustworthy.

We arrived at the restaurant, walking in the rear entrance and through the kitchen like that movie *Goodfellas*. A back booth was waiting on the other side, curtained off just as Harry said it would be. He was already seated, having a drink by himself and doing something on his phone. The gist of the meeting was this: Harry liked the site, liked me. He saw the humor in it, but he also saw all the untapped potential in it as well. It was something he wanted to invest in, but he had to pitch it to his dad because Peter Morton was the money man. They had flipped another site for $200 million and that's what he wanted to do with mine, so I left the meeting on cloud nine because it looked like I was finally going to get a serious investor.

This is when I learned that you never get excited about money until the contracts are signed and the check has cleared your bank account.

◆ ◆ ◆

Harry Morton really had no interest in turning Nik Richie into a profitable business. It was more about bragging rights for him. It wasn't enough that he was banging Lohan. He wanted to be able to say that he owned *The Dirty*, owned Nik Richie. The problem was that he couldn't convince his dad to get on board with the idea, and without Peter, there was no deal. It fell through and everything was rocky again.

I had a cushion, but the cushion was running out. The site made no money, had no infrastructure, which gave my wife all the more ammunition in her argument that I had pissed away twenty-five grand. We were already in a bad place, but the site's inability to capture an endorsement put an even bigger strain on our marriage. The love was gone. I was sleeping on the couch with my dog and we had become more like roommates than husband and wife. She hated Nik Richie, so by extension, she started to hate Hooman Karamian. They were the same person in her mind.

This was right around the time I got an e-mail from Jay Grdina. He was famous for being married to Jenna Jameson, and those two pretty much ran Scottsdale together right up until they decided to split up. Before that, anytime they walked into a club people would just start giving them bottles of Cristal or Dom, all for the sake of being able to say they partied with Jenna. So Jay said he wanted to meet but didn't give any specifics beyond that. After the Harry Morton deal fell through, I wasn't as optimistic that it would be about anything beneficial to me or the site. For all I knew, he just wanted to get a drink with me and bullshit. Back in those days, some of the more affluent people in town wanted to meet Nik Richie just to be able to say they met him. It was being part of some secret club.

I brought David Gingras along again, this time to a place called Mastro's in North Scottsdale. No backdoor this time. No partition. I wasn't as paranoid anymore. Jay showed up in a $250,000 Bentley, which made Gingras and me feel like we were at the kids' table. We were out of his league. Jay gave pretty much the same pitch Harry Morton did: loved the site, saw the potential, was interested in investing so he could flip it later for more money. Jay had followed the same business model before with Club Jenna, and they sold it to *Playboy* for nine figures.

"I think we could flip *The Dirty* for $100 mill," he said.

It sounded good in theory, but I could tell that Jay's idea was to make Nik Richie a celebrity like Jenna, and I didn't want that. In fact, all I was looking for was a $5,000 per month salary. That, and keeping my identity a secret, because I only wanted to be Nik Richie for a few years. It was fun, an escape, but I ultimately wanted to sell everything off for nine figures and retire somewhere down in Mexico. Maybe open a little beach bar. I could train some kid, some young version of myself, to do the job and hand the legacy over. That was more or less my plan: sell high, retire young, pass on the persona.

In order to bring that plan to fruition, I was going to need an investor.

The Grdina brothers put up $500,000, and *The Dirty* finally had funding.

◆◆◆

We moved into the old Club Jenna offices at the air park in Scottsdale, which we referred to as the Pentagon. Everything was brushed steel. There were phones and computers in every cubicle. We had a break room, a conference room. A parking lot. We had everything a real office was supposed to have. Essentially, Nik Richie finally had a real infrastructure and *The Dirty* became less of a garage operation and more corporate.

Jay sat me down and said, "We're going to take care of the business side. All you need to do is blog. Just be Nik Richie and we'll take care of everything else."

We had sixteen employees that checked submissions all day and put together the posts for me to review, comment on, and publish. For $5,000 a month we paid a publicist to get the brand out there, scheduling radio interviews for Nik Richie and getting press. We finally got ads: from clubs, plastic surgeons, and titty bars. For twelve hours a day I was reading and commenting as Nik Richie. He came up with new local vernacular and terminology. He broke down your clubs, your fame-chasers. His reputation was spreading beyond the five markets, but the work was too much.

There were far too many submissions for me to get to, and the investors became aware of it.

Jay said, "It's going to be impossible to keep up with two hundred cities at this rate. We're going to need more Nik Richies."

I said, "Jay, that's perfect. No one knows it's me."

We got two guys to be Nik Richie clones, and I thought they had read enough of the posts to become familiar with the language: the syntax, the tone, the vernacular. The two clones and I were posting as Nik Richie, but it didn't take long before we started getting called out in the comments section.

People were saying: "That's not Nik."

They could tell it wasn't me because I had a particular level of bad grammar and a certain way I arranged my words, and the clones weren't doing it quite right. Something was off. The voice had changed. It was the difference between the real band and a cover band: people can always tell which one's the original. Then I started to really freak out when people were saying I wasn't Nik Richie on my own posts.

We scrapped it after a day.

I told the investors, "We're going to need to convert over to the hub site and I'll just do as much as I can."

The hub site was going to bring all the markets together, the original five (Newport, Dallas, Vegas, Chicago, and Scottsdale) and every other major city. Every market under one universal banner. So we needed another domain to unite them under. We went after *dirty.com*, but the guy wanted $700K so we told him to fuck off. After that we approached *thedirty.com* under the premise that we were a small cleaning company. The broker wanted $5,000 but we managed to negotiate him down to $1,500. The investors locked it in and we started the hub site. Nik Richie was everywhere now: the coasts, the Midwest, the South. He was in Canada. Jay had all of his old Club Jenna people in our office, either checking comments or fixing the graphics or deleting spam. Everyone had a little job to do so that Nik Richie could focus on being Nik Richie. If I wasn't busy doing comments, I was on radio pushing the brand.

We were getting a ton of posts, but then we started getting pickier about the content. More exclusive. We started figuring out who "the cool kids" were, the local celebs. All we had to do was follow the Scottsdale model. Every city had its own version of G-Girl or Brock's Chick. Didn't matter if you were in Dallas or Vegas or Detroit, each one had its own resident group of douchebags and sleazy club promoters. From Newport to

New York, all variations of nightlife and fame-chasing were roughly the same. The difference was in the details.

For months it went on like that: going to the Pentagon, posting all day, being Nik Richie more and more, and in between there were radio interviews and meetings with the investors, but for the most part, it blurred. I was plugged in while the investors spent money to make the site grow. We were shelling out $30K in payroll. Jay was spending money like crazy and the cushion was running out again. The expenditures far outweighed the advertising income, and it was finally starting to catch up. Jim and Jay had even begun to openly argue about how to run the thing, sometimes placing me right in the middle of random feuds.

It all came to a head when Jay said he was leaving the company, and this was soon followed by Jim telling me we had to shut down the site.

The money had officially run out.

We were finished.

20/20 (Part 1)

Scooby gets an e-mail from ABC News.

This guy, Richard Brenner, who's a producer over at *20/20* apparently, is pitching us on some new show about Internet entrepreneurs called *Web Life in America*. He says that he wants Nik Richie to be the pilot episode, so in my mind I'm thinking it's a good opportunity to get some exposure and let a wider audience know how the site works. Up until this point, we had taken a lot of flak in the press, but people still remained ignorant as to exactly what the site does beyond "ruining lives."

So we do the pre-interview: Richard asks me a bunch of questions about *The Dirty* and my background. Basic questions. A few technical ones.

How did you start this?

How long have you been doing it?

What's the process of a submission?

It's nothing I haven't heard before.

Then Richard has one of his film crews follow me around for a couple days, reality TV-style. They follow me everywhere: around the apartment, in my car, everywhere except the bathroom. If I'm sitting in one place for too long, I get the feeling like I'm supposed to do something because there are two cameras on me with a boom mic overhead. We're all wired for sound. Everyone: myself, Shayne, Scooby and JV. Shayne is fine with it because she's done *The Bachelor*, so this is nothing new for her. She's got a gift for tuning things out. The guys hate it, though. Their nerves are shot from being under the microscope. JV wants to sneak off and smoke weed, but he's afraid the camera is going to follow him back to his place. I keep telling them to relax but they're both paranoid.

"I don't even know what the hell you're worried about," I tell them. "They're following *me*. Fucking chill out."

Day one of the filming captures the day-to-day business: posting sub-missions, blogging, doing Photoshop, moderating comments. The crew fucks with the lighting so that everything is dark except for the computer screen and my face (which now has a thin coat of makeup). They say this will make things easier to work with in post-production, and then they'll do things like film my hands or film my face, trying to capture my mood or expression. It's creepy and voyeuristic but I get used to it after a few hours.

Nik Richie during an ABC News interview at the Valley Ho in Scottsdale, Arizona.

Day two we have to go to Tampa Bay for an event at Venue. JV is extra nervous this time and overcompensates by drinking too much. We get hammered. That feeling of being obligated to do something because we're being filmed manifests in the form of too much alcohol. Scooby and I get up on the bar and pour it directly into the open mouths of girls. We spray champagne. I do The Rock. The feeling of having to act out, to perform for the cameras—it's so infectious that everyone in the club gets extra crazy.

We live. They document.

They've seen my personal life up close. They've filmed me working, filmed me and my team out on the road. They've asked us questions. By the time I'm flying out to New York for my one-on-one interview with Chris Cuomo, I'm thinking this is shaping up to be a decent little documentary. People are finally going to understand my side of the story.

Chris Cuomo is a nice guy. We joke around on the set when the cam-eras aren't rolling. The Kardashians come up and Chris can't understand how the hell they became so successful without any talent. I explain that this is more or less what my site does, that even without talent or person-ality or any redeeming qualities, people can still be famous simply through attention-seeking behavior. Everyone loves a trainwreck. If they're a rich trainwreck, even better.

The interview lasts about an hour, and during that time Chris is in his interviewer persona: rigid, professional, all business. I turn on Nik Richie and play the game back. It's mostly a puff piece, but sometimes Chris gets a little aggressive with his questions. Pushes me. It's his job so I don't take it personally. Chris knows just as well as I do that *The Dirty* exists in a gray area of morality, which is probably why it's such a topic of debate. When something isn't clearly right or wrong, it can be continuously discussed with no clear conclusion.

Some people like what I do.

Others hate it. Really hate it.

We talk about that. We talk about the power of rumors. At one point Chris asks about what's going on with me legally, briefly touching on Sarah Jones. It's the first time her name has come up, but the reality of the situation is that this is all about Sarah. The cameras and the questions and being followed around for two days—it's all about Sarah Jones.

Deposition[75]

The lawsuit starts over.

I fly out to Kentucky to do the depositions, and it's amazing how long they can drag these out. The lawyers and legal teams coop me up in a tiny room, microphone on. Wired for sound. They sit me down in an uncomfortable chair and start up with the questions about the site and my team and Sarah Jones. Question after question. Everything's recorded and transcribed, right down to the pauses and breaks in speech.

What's your name?

Where do you live?

It starts off simple like that and slowly escalates. Deters asks me about my wife, my investors, my LLC. He asks about all my names: Hooman, Corbin, Nik. Same guy, different roles in different periods of my life. The beginning of the deposition feels a lot like Deters confirming his information, perhaps so he knows he's not suing the wrong person again. He's trying to redeem himself for his fuck-up. It's personal. He's fighting for his reputation and I'm fighting for my First Amendment rights.

When you get right down to it though, the deposition is a game. Deters wants me to slip up and say something stupid. Something incriminating that he can use against me in court. This is why depositions are so dangerous. One wrong move and you can lose everything.

◆◆◆

Q: Sarah Jones—it was posted on theDirty.com that Sarah Jones had two sexually transmitted diseases that she had gotten from her boyfriend that cheated on her.

---

75 The following dialogue is between Nik Richie and Sarah Jones' attorney, Eric Deters. Deposition excerpts are taken directly from their transcript.

As the editor of theDirty.com, would you not—would you not agree with me that a young woman to be falsely excused [sic] of having sexually transmitted diseases is a godawful thing?

A: Not if it's true.

Q: All right. What if it's false?

A: Well, if—if there is something to back it up, I guess, but that wasn't—in her situation it wasn't about that, it was more that she's a public figure and was fraternizing with players, with the Cincinnati Bengals. I was—when I looked at that post it was more—it wasn't geared toward her, it was a situation.

Q: All right. Who submitted the post?

A: No idea.

***

Q: All right. Now I've gotta ask you this. Sarah Jones—the record is clear as day that Sarah Jones requested repeatedly, repeatedly, repeatedly for these postings to go down. Why didn't you do it?

A: Like—once again, like I said, she's one of many, but the situation was more that she was a public figure and she was, you know, claiming—I think she was a cheerleader or something like that, and she was claiming—I thought, in my opinion, she was claiming that she was, you know, I'm not this bad person. You know what I mean? I'm a role model citizen. And the situation, with her boyfriend and the whole thing, it was—you know, it was submitted by someone who truly believed it. So when I was reading the post, in my opinion, I thought it wasn't something that, you know, needed to be removed at the time.

***

Q: I've gotta ask you this question. Can you—how did you—how did theDirty.com, you and your team, verify that what—the posts about Sarah Jones were true?

A: We didn't, there's—it's impossible. I can't fact-check every single post.

Q: **But after the posts went up, did you verify that she had ever had sexual relationships with a single Bengals football player?**

A: I read what was submitted and I posted it.

Q: **So you didn't?**

A: There's no way of me doing that.

Q: **Isn't it true that after the post went up, you never verified whether or not she had had sex at the high school where she taught with her boyfriend?**

A: It's not my job to verify posts. My job is to put up the stuff that I believe is truthful.

Q: **Isn't it true that—**

A: You're looking at this like this is my opinion of what I think of the situation. You know what I mean? So if I was to say, hey, this post is not believable, like this girl has herpes or it's a gang bang or something like that, I don't—it doesn't even see daylight.

***

Q: **All right. Now the other question I have because I don't want to—I want to verify it without going through a whole transcript, you spoke about this case on Dr. Phil and we got the transcript.**

A: This case?

Q: **Well, no, I take that back. You spoke about your work on Dr. Phil, you're aware of that?**

A: Yeah.

Q: **All right. Have you seen the transcript from that public interview?**

A: No.

Q: **All right. Do you stand by everything that you said—**

A: Well, Hollywood edited it.

Q: **I understand.**

A: You know that.

Q: **I know that, but I'm talking about what was**

actually shown on television. Do you—are you willing to acknowledge—

A: Do you have a copy of it?

Q: Uhm, I've got—I've got a copy of it.

A: Well—

Q: I'm not talking about—I'm not talking about what was not shown on television. I'm talking about what was spoken by you, that was aired on television. Here's my question: I just want to get this on the record.

A: But, Bulldog, you're talking about—

Q: Did you—

A: —Dr. Phil, like the most—this is like Springer. You know what I mean? They edit it, like, cut, he said this, cut the word, cut the—like, there was applauses that they edited out.

Q: Okay. Okay. I'm—this is why I'm asking the question. So you're saying Dr. Phil was highly edited?

A: He basically—he painted me out to be the bad guy, which is fine, it's Hollywood, that's—

Q: You are the bad guy, aren't you?

A: No.

Q: You're not?

A: No.

Q: All right.

***

Q: I gotta ask you this question. There was a post that said that she had had sex with every member of the Cincinnati Bengals professional football team. When that was posted, did you reach the conclusion that Sarah Jones had had sex with every member of the Cincinnati Bengals professional football team?

A: I didn't post that.

Q: All right. But you did—you reviewed it and you left it up. I'm just asking you—

A: Where, was it in the comments?

Q: I'm asking you what you decided. Did you decide that Sarah Jones had sex with every member of the

Cincinnati Bengals professional football team or—

A: How would I decide that? That makes no sense.

Q: Well, you could—I immediately would say that's obviously not true, can't you—

A: Well, was I comment—

Q: Can't you—can't you say that's not true?

A: Was that in the comment?

Q: Here's my question. Did you believe Sarah Jones had had sex with every member of the Cincinnati Bengals professional football team?

A: No.

Q: Okay.

A: I hope not.

***

Q: Umm, Sarah Jones maintains that she sent e-mails October 29th, November 1st, '09, November 6th, November 8th, November 9th, November 11th, November 12th, November 13th, November 14th, November 15th, November 19th, November 19th, December 8th, December 9th, December 28th, December 28th, December 28th, December 28th of '09, asking you to remove these postings about her having sex with every single Bengals player and the fact that she had had these STDs and had sex at work. Isn't it true that you—

A: These are third-party postings. I didn't write—I didn't say any of that stuff.

Q: But you—isn't it true that in response to these e-mails you—

A: Can I see the e-mails, because I don't—you have to understand, I have 30,000 e-mails I haven't even opened. I get thousands of e-mails a day.

Q: Well, here's one. This is December—uh, this is December 9, 2009—

A: Can I see that?

Q: Yeah, you can see it. I'm going to read it.

A: Okay.

Q: *I*—this is Tim Jones. "I e-mailed the other night

and asked you to remove the post for Sarah J., the Bengals cheerleader."

A: Who's Tim Jones?

Q: **Her dad. "I don't know if you have kids or even if you care, but please understand that your website in [sic] ruining the career and a beautiful young woman. Maybe in your mind she's not very pretty. Pretty on the inside is much more important than on the outside. This girl has lived her life building a strong moral reputation. She's never had a drink in her life. She's a strong Christian with high morals and values—"**

A: She's never had a drink in her life? She was at the Pavilion last night.

Q: **That's what the e-mail says.**

***

Q: **Do you know, uh, what Sarah Jones had to go through in order to remain as a Bengal cheerleader, as a result of the posts?**

A: No, I don't. I don't live in Cincinnati. Like I said, I don't even know Sarah Jones.

Q: **Okay.**

A: But I do know, from what I've heard, that she's the captain, or something like that, and she's actually trying to cast herself to be famous on reality shows.

Q: **All right. Do you know who onlinecityguide.com marketing is?**

A: No.

Q: **All right. This says, "Dear Sarah"—this is dated January 10, 2010—"Dear Sarah, theDirty.com WILL NOT," bold all caps, "be removing those photos and stories about your client, Sarah Jones. Advise your client to get tested for STDs and send theDirty.com results. You can sue theDirty.com, but you will not win. Many have tried and all have failed. We suggest you find something else better to do with your time. You're nothing but some punk lawyer who thinks they're tough for bringing a lawsuit against theDirty.com—"**

A: Who's writing—I don't—

Q: **This is onlinecityguide.com.**

A: What does that have to do—

Q: **That's why I asked you if you knew who it was.**

A: No.

Q: **"I've seen your pictures on the website. You look like someone who was raped up the ass by their father when they were a child. By the way, there's a brand-new story about Sarah Jones on theDirty.com." Now, you don't know anything about onlinecityguide.com marketing?**

A: No.

***

Q: **Is it fair—it's a fair statement, isn't it, that you—based on what I've discerned here today, that you play a significant role in creating, developing and transforming relevant information on theDirty.com?**

A: No.

Q: **You don't?**

A: No.

Q: **As the editor, you don't involve—you don't play a significant role in creating, developing—**

A: I don't create or develop anything. It's a third-party platform. People submit stuff and I get it published.

Q: **And you edit it, correct?**

A: No. I put my line at the end of it. I don't edit posts.

Q: **So you—so you put your line at the end of it?**

A: The only thing I edit, I'll put an asterisk and like if someone says fuck or shit, I'll put a star and a vowel.

Q: **Okay. So you are—you are commenting on this platform about the post?**

A: I put my opinion to what I think of the image, yes—

Q: **Okay.**

A. —or the situation.

***

Q: One of the comments that's under Nik in the Sarah Jones matter is, "Why are all high school teachers freaks in the sack?"

A: Um-hmm.

Q: Why did you post that?

A: Just, it was my opinion, you know, watching the news and seeing all these teachers sleeping with their students and, you know, just my opinion on all teachers just from, like, what I see in the media.

***

Q: I know that you're saying that you never did, but you know, Nik, you know that your site, theDirty.com, had a post that said that Sarah Jones had chlamydia and gonorrhea, you know that for a fact, correct?

A: Third party, someone else said it and I posted it [sic] theDirty.com.

Q: I am going to produce evidence at this trial, Nik, that Sarah Jones never had chlamydia and gonorrhea—let me finish the question.

A: Yeah, but that was before the post.

Q: Well, we'll sort out all the timing and everything else.

A: Okay.

Q: There's going to be no evidence that Sarah Jones ever had chlamydia and gonorrhea. There's going to be evidence—

A: But I never said that.

Q: There's going to be evidence that she doesn't and never did have chlamydia and gonorrhea.

A: Okay.

Q: How can you leave that up on a website for the— how many people hit in a month, 600,000, potentially 600,000 people to see on a daily basis, how can you leave that up there, knowing that that is false or not

knowing that it's true?

A: It's not my job to fact-check every single post, I can't do that. It's impossible.

Q: **Then why do you let them all come up?**

A: I don't.

Q: **You did—you did fact-check these posts, though, because you are the editorial committee of the people—**

A: I didn't fact-check—I can't fact-check. I don't even know Sarah Jones.

Broadcast

My episode on Dr. Phil airs.

I don't watch it. I had been seeing previews for it, most of them painting me up as the bad guy with the mentions of suicide and whatnot. Unlike most people, though, if I think someone is saying bad things about me, I can stifle the urge to investigate. Self-torture has never been my thing, which is why I avoid the comment boards if the article is about me. Same with the show. I intentionally miss it, but people are calling and texting. I'm getting recognized on the street. The reactions are mixed, but I'll take that over the definitive negativity I got from the studio audience. Most importantly, the site hits record numbers.

All those *Dr. Phil* people that had never heard of *The Dirty* before are checking it out now. It's cross-promotion at its finest. The episode, I'd find out later, is one of Dr. Phil's highest-rated. It would air again a month later, and I would sit down and watch it only to find out that it's as chopped up as it could get.

During the filming, Dr. Phil had given me a ton of flak for my editing (or lack thereof) on the site, so it's interesting that his episode uses little editing tricks. For the most part, there's not a lot of dialogue cut out. That's not the issue. With television, you change the mood of things using the audience. I only realize this because I can compare the show with what happened on the set, but what I'm noticing is that certain points of the interview that were once silent are peppered with applause or "boos" or people laughing. Post-production doesn't need the audience to do much more than sit there. If things are too quiet or the mood isn't right, they can mix in the sounds that suit Dr. Phil's agenda.

So I end up on the receiving end of "the magic of television," but I can't deny that Dr. Phil brought in the business for me. He was nice, and he gave me an open invitation to come back. It pushed *The Dirty* more into the mainstream. Honestly, I get the feeling that Dr. Phil is a little bit of a fan. But this show is merely a prelude for the clusterfuck that is *20/20*.

20/20 (Part 2)

A couple things happen with the 20/20 people.

Richard Brenner reaches out to Scooby to let us know that he has great news. He says that the pilot is still ongoing for *Web Life in America*, but they want to feature my episode on *20/20*. So I'm fucking stoked about it up until David Gingras calls me, mentioning in passing that during the Sarah Jones deposition the topic of interviews came up. The legal team asked who (if any) networks or interviewers she's sat down with, and one of them was *20/20*. She met with Chris Cuomo, David tells me. The same Chris Cuomo I sat down with.

"She flew out to New York and everything," he says, but I write it off as a weird coincidence up until I'm watching myself on *20/20*.

Chris Cuomo says his opening line: "The name alone makes you want to take a shower: *TheDirty.com*, but wait till you see what this website can do to innocent people," and from that point on, I know this is all going to be about me getting fucked. It's all about Sarah Jones and her crusade against me because she's actually the feature. Not Nik Richie. All that time being followed, the cameras and microphones and the interviews, it was all about getting B-roll footage to make me look evil and indecent.

They play up the teaching angle for Sarah. *20/20* shows her running her class. They play up the cheerleading captain angle. *20/20* has her dancing in uniform and going on a USO tour to support the troops. The idea is to sell to the public that Sarah Jones is a role model, a decent person. Sarah Jones is not only the opposite of Nik Richie, but also a victim. That's what they're getting at.

I'm fucking mortified. Shocked. They're talking about me, the site, referring back to the Carrie Prejean scandal and how she lost her crown. They showcase blurred-out screenshots of the Matt Leinart post partying with young girls. Both are cast in a negative light, as if I went looking for nude photos of Prejean posing topless, as if I forced Matt Leinart to party with underage chicks in a hot tub. The angle is that Nik Richie is the villain. He's the one that ruins lives, Sarah's being one of them.

During her part of the interview, Sarah explains that she sent at least thirty emails to me trying to get her post down. *20/20* takes her word for it. The issue of how that's a fabricated number never comes into question. When you're the victim you don't get cross-examined, so when the second Sarah Jones post is addressed (the one regarding her having sexual diseases), Chris Cuomo never asks her if she actually does. Lawyers do that, not talk show hosts. They're just trying to make good TV.

Sarah's the good guy. Nik's the bad guy.

If there's anything that sells better than sex, it's conflict.

It's the sweet innocent teacher versus the big bad Internet blogger. It's being televised nationally, me answering Chris Cuomo's questions as they overlap it with B-roll of us out at the club in Tampa, me typing in the kind of dark lighting that makes me look like I have cancer. Like I'm inside a fucking bunker planting Internet WMDs.

Nik Richie is a sociopath. He's a terrorist.

He's defaming the all-American girl, Sarah Jones.

This is essentially the entire non-pilot episode of *Web Life in America*. They snaked me. Tricked me. Chris Cuomo brings up the $11,000,000 default judgment, completely brushing over the part about how Sarah's lawyer sued the wrong website. Instead, they cut to me saying that I'm going to fight this thing in court. To the casual viewer, Sarah's already had her way with me in the legal system. Yet, the experts of *20/20* maintain that the site has stained her, that she's going to carry around a scarlet letter forever.

"The Internet has no delete button," they say.

It's the only part of the show I agree with.

Anderson: Episode 1

After a couple of television appearances, The Dirty is picking up speed in the talk-show circuit. It's a no-brainer, really. Nik Richie equals controversy and controversy equals ratings. After the *Dr. Phil* and *20/20* spots, the networks are figuring this out. They may not like me or what I do, but they can't argue with viewership. The only way to up the ante now is to confront me with the person I'm currently in the middle of a legal battle with. This is where Anderson Cooper comes in.

I'm being conferenced in via satellite for my first official one-on-one with Sarah Jones, and it's obvious she has a lot of pent-up aggression. Anderson asks the leading question, what she wants to ask me, and she says, "I just—I just want to know why. Um, why me? You keep saying I'm a little example but this is my life. So forever, on the Internet, it's gonna be posted on there, and I just don't understand what—that I lived my life according to the way y'know, that I want, that my parents raised me, the character that I have, I've set for myself. And one posting in one day—I understand that you're the moderator and somebody sent that in, but you didn't take it down. It was your choice to comment "All high school teachers are freaks in the sack.' Y'know, I work my butt off to have a great reputation and a good character, um, to provide the girls and the boys that I teach a strong foundation. Some of my students don't have that stability at home. They have a bad home life. We see these people that—sometimes teachers are the only solid foundation in their life and that's what I am to them."

Applause. She keeps going, "And because of you that's been taken away from me. These girls can't look up to me and they can't—they feel, they see these things on the Internet and they assume that they're true. They're fifteen so in their mind it's true, and I just don't understand how you could do that, and to say, as a father, as, y'know, you're about to have a child, to say that you don't mind if your daughter would have to go through this, I am just very nervous for the way you're going to raise your child in your home."

More applause.

"Thanks for being very hypocritical right there. I've never attacked you personally and you just attacked me, which is awesome."

"It's not an attack. I'm not being hypocritical."

"How are you not? You just verbally attacked me and I've never attacked you once. Even after your husband—I think you're married now—admitted that he cheated on you."

"Which is true, so not only did I have to deal with that in my own life, I had to deal with that on the Internet."

"And it was true."

"Not by my husband, by my boyfriend in high school, but, yeah, I guess, yeah, and that's one of those things where you live and you learn. You make mistakes, you learn from them. I was with a cheating boyfriend, therefore, I deserve to be on a site?"

"You act like I didn't take this stuff down," I say.

"You did not take those things down. You did not them down until I got my default judgment in August of 2010."

Oh, this shit again?

"That is not true," I say.

"I have the documents."

"You didn't get a default judgment. You never got a default judgment, you sued the wrong person and the wrong company. We came to you saying "hey,' we—I actually came to your legal and said, "Hey, I'm the right guy.' We apologized and said, "Hey, what else do you want from us?' and you said you want money."

"An apology—y'know, an apology, I appreciate your apology."

"You just want to be famous."

"But—I just want to be famous, no."

"You just want to be famous."

"I would love for my—if I could, right now, go, take all of this thing back, if anything, if I could take it back, I just want to wake up and be a teacher."

Sure you do.

"I already gave it back to you."

"It's tarnished! It's gone. It's done. You can't go back from that. You can't recover."

"Sarah Jones, you're painting yourself as the totally wrong person that you are, but it's fine. Whatever."

Verdict

Gingras and I fly back to Kentucky to present our case.

The presiding judge is William O. Bertelsman [76], and what we find out about him is that he's old-school. He's not fully versed in the Internet or Internet law, specifically the Communications Decency Act. He's also got a soft spot for Sarah Jones. She's a local, a teacher, a cheerleader for the home team. Also, when Sarah and her lawyer were going after the wrong site, she did what she does best: cried. She cried for the judge and got super emotional, so this guy is looking at me now like, *This is the son of a bitch that made this little girl cry.*

David does his spiel about the CDA, how it works, and how it applies to *The Dirty*. It's all the stuff he said on *Dr. Phil* but a little bit more formal and intercut with various legal jargon. He makes sure to point out that I'm not the one that wrote all this shit about Sarah Jones. It's third-party. I'm just the billboard. Judge Bertelsman gets hung up on the name of the site, saying that it indicates we're looking for dirt. We're looking for scandal and lies and Sarah Jones is just another victim of that.

I fail to agree with him since practically anything can be called "dirt" these days. You can call the news dirt. Celebrity divorce is dirt. *TMZ* and Perez Hilton dish dirt. It's everywhere. I'm not looking for dirt. I'm looking for whatever is relevant at that particular moment. I'm looking for the stir, the wake-up call. I'm looking for the cheating spouse. The athlete not paying his child support. I'm looking for whatever the audience wants to see, and that's the reason we do everything third-party. It's your posts, I'm just publishing and making a comment. Then someone decided to put up Sarah Jones.

And in this case, the comment was: "Why are all high school teachers freaks in the sack?" He gets hung up on that, too. According to the judge, this implies that Sarah Jones is a freak in the sack. It's another way

---

76 Appointed to federal bench in 1979 by President Jimmy Carter.

of saying she's "a slut" or "a tramp" or "a whore." Any degree of sarcasm is lost on the judge. You can't use the "I was kidding around' defense in court. When Bertelsman looks at me, it's obvious that Nik Richie is a malicious man posting nasty rumors about innocent girls. He wants to make them cry.

So even though David does a good job of explaining the CDA and how it relates to me and the case, it's not enough. What's right isn't always legal and vice versa.

We lose the case.

TheDirty.com lawyer David Gingras and Nik Richie (in mirror) in the green room at Anderson Cooper's show *Anderson Live* in Manhattan, New York.

Anderson: Episode 2

This is my second attempt at Anderson.

The first time was via satellite regarding Sarah Jones, and it was obvious from the get-go that Anderson saw a crying girl and decided to play the role of the protector. I'm okay with that. Anderson has an audience he plays to the same way that I have an audience that I play to. Any attempt on his part to appear unbiased wouldn't have gone over well with the crowd, so I can understand why he took her side. It was the easy choice.

What bothers me is, unlike Dr. Phil, Anderson never let me talk. That, and he edited me to death. When you appear via satellite, you put yourself at a distinct disadvantage in that you can be turned off at any point in the interview. It really is as easy as pointing the remote at the TV and pressing the "power" button, so not only did he cut me off, his people cut up the interview after the fact in editing.

Nothing really got accomplished between Sarah and me since it was more of an argument than a conversation. And yet again, these television hosts failed to see my side of it because they didn't want to see my side of it. This is my principal reason for agreeing to do *Anderson* for a second time.

What happened was that Anderson's ratings were so high after my appearance the people running the show thought it would be a good idea to have me back, but in the actual studio this time. My hits to the site went up as well, but failed in regard to getting my point across. This time, I thought, he's not going to be able to control the interview by patching me in via satellite. He'll have to let me talk.

◆ ◆ ◆

The producers of Anderson Live are awesome.

They're asking me if I'm comfortable, if I've got everything I need, if they can get me coffee or water or a soda. They're asking me if the temperature in the green room is to my liking.

"Can we get you anything to eat, Mr. Richie? Bagel? Donut?"

"No, I'm good."

"Candy bar? We got a candy machine down the hall."

This is my first official warning: when you go onto a nationally televised show and the host hates your guts, pay attention to the producers. If they're being all extra nice like this, that means you're about to get motherfucked.

"Smoothie, Mr. Richie? There's a smoothie place just off the grounds in Central Park."

"No, I'm fine," I tell them. "Can you tell me anything about the show? Anything I should be worried about?"

"Oh, it's just pageant stuff. You should be fine."

The producers leave me alone with my lawyer, convinced that my guard is completely down now. Moments later, Anderson Cooper walks by the green room and gives me the check. The smirk. He gives me this look like, *oh yeah, just you wait, you little shit. You're mine.*

That's the second warning.

I ask David some last-minute questions, if I can call Anderson the thing that I'm thinking. Speak my mind. I ask him, "If it comes down to it…if we get into some sort of battle and we're in a position were he wants to know what *I* think of *him*…I want to know if I can call him a gay communist?"

I want to know because:

a) Anderson is, in fact, a homosexual. Whether or not he wants to formally admit it, he is.[77] The fact that he doesn't admit it indicates a certain level of dishonesty, and I'm of a mind that dishonest people shouldn't be put into a position to judge.

b) He wants to censor the 1st Amendment. Actually, he supports freedom of speech, just as long as he agrees with what's being said. He wants to pick and choose who gets to talk and who doesn't. I'm one of the people that shouldn't get to talk, according to Anderson.

I run this by David, and with very little deliberation he says, "Go fuck yourself. No, you can't say that."

◆◆◆

---

77 Anderson would formally come out on July 2nd, 2012, in a letter to Andrew Sullivan of TheDailyBeast.com.

Anderson refuses to meet with me, refuses to even sit down next to me on the set. The entire time he's in an elevated position, high above in the stadium of the audience so that I have to look up to him. It's a little psychological.

It's him saying: *you're beneath me, and I'm going to make an example out of you.*

It's yet another red flag in the series of red flags.

Today's girl in question is named Kelly. She's from Texas. Does pageants, and Kelly is one of those girls that has to appear perfect because that's what's expected of her in the pageant world. The problem is that I kept getting submissions of her being out in the clubs, drunk. Naked pictures of this girl kept rolling in.

Kelly is blaming me for tarnishing her reputation. She says that when you're a pageant girl, the judges research every single contestant. Facebook, Twitter, news articles, etc.

"They disregard everything that is positive," she says.

In other words, these judges go looking for dirt[78]. Kelly is alleging that her pageant career was ruined due to my site, and I'm the reason she didn't win Miss Texas. We don't talk about how I'm not the one that took her photo or submitted it. In her mind, I'm at fault because my site made her irresponsibility public.

Anderson asks me why I want to be *this* guy. As in: the guy that runs a site that "tears people down," as he puts it. He asks me how I can look myself in the eye. He asks why I couldn't have come up with something else.

Of course, the moment I try to answer one question he cuts me off with another. That, or the audience starts applauding one of his little comebacks.

Once again, things aren't going well for me on TV.

◆ ◆ ◆

It's impossible to finish a metaphor with Anderson.

I say I'm not the author of these posts, and that's absolutely true: I don't title it or write the body of them, I don't choose which picture(s)

---

78 Whether or not this is a common practice among pageant judges is arguable. It's entirely possible that part of their job is contestant research. It's equally possible that this was something that was brought to their attention by a third party or even another contestant. If the common belief is that *The Dirty* publishes nothing true as Kelly and Anderson continue to point out, then I fail to understand why a pageant judge would see otherwise.

are attached, and more often than not, I have no idea who the subject is personally. I'm the guy that puts it up for public consumption and gives a little one- or two-line reaction. That's it.

"I'm just the librarian," I tell Anderson.

Metaphorically speaking, that means that I have nothing to do with the actual writing of the book. I simply put it on the shelf. If the book offends you, don't read it.

This is when Anderson tells me that someone in his family is a librarian and they'd be very sorry to hear that I'm comparing myself to them. Once again, the point that I'm trying to make is lost to a storm of applause.

◆ ◆ ◆

Sometimes our exchanges were cut out in editing:

"I didn't want you here. We don't want to give your site more traffic."

"Anderson, my site gets more traffic than your show. Your show is failing. I'm here for a reason."

And then later:

"You're not a good person, Nik."

"You're not a good person, either. You judge people more than I do—and you're judging me right now."

No applause.

No airtime.

◆ ◆ ◆

"You're clearly a smart guy. You know how to use the Internet. You have creative ideas. Why not create a site that actually does good?" Anderson asks, right before he decides to put words in my mouth. "We know the answer is money. A site for troubled teens is not gonna—"

"—It's not money," I cut in. "I'm actually getting involved—"

"—It *is* money," he cuts back.

I'm thinking, *oh Anderson, if only you knew how long I've done this* without *getting paid.*

He says, "You keep saying there's a market for this. A market means money."

"Okay, well, Anderson, what's this show? What's this show for you? It's for money?"

"Actually, no, it's not."

Bullshit.

"It's not? You mean you're actually doing something positive by doing the show or you're doing it for money?"

"Yeah, I'm actually trying to. Yeah."

Bullshit.

Applause.

♦ ♦ ♦

Anderson doesn't want to meet me after the show.

As a joke, I ask for an autographed headshot but the producers say there's no way in hell that's happening. He's not like Dr. Phil. Anderson brings his emotions into the show. He's actually convinced he's some kind of messiah, saving the planet by facing all the Nik Richies of the world. The reality of the situation is that Anderson is more like me than he's willing to admit. He judges. He pokes fun. He's done his fair share of satire.

The show is called The *RidicuList*, which is kind of a *TMZ* bit where Anderson rips on people in his own snarky little way. So all that talk about doing something good and not tearing people down is a bunch of bullshit. He's guilty of playing the tabloid game, too.

More than likely he'd say, "But these are celebrities. These are public figures."

When does someone officially become a public figure: when they start asking for attention or when they actually get it?

Anderson was born into fame and money.

He hasn't seen what I've seen.

Billboards

The site and all the controversy it inspires can be illustrated in billboards.
We see these everyday: for fast-food restaurants, vehicle repair, fashion.
Pick any major highway or interstate and more than likely you're going to
be bombarded with some kind of advertising or influence you didn't ask
for. Or perhaps you just didn't know you were looking for it.

On I-5 you pass by billboards for McDonald's, the San Diego Zoo, an
abortion clinic. Each one serves a specific function for a particular market.
Each one has a detractor. An opponent. Something to keep it in check.

McDonald's: FDA.

San Diego Zoo: PETA.

Abortion clinic: pro-lifers.

At all times there's a lawsuit pending for the adverse effects of the Big
Mac and the unethical treatment of panda bears. A cheeseburger is no
longer just a cheeseburger. It's a murder weapon, some kind of delicious
poison that's being snuck into Happy Meals. It's on the menu and it's towering over a hundred feet above ground, luring you off the road into one
of their nearest locations.

We hear it all the time:

"Fast food is bad for you."

"The animals don't look happy."

"Abortion is against God's plan."

They all have billboards, advertising, pulling you away from your everyday routine. Some of them are considered socially acceptable. We pass
them all the time without giving them a second thought. Others, like the
abortion clinic, are considered immoral. Unlike the fast-food restaurant or
zoo, there's no sheen of good intentions.

So these people, the pro-lifers, they go after the billboard company.
They call the 1-800 number and make their demands, their threats. They

keep bombarding them with their moral fortitude and guilt until the ad gets pulled from the side of the road. In this day and age, if you cry and complain long enough, more often than not, you can get what you want. Temporarily, at least.

The Dirty functions much the same way as a billboard company. The difference is that we're putting up coke dealers, Vegas escorts, and fame-chasers. We're putting up socialites and guys who are cheating on their spouses. And just like any cheeseburger or cosmetics line you see towering by the highway, you can choose to ignore it. Drive on. Don't pay it a second thought if it offends you. That's what I keep telling people.

"If you don't like it, don't come to the site."

No one is forcing you to buy a Coach purse, the same way I'm not forcing you to come to *The Dirty*. Every post is a billboard submitted by someone else: a friend, an ex, a family member. It's submitted by an enemy or someone you've fallen out of favor with. It's not Nik Richie. It's not the staff. We hit "publish" and move on. Nine times out of ten, we have no fucking clue who you are. We're just the billboard company.

And people like Anderson and Dr. Phil are always suggesting that I shut down *The Dirty*, as if that would really clear up all the so-called "problems" they have with my site and what it does. They make it sound so easy. So simple. The problem with that logic is that there are plenty of billboard companies. There are numerous sites trying to do what I do, and the moment I shut down, ten more would rise up in an attempt to fill the void. You can take down a billboard for something you don't agree with, but that doesn't mean it won't crop up on another interstate the next week. There's always another company, another website. Someone is always waiting to step in, and that applies with *The Dirty* too.

Shutting it down wouldn't fix a fucking thing. I know this because there's a demand for the platform. It's a demand that I can numerically measure with analytics and track in hits, and as the years go on, the consumer base gets larger and larger. Closing the door on *The Dirty* would open up ten windows for the next wannabe Nik Richie.

And one Nik Richie is enough.

Origins (Part 5)

It was a bad situation.

One of my investors had quit. The other one was telling me that all the money was gone and we had to close up shop. Shut down the site. Meanwhile, my wife and I were on the verge of divorce. We barely spoke. She resented me as a person and gave up on me as a husband. Being Nik Richie was literally the only joy I had left in my life, so once again, I had to fight for it.

I sat Jim down at one of the laptops, opened up a browser window and asked, "When you look at this site, what do you see?"

He leaned toward the screen, pointing to different parts of the page, saying, "The colors are off here on this graphic, and we need to reformat this part—"

"—Jim, I'm not talking about the graphics or the colors," I cut in. "I'm asking you, when you go to this site, what do you see?"

He paused, thought it about. Jim said, "I see Nik Richie."

"Why do we have sixteen employees, Jim?"

He looked at me, not speaking. I really didn't want him to say anything since there was no right answer.

"Why are we spending all this money? This isn't Club Jenna," I told him. "We're not trying to be cool and down. We already are cool and down."

"What are you telling me? That you've got a solution?"

"Tomorrow I'm coming in and I'm firing everyone. I'll keep Gayden, but everyone else is gone," I explained. "We'll cut the overhead, we'll cut my salary down to 5K a month. All I need from you is to make it so the existing ads can cover the payroll."

"Okay..." Jim said, as if he wanted to hear more of the plan.

"Give me two months. Let's see what I can do in two months."

"Fine," he nodded. "Two months. I think you know what happens after that if this doesn't start turning around."

I knew exactly what would happen.

Nik Richie would die.

◆◆◆

The next morning I did what had to be done.

I gathered everyone up and told them that due to the financial situation, we were going to have to let everyone go. It wasn't a long dragged-out speech. Even though some of the girls were crying, I knew they understood it wasn't anything personal. Gayden was informed that he'd made the cut (purely out of nepotism).

The Dirty resigned from the Club Jenna offices and moved into one of Jim's condos in Phoenix. The place had been empty for months, so we turned that into our new headquarters and saved even more money on our overhead. We found our groove. Jim handled the business stuff, tracking our expenditures and trying to fetch more ad revenue. He put in an additional $100K to keep everything alive. Gayden went over posts. I made my comments on the bottle rats in New York or the pretend models in L.A., hit publish, and moved on to the next thing. It made me happy. Doing this, being Nik Richie, it didn't feel like work. I got to say what I thought all day, but I had just gone from a staff of sixteen to just myself and Gayden. Two guys combing through thousands of submissions. We literally could not keep up, so I had to make the call.

I had been receiving emails. For months, these things had come in, and they all pretty much said the same thing: that he couldn't believe I cut him out, that he had always been there for me. He was there for me through thick and thin. Sometimes it was a guilt trip. Other times it was a death threat. Not a for real-death threat. Anthony was telling me that he was disappointed in the way that Anthony does, and I ignored the guy. Ignored the emails and calls. There was one instance where we talked about *The Dirty* and how it wasn't my decision on who got hired. I blamed it on the investors, but it was bullshit. Anthony had been around in some capacity for the CIG and NPMG scams. I didn't want him around for this. *The Dirty* wasn't a scam or a way to fuck people out of money, so in my mind, Anthony wasn't right for it. That didn't stop him from reaching out. Like clockwork, the guy either emailed or called, telling me that he deserved a spot after all the shit we've been through. This isn't how you treat your friends, he said. I ignored it. All of it.

I put off Anthony until I absolutely couldn't anymore: this particular moment in which I was trying to run a site that's understaffed and over a half-million dollars in the hole. It was the situation in which I would have accepted anyone's help, but I needed a guy that I could trust, and that truly wanted to be here with me. So I finally called Anthony. It had been close to two years since I had last reached out to him.

He picked up, and the first words out of his mouth weren't hello.

He asked, "Where do you want me, boss?"

♦ ♦ ♦

Anthony came on board. I told him I wasn't paying him shit for like five months. He was going to have to prove himself as an intern first, which was fine by him. All the guy ever wanted was to be included, and he made plenty of money selling drugs and painting houses on the side. I only had one rule: the minute we put him on payroll, he couldn't sell drugs anymore. I didn't care if he did them, but I refused to employ a guy that dealt. Until then, he could do whatever he needed to make ends meet.

So he started working out of the condo with Gayden, but it came to light pretty quick that the kid didn't know shit about computers or Photoshop or anything that would have been considered useful for the job. We had to train him from scratch on everything. Literally everything, and this is how Anthony came to be called Junior Varsity.

The phone call proved something to me, and I think I had known it for quite a while, but when I reached out it was confirmed: JV would take a bullet for me. I could not talk to the kid for fifty years, but if I was in Russia with a gun to my head, he'd be on the first flight out with a million dollars in ransom money. He'd find a way to get me out of the situation. If he couldn't, he would find someone that could. JV is a jammer, but the problem is that everything he does is junior varsity [79] level. He'll get the job done, but it's going to be slightly janky and fucked-up. That's the thing Gayden and I learned when he started working for the site: the work ethic was there, but it was fucking junior varsity.

♦ ♦ ♦

I remembered something that happened in Hawaii: Amanda and I were hiking, and we had gotten to a spot on the island where we were elevated

---

79 Refers to when something, typically a job, is done less than ideally.

enough to get a great view of everything. I remember my eyes tracing the place where the ocean and the beach met, taking in clean air and feeling calm for once. There was this beautiful view in front of us, and my wife broke the silence and told me, "I don't know what the fuck it is, but every time I do something good you top it."

It was an out-of-the-blue comment, yet I knew exactly what she was talking about. The thing about Amanda is that she tried. She worked hard; she had the credentials. She was a smart businesswoman. All things considered, she should have been making six figures by now. Yet somehow this college dropout scam artist of a husband had made something bigger than what she could. I was successful by accident. That's what bugged her. I wasn't even trying and I still overshadowed anything she had ever done.

"I'm going to be honest," she said. "I'm jealous."

That was her way of saying: "I resent you."

I think that was the first time I realized this wasn't going to last.

◆ ◆ ◆

I started taking more of an interest in the things Amanda was working on, asking about her career and her plans. I tried to be encouraging, communicative. I tried to be the guy she met all those years ago, and it started to work. She smiled more, and we were kissing good-bye again rather than simply parting ways in the morning. We were intimate. For the first time in forever, we were having sex and sleeping in the same bed. Most importantly, I never mentioned *The Dirty*. If she asked how things were going (she usually didn't), I kept it short and said either "fine" or "good" or "okay." There was no need to brag or rub salt in the wound. I had learned a long time ago that despite her emotions toward me, she was still a competitive person that didn't like being outshined. The least I could do was keep it to myself, so I did.

We went to movies.

We went on dates.

Hooman Karamian and Nik Richie started to become separate people again. She saw her husband, not the blogger or the chicks he ragged on. She was starting to be happy again. We both were.

And then she got pregnant.

Amanda had been pregnant for about a month, but it was confirmed around Thanksgiving. We had never planned on having kids. Not at that particular moment, anyway. Amanda and I were finally getting along again, but the idea of having a kid reintroduced a certain amount of stress into our lives. She had things that she wanted to do with her business that would need to be put on hold. I was more concerned about the idea of Amanda and I raising a child together. Our relationship as husband and wife was rocky. Adding a kid would introduce a whole other level of complication. That, and Amanda still didn't approve of what I did all day with the site. Quite honestly, I had a suspicion she'd use the kid to get me to discontinue my involvement, either by selling it to the first bidder or shutting it down completely.

And I was also worried about being a good father.

I was having a lunch with Jim and told him about all these issues, but he insisted that this was going to be good for me. This baby would bring a lot of joy into my life, he said.

So Amanda and I had a series of talks over the next few weeks, more or less preparing ourselves for the changes that we were about to face. We were both going to have to scale back on work. We'd have to rearrange our finances, set up doctor's visits, and start reading books like *What to Expect When You're Expecting* because we were both fucking clueless when it came to kids. The two of us needed to mentally prepare for this, because up until this point, we were both all about our careers. We were going to have to stop being so selfish, and right around the time we finally accepted this new reality is when it happened.

She lost the baby.

◆ ◆ ◆

It was December. I'm not sure which day.

What I remember is that my wife was screaming out in pain from the bed, clutching her stomach. There were faint blotches of blood coming through the sheets, so I was already starting to feel faint. Light-headed. The old phobia was kicking in, but the situation was making my adrenaline pump. It kept me conscious. I helped her walk from the bed to the bathroom, and she was crying, telling me how much it hurt. Her stomach was in pain. Sharp pain. And there was blood coming out of her vagina into the toilet. I couldn't see anything, just kept hearing drop upon drop of it coming out of her. She cried and cried, and it was like this for I don't know how long. I just squeezed her hand until she felt like she was ready to try and move, try and go to the hospital to see what was the matter. We already knew, but we had to hear it from a doctor to be sure. As if to make it official, they had to run their tests and take their samples.

Before we could confirm that we weren't going to be parents, a doctor had to tell us, "I can't find the baby."

♦ ♦ ♦

Amanda blamed me.

For some reason, I couldn't say why, it was my fault that we lost the kid. We lost. The both of us. Not just her. I had to keep repeating that it was my kid, too. She wouldn't listen, though. It was easier to make me the scapegoat. The villain. The bad guy.

After she miscarried, the air in the apartment became something worse than it ever had before. She started resenting me again. Hating me. Hating me for being Nik Richie and hating Hooman Karamian for killing her baby. I disgusted her on so many levels that she couldn't stand the sight of me, and so I went to the place where I was accepted. Wanted.

I lost myself in my work.

Relished it. Needed it.

I wanted to be Nik Richie all the time now because my other life was in shambles. Broken beyond repair. Hooman Karamian slept on the couch and was hated by his wife. Nik Richie was loved, feared, adored, funny. He was all these things that Amanda didn't see, or didn't want to. He started out as the escape from work, and then he became the escape from my marriage. My life.

All day I would go over posts that Gayden and JV sent.

All day I got to be Nik Richie. I got to escape myself.

People had been asking for years how I could stand being Nik Richie, and my answer was usually along the lines of how this kind of figure was warranted. Needed. There needs to be a guy like this to call people out, keep them in check. This answer is true, but not the whole truth.

The reality is that compared to how bad things got in life, being Nik Richie is easy. Nik Richie didn't have the same problems that Hooman Karamian had. He was above it. Beyond it.

That all changed on January 23rd.

I was about to have my own dirt.

☐ Domestic Violence ☐ Child Abuse ☐ Arson ☐ Homicide ☐ Hate Crime ☐ Elderly ☐ Gang Related ☐ Liquor Establishment

Agency: SPD	**Incident / Investigation Report**		Case Number: **0802405**
	EXTREME DUI-BAC .15 OR MORE		
Reported 01/23/2008 03.31	Found 01/23/2008 03:55	Occurred 01/23/2008 03:31	
Location N HAYDEN RD / E INDIAN BEND RD , SCOTTSDALE, AZ		Original Officer (1183) NAVARRETE, R.	

Original Information	original page 4
Date added: 01/23/2008	Added by: (1183) NAVARRETE, R.

Narrative

On 01-23-2008 at approximately 0331 hours subject drove his motor vehicle recklessly by exceeding the posted speed limit by 37 MPH in a construction zone, was DUI Extreme .15% or more, DUI .08% or more, and DUI impaired to the slightest degree. Additionally, he did not have proof of insurance. This occurred at approximately 7800 East Indian Bend Road in Scottsdale Arizona.

On 01-23-2008 at approximately 0331 hours I was on patrol in a marked patrol vehicle in regulation uniform in Scottsdale Arizona. I was headed west on Indian Bend Road just west of Hayden street. I was monitoring traffic flow using moving radar for eastbound traffic on Indian Bend Road. The area between Scottsdale Road and Hayden on Indian Bend is designated a construction zone with numerous flashing signs and speed limit signs posted at 25MPH with an additional orange sign designating the area as a work zone. Additionally, there is a large informational lighted sign that informs drivers of the construction zone area from both directions of travel as they enter the construction zone. This area is a business area, in addition to several housing communities along Indian Bend road. The 25MPH speed limit signs at the location for eastbound travel were clearly posted and operational. I was in patrol vehicle 206915 using the Talon II model radar unit serial number T03229 which I checked at the beginning and end of my shift using KA Band tuning forks serial #34992 and #32993. Both checks indicated the radar unit was operating within standards. I am trained and certified to use both moving and stationary radar and to visually estimate speeds within + or - 5MPH.

At approximately 78th Street and Indian Bend, I observed a dark gray Porsche Boxster, traveling east at a high rate of speed. I visually estimated the speed of the vehicle at approximately 60 MPH in the posted 25 MPH construction zone. As I observed the vehicle, the radar unit produced a high pitched audible clear tone and I observed the digital readout of the Talon radar unit which indicated the vehicle was traveling at 62 MPH. I immediately engaged my emergency lights, made a U-turn and accelerated my vehicle. I caught up to the vehicle which was stopped at Hayden and Indian Bend for a red light. When the traffic light changed green, the vehicle continued through the intersection and pulled over at the Albertsons shopping center complex located on the southeast corner of the intersection. I observed the Porsches' license plate was California

I approached the driver and asked him why he was driving so fast in the construction zone. The driver of the Porsche, identified by a California Drivers license as Hooman Abedi Karamian, stated, "I wasn't going that fast." I told Hooman I had him on radar doing 62MPH in a posted 25MPH Construction Zone. Hooman again told me he didn't think he was going that fast. I asked Hooman how fast he thought he was going. Hooman told me he thought he was only going 53MPH. I asked Hooman for his license, vehicle's registration and insurance card. Hooman told me his brother owned the vehicle and began searching for the documents in the center console. Hooman found the California registration and his California Driver's license. However, he was unable to produce an insurance card. Hooman assured me he paid the insurance on the vehicle and was covered, but was unable to provide proof.

While I was speaking with Hooman, I detected the odor of intoxicating liquor emanating from his breath. Additionally, I noticed Hooman was slurring his words, and had bloodshot and watery eyes. I asked Hooman how many drinks he had consumed prior to driving. Hooman told me he had 3 drinks of Redbull Vodka about 2 to 3 hours prior to the stop. Hooman told me he had tried to sleep it off, and was now headed back to his home. I immediately requested a backup unit to the scene.

Upon backup unit arrival, Officer Metz, I returned to the Porsche and asked Hooman to step out of his

☐ Domestic Violence ☐ Child Abuse ☐ Arson ☐ Homicide ☐ Hate Crime ☐ Elderly ☐ Gang Related ☐ Liquor Establishment

Agency: SPD   **Incident / Investigation Report**   **Case Number: 0802405**

EXTREME DUI-BAC .15 OR MORE

Reported 01/23/2008 03:31   Found 01/23/2008 03:55   Occurred 01/23/2008 03:31

Location N HAYDEN RD / E INDIAN BEND RD , SCOTTSDALE, AZ   Original Officer (1183) NAVARRETE, R.

Original Information   original page 5

Date added: 01/23/2008   Added by: (1183) NAVARRETE, R.

Narrative

vehicle so I could make sure he was able to drive his vehicle. I directed Hooman to the sidewalk on the north side of the Albertsons main entrance. As we walked to the sidewalk I noticed Hooman was walking slowly but he did not stagger. I asked Hooman if he had any head injuries or vision problems and he responded, "No." Next I performed HGN on Hooman. I have completed the HGN training course and currently in training to complete HGN certification. After completing HGN, I observed 4 clues of impairment.

Next, I asked Hooman if he had any medical conditions that would prevent him from performing a few simple tests and he replied, "No." I noticed Hooman was wearing light dress flat non-heeled shoes which he did not remove during the SFSTs.

As I began to administer the "Walk and Turn test", I noticed Hooman was having difficulty standing with one foot in front of the other. Hooman lost his balance and broke the instruction stance while I began explaining the Walk and Turn test. Additionally, while I was explaining the instructions, Hooman immediately began walking and I had to tell him to stop and re-acquire the instruction stance. I used a real line when administering the Walk and Turn test. I used a line that was between two columns in the side walk. While in the performance phase of the Walk and Turn, Hooman took several large steps not touching heal to toe and consequently ran out of room on the 9th step of the test. Hooman ran into the column and I had to redirect Hooman to the sidewalk so he could complete the test. While performing the test, he had to be given instructions, not to raise his arms and to look down at his feet (See AIR for further). Additionally, Hooman completed 9 steps forward, 9 steps back and then tried to complete another 9 steps and had to be told to stop.

While performing the one leg stand, Hooman was told 3 times to look down at his feet while he was counting. At the number 1007, Hooman counted this number twice. At number 1015 Hooman stopped counting, looked in my direction and told me, "I can do this all day." I had to instruct Hooman to continue counting as the test was not over. When Hooman reached the number 1020, he did not count in the prescribed manner and just stated 21,22,23.ect. (See AIR for further on all SFSTs).

After completing the field sobriety tests, I asked Hooman if he would be willing to provide a sample of his breath using a preliminary breath test (PBT) device. Hooman told me he had a website where he posted DUI results and agreed to provide a sample. At approximately 0354 hours Hooman blew into the PBT and the results indicated Hooman's BAC was at .152%.

At approximately 0355 hours, I placed Hooman in double-locked handcuffs to the rear, and told him he was under arrest for DUI. I immediately took Hooman to my patrol vehicle, where I searched him incident to arrest with negative results. After the search, I placed Hooman in the back seat of my patrol vehicle and rolled the rear window down.

At approximately 0407 hours, I read Hooman the Admin Per Se/Implied Consent Affidavit. After reading the Admin Per Se, I re-explained the Admin per Se in laymen's terms and told Hooman the Scottsdale PD Policy was to obtain a sample of his blood to determine his alcohol concentration. I told Hooman the procedure would be completed at the hospital. I asked Hooman if he would be willing to provide a sample of his blood and Hooman replied, "Yes." While I was reading Admin per Se, Officer Metz inventory searched Hooman's vehicle and impounded his vehicle in accordance with ARS 28-3511 and was removed from the scene by All City Towing.

9/3/2008 10:48:01 AM   Page 5 of 7

☐ Domestic Violence ☐ Child Abuse ☐ Arson ☐ Homicide ☐ Hate Crime ☐ Elderly ☐ Gang Related ☐ Liquor Establishment

Agency: SPD	Incident / Investigation Report	Case Number: 0802405

EXTREME DUI-BAC .15 OR MORE

Reported: 01/23/2008 03:31   Found: 01/23/2008 03:55   Occurred: 01/23/2008 03:31

Location: N HAYDEN RD / E INDIAN BEND RD, SCOTTSDALE, AZ   Original Officer: (1183) NAVARRETE, R.

Original Information

original page 6

Date added: 01/23/2008   Added by: (1183) NAVARRETE, R.

Narrative

I then transported Hooman to the SHC Shea Hospital for the blood draw procedure. While I was explaining the SHC Hospital consent form. Hooman asked me what would happen if he did not consent to the blood draw procedure. I re-explained the Admin Per Se affidavit and told him if he refused or delayed the process his license would be automatically suspended for 1 year. Hooman told me, I did not know the things he did for the community, and that a DUI would not be a good thing for him. He paused for a few seconds and told me he did not want to sign the form and told me he wanted to speak to an attorney before giving consent to the blood draw. Hooman told me he had 3 attorneys he knew. I told Hooman If he wanted, I could bring him his cell phone from my patrol vehicle, and he could call his attorneys and speak with them from the Hospital. Hooman told me he didn't have his attorney's number on his cell phone. I told Hooman, I would take him to the station, where he could speak with an attorney.

I transported Hooman to the District 2 Jail and placed him in the designated phone booth with a phone book next to the phone. I told Hooman to select an attorney from the phone book and to make his phone calls. Hooman told me he needed his cell phone to call his agent. I told Hooman what number he wanted from the cell phone and I would gladly retrieve the number. Hooman told me he needed Frank Demaggio's number on his cell phone. At approximately 0442 hours I went to Hooman's property, retrieved his cell phone and located Frank's number and wrote it on a piece of paper. I then went to the phone booth and gave Hooman the number he requested. After approximately 5 minutes, Hooman began knocking on the door to the phone booth. I opened the door and Hooman told me his attorney was in bed and could not talk with him. I asked Hooman if he wanted to make contact with other attorneys listed in the phone book. Hooman pointed to the open phone book which was on an ad to Phillips and Associates and stated, "Phillips and Associates? You gotta be kidding me." Hooman told me he would not consent to the blood draw until he spoke with his attorney. I explained Admin Per Se once again to Hooman and told him the consequences of not providing an affirmative response to the blood draw consent. Hooman told me once again he did not want to speak to any attorneys in the phone book. I told him he could not delay the process any further and by not giving a "yes" response to the blood draw it would be considered a refusal. Hooman told me, "I can't say yes until I talk to my attorney and he's asleep." I told Hooman there were attorneys in the phone book who worked 24 hours a day, and seven days a week that would provide him advice with a call. Hooman again told me he would only speak with his lawyer and walked out of the phone booth room..

At this point I directed detention staff to place Hooman in a cell and provide him with phone access if he desired. Since Hooman had not consented to the blood draw, and I felt he was trying to delay the process, I began the procedures to obtain a Telephonic Search Warrant for his blood.

I completed the night-time telephonic search warrant documents at approximately 0507 hours, to obtain a sample of Hooman's blood and faxed them to Judge Arnold at the Maricopa County Superior Court. At approximately 0515 hours, Officer Oliver who was my witness on the search warrant, called to confirm receipt of the TSW. Officer Oliver told me Judge Arnold was still on the bench and would complete the TSW as soon as possible. On call phlebotomist Adell, was contacted and stated she would respond to the jail. At approximately 0546 hours I called the court again and was told the Judge was now off the bench and would be calling me shortly. At approximately 0556 hours Judge Arnold called me at the District 2 Jail and swore me in and told me the TSW would be faxed immediately. At approximately 0557 hours, I went to the detention cell where Hooman was located and read him the Admin per Se Order of Suspension. Hooman told me he did not want to sign the suspension notice and told me his lawyer was on the way to the District 2 Jail to assist him. I noted his refusal to sign on the Admin per Se affidavit. At no time did he state he would submit to the blood draw again.

9/3/2008 10:48:01 AM   Page 6 of 7

☐ Domestic Violence ☐ Child Abuse ☐ Arson ☐ Homicide ☐ Hate Crime ☐ Elderly ☐ Gang Related ☐ Liquor Establishment

Agency: SPD	Incident / Investigation Report	Case Number: 0802405

EXTREME DUI-BAC .15 OR MORE

Reported: 01/23/2008 03:31	Found 01/23/2008 03:55	Occurred 01/23/2008 03:31
Location N HAYDEN RD / E INDIAN BEND RD , SCOTTSDALE, AZ		Original Officer (1183) NAVARRETE, R.

Original Information	original page 7
Date added: 01/23/2008	Added by: (1183) NAVARRETE, R.

Narrative

At approximately 0559 hours Hooman was taken out of the detention cell and was seated in a restraint chair. After Hooman was seated, Sgt. Henderson was notified about the granting of the search warrant. I then read Hooman the refusal statement. Next, I served Hooman with the search warrant issued by Judge Arnold and told him I obtained a telephonic search warrant from an MCSO Judge to obtain a sample of his blood and was granted the search warrant and he could no longer refuse to provide a sample of his blood. When given the choice of voluntarily extending his arm, Hooman told detention staff would not give his blood voluntarily. At this point, detention officers had to strap Hooman down to the chair and restrain him so phlebotomist Adell could complete the blood draw procedure. While Hooman was being restrained he began to yell out. Detention officers told him to relax and not fight and Hooman stated, "I'm just doing what my Lawyer told me to do; to not comply."

At approximately 0601 hours while strapped to the restraint chair, phlebotomist Adell completed the blood draw procedure from Hooman's left arm while I witnessed the procedure. The phlebotomist Adell is a certified City of Scottsdale contracted Phlebotomist. Adell appeared to be familiar with the blood draw kit and there did not appear to be any problems during the performance of the blood draw. I noted the expiration on the kit was 05-31-2009 and also noticed the same date on the vials used to collect Hooman's blood. Additionally, when I received the blood vials Adell extracted from Hooman, I inverted each vial 10 times to ensure the anti-coagulant powder in the vial mixed properly with the blood. Then, I sealed the vials with the tamper proof seals.

At approximately 0619 hours, after the blood was obtained, I took Hooman to the Jail interview room and read him the blood destruction notice. Hooman refused to sign the blood destruction notice after the explanation. At approximately 0621 hours I read Hooman his Miranda Rights using my Scottsdale issued Miranda rights card. I asked Hooman if he understood his rights, and he stated, "Yes". Hooman told me he did not want to answer my questions without speaking with his attorney (See AIR for Further).

I completed citation #1726482 and booked and released Hooman for the following ARS charges: ARS 28-1380A Extreme DUI .15% or more, ARS 28-1381A2 DUI BAC of .08% or more, ARS 28-1381.A1 DUI Impaired to the slightest degree, ARS 28-693 Reckless Driving 30 MPH over speed limit and ARS 28-4135C No proof of insurance.

Hooman was given a copy of the blood destruction notice, search warrant copy, citation copy, Admin per Se MVD Suspension notice (Pink and Yellow copy), and impound intent notice.

Next I completed the impound procedures for Hooman's blood evidence and placed them in the District 2 refrigerator evidence slot at approximately 0630 hours.

Since Hooman had a California Driver's license, it was not impounded or submitted to MVD.

This concludes my involvement in this matter.

9/3/2008 10:48:01 AM   Page 7 of 7

JMS Internal Booking Number 2008-001053	Alert/VP	CITY OF SCOTTSDALE	DNA previous	DNA taken	Fingerprinted	Photo
AJAPIS PCN Number 2301035478	VP9	ARREST REPORT			B	Y

ORI #: AZ0072500	Agency: SPD		Arrest: 2008-001426	Case #: 08-02405

Last, First, Middle Name		Sfx:	Alias / AKA	Citizenship	Resident	Interpreter
KARAMIAN, HOOMAN ABEDI				US	R	

Race	Sex	Height	Weight	Eye	Hair	Scars, Marks, Tattoos, Amputations
W	M	508	140	BRO	BLK	

Place Of Birth (City, County, State)		SSN	Date Of Birth	Age	DL #	State
NJ				28		AZ

Relative Name	Relationship	Relative Address / Phone

Home Address (Street, City, State, Zip)	Residence Phone	Occupation
SCOTTSDALE AZ 85260		WEBSITE WRITER

Employer (Name of Company / School)	Business Address (Street, City, State, Zip)	Business Phone
DIRTY SCOTTSDALE		0

Location of Arrest (Street, City, State, Zip)	Dist / Beat	Date of Arrest	Arrest Time	Day of Arrest
8000 E INDIAN BEND RD SCOTTSDALE	D2/10	01/23/2008	03:55	Wednesday

#	Fel	Cnt	Charge	State/Local	Citation/Warrant#
1	M	1	EXTREME DUI-BAC .15 OR MORE	28-1382A	1726482

Case#	Bond	Dispo	Release Date	Violation Date	Court ORI
08-02405		CR	01/23/2008	01/23/2008	SCOT

#	Fel	Cnt	Charge	State/Local	Citation/Warrant#
2	M	1	DUI-BAC OF .08 OR MORE	28-1381A2	1726482

Case#	Bond	Dispo	Release Date	Violation Date	Court ORI
08-02405		CR	01/23/2008	01/23/2008	SCOT

#	Fel	Cnt	Charge	State/Local	Citation/Warrant#
3	M	1	DUI-IMPAIRED TO SLIGHTEST DEGREE	28-1381A1	1726482

Case#	Bond	Dispo	Release Date	Violation Date	Court ORI
08-02405		CR	01/23/2008	01/23/2008	SCOT

#	Fel	Cnt	Charge	State/Local	Citation/Warrant#
4	M	1	RECKLESS DRIVING	28-693A	1726482

Case#	Bond	Dispo	Release Date	Violation Date	Court ORI
08-02405		CR	01/23/2008	01/23/2008	SCOT

Release Notes: REL TO AAA CAB 307

Date of Booking	Booking Time	Day of Booking	Cell	Jailer Name #
01/23/2008	04:37	Wednesday		(B1359) KLEINHEINZ, J.

Property Locker: DISTRICT 2 | JAIL AREA | LOCKER 109 |

Date of Release	Release Time	Releasing Officer's Name	Agency / Division	ID#
01/23/2008	6:52			

Released To	Agency / Division	Agency Address
TAXI		

Property Taken:
cellular telephone, misc papers, key, watch - white, ring - white, wallet, credit card, other, purse

Date Taken:	Taken By:	Date Returned:	Returned By:
01/23/2008	(B1359) KLEINHEINZ, J.	01/23/2008	(B1242) HAZEL, L.

Receiving Officer	Releasing Officer
	(B1114) LOVELADY-JR, E.

Related Cases

Alias/AKA

Scottsdale City Court	700 N. 75th St. ○ Scottsdale, AZ	251 ○ 480 312-2442	
STATE OF ARIZONA VS. KARAMIAN, HOOMAN ABEDI	**Case #:** M-751-TR-2008003956 **Complaint #:** 01726482	**Judgment and Sentence**	
		Violation Code: 28-1381A1	
		☒ First Offense ☐ Second Offense	
Courtroom: 1 Judge: B. Monte Morgan		Classification: *IM*	

Date of Birth: 2/12/1979 Attorney for State: _MarBeller_ Attorney for Defendant: _Larry Kazan_

The State is represented by the above named Attorney; the Defendant is present with above name counsel.
The Defendant is advised of the charge(s), the determination of guilt, and is given the opportunity to speak.

Pursuant to A.R.S. §13-607, the Court finds as follows:

☐ Waiver of Counsel - The Defendant knowingly, intelligently, and voluntarily waived his right to be represented by counsel after being advised of the right to be represented by counsel, including the right to have counsel appointed free of charge if the Defendant is indigent.

☐ Waiver of Jury Trial - The Defendant knowingly, intelligently, and voluntarily waives his right to a jury after having been advised of his right to same. The determination of guilt was based upon a trial to the Court.

☐ Waiver of Trial - The Defendant knowingly, intelligently, and voluntarily waived his right to a trial with or without a jury, his right to confront and cross examine witnesses, his right to testify or remain silent, and his right to present evidence and call his own witnesses after having been advised of his right to same. The determination of guilt was based upon plea of guilty/no contest.

☐ Jury Verdict - The determination of guilt was based upon a verdict of guilty after a jury trial.

Count	Charge Code	Charge Description	Current Disposition	Dispo Date
1-1	28-1382A (1ST)	EXTREME DUI .15 AND ABOVE		

Disposition Codes: 10 11 20 21 30 43 (44) 45 59 67____ New Dispo Date: 9308 Sentence Code: ____
Amended Charge: ____ Prejudice: ☐ With ☐ Without Fine Amount $____

Count	Charge Code	Charge Description	Current Disposition	Dispo Date
2-1	28-1381A2 (1ST)	DUI W/BAC .06 OR MORE		

Disposition Codes: 10 11 20 21 30 43 (44) 45 59 67____ New Dispo Date: ____ Sentence Code: ____
Amended Charge: ____ Prejudice: ☐ With ☐ Without Fine Amount $____

Count	Charge Code	Charge Description	Current Disposition	Dispo Date
3-1	28-1381A1 (1ST)	DUI LIQUOR/DRUGS/VAPORS/COMBO		

Disposition Codes: (10) (11) 20 21 30 43 44 45 59 67____ New Dispo Date: ____ Sentence Code: T
Amended Charge: ____ Prejudice: ☐ With ☐ Without Fine Amount $ 488.40

Count	Charge Code	Charge Description	Current Disposition	Dispo Date
4-1	28-693A	RECKLESS DRIVING		

Disposition Codes: 10 11 20 21 30 43 (44) 45 59 67____ New Dispo Date: ____ Sentence Code: ____
Amended Charge: ____ Prejudice: ☐ With ☐ Without Fine Amount $____

Count	Charge Code	Charge Description	Current Disposition	Dispo Date
5-1	28-4135C (1ST)	FAIL TO PROD EVID FIN RESP (1ST)		

Disposition Codes: 10 11 20 21 30 43 (44) 45 59 67____ New Dispo Date: ____ Sentence Code: ____
Amended Charge: ____ Prejudice: ☐ With ☐ Without Fine Amount $____

☐ ____ Months unsupervised Probation
☐ ____ Months supervised Probation
☒ 10/14 Days in jail (SCOJ/LBJL)
☐ ____ Days given for credit time served
☒ 5 Days suspended upon completion of probation/programs
☐ Alcohol Screening/Program (5148) JS / CC / ACC / STI
☐ Domestic Non Violence Prog (5132) JS / CC / ACC / STI
☐ Peace Program (5103) JS / CC / ACC / STI
☐ MADD Impact Panel (5260) JS / CC / ACC / STI
☐ 13-3601(M) Diversion (S902)
☐ Ignition Interlock
☐ Community Restitution

☒ $1188.40 Fine and Surcharges
☐ $____ Time Payment Fee (T3)
☒ $500 PCoP (PS) ☒ $500 Xtra DUI (X5)
☒ $34 Blood Costs (BA)
☒ $22 Jail Costs (JF)
☐ $____ Default Cost (DC)
☐ $____ Restitution (R1)
☐ $____ Court Costs (CC)
☐ $____ Probation Costs (P)
☐ $____ DUI Abatement Costs (DU)
☐ $____ Public Defender Costs (PD)
☐ Reduce Fine(s) if ____

I certify that the Defendant's fingerprint was permanently affixed to this document at the time of sentencing and in open Court. Required for violations of Domestic Violence or A.R.S. §13-3415, §13-1602, §13-1802, §13-1805, §28-1381, or §28-1382.

Revision 3 6/2004 Case Number: M-751-TR-2008003956 Page 1 of 2 9/3/2008 9:01:01 AM

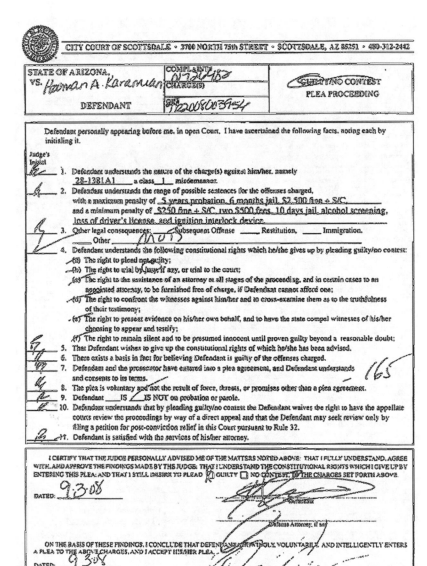

CITY COURT OF SCOTTSDALE • 3700 NORTH 75th STREET • SCOTTSDALE, AZ 85251 • 480-312-2442

STATE OF ARIZONA,
VS. Harman A. Karamian
DEFENDANT

COMPLAINT:
CHARGE(S)

GUILTY/NO CONTEST
PLEA PROCEEDING

Defendant personally appearing before me, in open Court, I have ascertained the following facts, noting each by initialing it.

Judge's Initial

1. Defendant understands the nature of the charge(s) against him/her, namely 28-1381.A1 a class 1 misdemeanor.
2. Defendant understands the range of possible sentences for the offenses charged, with a maximum penalty of 5 years probation, 6 months jail, $2,500 fine + S/C, and a minimum penalty of $250 fine + S/C, two $500 fees, 10 days jail, alcohol screening, loss of driver's license, and ignition interlock device.
3. Other legal consequences: ___ Subsequent Offense ___ Restitution, ___ Immigration. ___ Other _____
4. Defendant understands the following constitutional rights which he/she gives up by pleading guilty/no contest:
   (a) The right to plead not guilty;
   (b) The right to trial by jury, if any, or trial to the court;
   (c) The right to the assistance of an attorney at all stages of the proceeding, and in certain cases to an appointed attorney, to be furnished free of charge, if Defendant cannot afford one;
   (d) The right to confront the witnesses against him/her and to cross-examine them as to the truthfulness of their testimony;
   (e) The right to present evidence on his/her own behalf, and to have the state compel witnesses of his/her choosing to appear and testify;
   (f) The right to remain silent and to be presumed innocent until proven guilty beyond a reasonable doubt;
5. That Defendant wishes to give up the constitutional rights of which he/she has been advised.
6. There exists a basis in fact for believing Defendant is guilty of the offenses charged.
7. Defendant and the prosecutor have entered into a plea agreement, and Defendant understands and consents to its terms.
8. The plea is voluntary and not the result of force, threats, or promises other than a plea agreement.
9. Defendant ___ IS ___ IS NOT on probation or parole.
10. Defendant understands that by pleading guilty/no contest the Defendant waives the right to have the appellate courts review the proceedings by way of a direct appeal and that the Defendant may seek review only by filing a petition for post-conviction relief in this Court pursuant to Rule 32.
11. Defendant is satisfied with the services of his/her attorney.

I CERTIFY THAT THE JUDGE PERSONALLY ADVISED ME OF THE MATTERS NOTED ABOVE: THAT I FULLY UNDERSTAND, AGREE WITH, AND APPROVE THE FINDINGS MADE BY THE JUDGE; THAT I UNDERSTAND THE CONSTITUTIONAL RIGHTS WHICH I GIVE UP BY ENTERING THIS PLEA; AND THAT I STILL DESIRE TO PLEAD ☑ GUILTY ☐ NO CONTEST TO THE CHARGES SET FORTH ABOVE.

DATED: 9.3.08

Defendant

Defense Attorney, if any

ON THE BASIS OF THESE FINDINGS, I CONCLUDE THAT DEFENDANT KNOWINGLY, VOLUNTARILY, AND INTELLIGENTLY ENTERS A PLEA TO THE ABOVE CHARGES, AND I ACCEPT HIS/HER PLEA.

DATED: 9.3.08

Judge

The Tour

Looking back on it, the details seem to stick out more than anything.

Hurricane Bay in Glendale, AZ: I start calling it Glentucky because the girls are trashy and have no teeth. Mansion in Miami, FL: smells like noodles. Venue in Houston, TX: steroids; every guy in the place is a roided-out juicehead sporting tribal tattoos. I'm drinking. Drunk. Privé in Las Vegas, NV: we're at table 69, which only celebrities are allowed to sit at. Barcelona in Scottsdale, AZ: I'm home but it's cougar central. Rich divorcées staring at me like I'm meat. And I'm still drinking. Drunk. Losing it. Flying to Republic in New Orleans, LA: it's my first Mardi Gras; girls flashing their tits for plastic beads. Me: stumbling through the French Quarter. Sometimes I get so drunk I puke, and then I wake up and go to Blonde in Kansas City, MO: the promoter has these terrible hair plugs and all the girls look too old. I celebrate my 30th birthday fifteen times and they pay me for this. $10,000. $15,000. $30,000. It depends on the market. A short flight to Lure in St. Louis, MO: get drunk and RichieRexic (*Dirty* Celeb) is waiting for me in the tub in my hotel room like she's Mena Suvari in *American Beauty*. I don't fuck her. Never fuck a *Dirty* Celeb, I tell myself. Then it's Primal in Atlanta, GA: I'm expecting it to be packed with blacks but it's totally vanilla. I understand my market a little bit more. Drink. Get drunk. Move on to Energy Night Club in Chicago, IL: it's sixteen-and-over night, and all I remember is a bunch of little kids waiting in line to take their picture with me like I'm Santa Claus. Sugar Night Club in Columbus, OH: not even memorable, but I'm still drinking. Getting drunk and waking up hurting and hungover, going to Dream in Sacramento, CA: the armpit of America where every chick is beat. Fly south to Wet Night Club in San Jose: hottest servers I've ever seen, but I get rejected by all of them. Get drunk, can't remember who I slept with. I'm sleeping with a lot of girls I don't remember. Forgetting them. Forgetting myself, and now I'm at llounge in Orange County, CA: Persian mafiaville; I'm home again. Leaving for Dolce Vendetta in Dallas, TX: break my own rule and fuck a *Dirty* Celeb. I break a lot of rules. Fly out of DFW to the Hard Rock in San Diego: talk shop with Andy Hirsh; it's a rare chill night. Move on to Playboy mansion in Beverly Hills, CA: Hefner is a geezer walking around in his jammies. The Shannon twins give me *Dirty* looks all night. Hot chicks with +2's everywhere wearing costumes and lingerie and body paint. It's not reality. Go back to Vegas for a Tao Group event. Go back to Dallas to do Kinki Lounge: 8-Belles is running the girls there. I don't fuck her. Have a threesome with some other girls instead, and I'm starting to lose it hard now, but I keep moving. Fly to Seattle, WA, for Last Supper Club: I get drunk and fuck a girl in my hotel while her friend watches us and masturbates against the wall. They get weird in the morning and I leave town. I disappear. I'm at Aura in Pleasanton, CA: pull a Janny on Amanda Reed, fall hard for her and make love like I never thought was capable. Go to PCL in Scottsdale: I'm back where it all started and I'm a god here. Drinking and drinking and drinking more with these AZ chicks. I'm at Glow in Long Island, NY: it's fucking guido country...like a *Jersey Shore* audition. Back to Vegas to do Pure Group: I'm limitless. In Vegas, Nik Richie can do whatever he wants. Fuck whoever he wants. Drink whatever he wants in any amount. I'll even spray champagne in the server's face. Then I move on to Crobar in Chicago, IL: it's the easiest place to get laid. Drink. Fuck. Leave. A pattern is emerging, and I'm getting on a plane to Charlottle, NC, for some event at Cans Bar & Saloon: I sit with Bobcat cheerleaders and get wasted. Do Bar Canvas in Austin, TX: total letdown. I'm expecting blonde, blue-eyed Texas girls and they're all beat. Keep drinking, moving, going to Empire Social in Sacramento: it's worse now. Everyone's offering me drugs (Pepsi, Molly, random pills) and I'm saying "no" but they keep coming with their dead eyes staring at me. Everyone's a vampire. Go to Jet Companies in Denver, CO: the mountain air clears my head, everyone is nice. Tons of snow-bunny blondes. Go to Velvet Dog and Barley House in Cleveland: double-duty. Get so drunk playing beer pong that I wake up at some girl's house. I'm not playing it safe anymore. Keep moving to Harrah's in Atlantic City, NJ: I'm out of control and swim across the pool in my underwear in front of everybody. Nobody tells me that it's against the rules. Nobody tells Nik Richie what he can or cannot do. I keep drinking, keep moving to Plush in Dallas: meet some friend of Sarah Wood's but don't fuck her. I'm at the VooDoo Lounge in Ft. Lauderdale, FL: hook up with Brock's Chick's cousin and she tastes like spray tan. Want to call

Quayle and tell him but we're on the outs. Move on to Status Lounge in Houston: I fucking hate Houston. It's so boring, or maybe I'm impossible to entertain now. A year has passed: drinking, flying, and fucking. I'm puking and blogging and eating on the run. I'm at the Hyde Lounge in Hollywood, CA: it's terrible; everyone is just staring at each other and sizing them up. Too much ego. Turn 31 at Vanity in the Hard Rock: watch young girls do too much coke. Almost participate but decide against it. Do Haze Nightclub in Vegas: pound a bottle of Patrón. Puke hard. Fly away to Pink Kitty in Cabo: my opinion of Mexico totally changes. Go back to Vegas: get married. Holy shit, I'm fucking married now. The media is eating it up but we've got to keep moving. I go to the Lucky Buddha in Richmond, VA: bring two chicks back to my hotel but ditch them in someone else's room by using the balcony. Shadow Room in Washington, D.C.: someone tries to jump me for the first time. The guy acts like he has a knife and security pushes me into a taxi. I almost relish the surprise. Back to Vegas, I give away +2's at Eve Nightclub. I randomly run into Amanda Reed at Wet Republic. She looks good. She grew up okay. At McFadden's in Pittsburgh, PA: get cuffed for taking a swing at a guy because he called me gay. No arrest. Move on to Club Elevate in Salt Lake City, UT: fucking bust. I'm expecting hot, blonde Mormon girls and they're all beat. Keep drinking. I notice I'm getting older. Losing my looks, my mind. It's starting to take its toll, but I keep going to Wet Republic in Vegas for a pool party. Go to Ivy Rooftop in San Antonio, TX: the city is romantic. Go to The Palms in Vegas for Halloween as Brad Pitt and my wife is Angelina Jolie: a power couple dressed as a power couple. We're in Aja in Tampa Bay, FL: we call it Trampa Bay, and there's a *20/20* film crew following me and Scooby and JV, so I'm showing off and doing The Rock[80] in the club. We go to Lunar in Cincinnati, OH: we can't find JV because he gets lost and some chick steals his clothes. We're at LIV in Miami, FL: hands-down best club in the world, but the problem is you can't communicate with anyone. They're all rich and foreign so there are two language barriers. I keep going. Keep drinking, but it's a routine now. We go back to the same spots in Vegas, L.A., Scottsdale. We go back to Dallas. I have my dinner, drink, sleep, fly away. Scooby and JV love it, but to me it's a paycheck. I don't even want to do it anymore but we need the money. For years, we're on this road of airports and the hot dark of the club and hotels that only look slightly different from each other. The details change so little from

---

80 Signature move in which I take two bottles of champagne, hit them against my chest, and spray them as I fall to my knees on the ground, waving them signal flare-style like Nic Cage does at the end of the movie.

place to place: the hairstyles and the clothing and the accents. Other than that, it's *Groundhog Day*. A cyclical nightmare. Purgatory. We're remixing the remix, but it's the same night over and over and over. It blurs together in ways you'll never forget but can't remember clearly in hindsight. When it all began, the high of being Nik Richie lasted three hours. Now I'm lucky if I cop a buzz for five minutes. The body, the mind, they've built a tolerance to it. The fun is gone. It's work. Money. Doing an event is almost painful now, and I can't wait to reach the end of the road.

I want to be done with it before it's done with me.

The Catalyst

In hindsight I can see that the DUI was the reason The Dirty became successful. Perhaps "successful" isn't the right word. The site makes very little money on its own, but it was able to survive due to my momentary lack of judgment.

My goal was to never let my identity become public. I was going to start this site and then flip it for however many millions of dollars and retire. Doing *The Dirty* forever was never in the cards. It's a young man's game, and people get older. They move on. I was going to open up a little beach bar in Orange County or maybe even Mexico, something to keep me busy in between boat trips and rounds of golf. I've always been the type of person that even when I'm on vacation or trying to relax, I feel like I need to be doing something. Always moving. Hustling. Looking for the angle. That's a trait of Hooman Karamian that translated over to Nik Richie: the ability to devote myself to something entirely for the sake of success. I discovered it when I wanted to become a doctor and was able to maintain it all these years.

Sometimes devotion isn't enough, though.

Sometimes you need to compromise.

In this particular case, I needed to make my identity public. Expose myself. I had to let this Nik Richie persona become a tangible presence that people could meet in the real world. An idea can only do so much on its own, and in this case, the man behind the curtain made more money than his idea ever did. All those trips to L.A. and Vegas and Miami—that's what kept everything afloat. The appearance fees. It started with Dolce Vendetta in Dallas and kept on going for years to come.

As much as the people over at The Smoking Gun don't like me or my site, the reality is that their threat to out me served as a catalyst for everything: the events and the money and that ever-growing reputation of Nik

Richie who seemed to crop up everywhere. I did the TV show circuit. I did the tour, a tour that almost killed me. I met people: industry people, people who were chasing fame, and girls. So many girls. Girls like Sarah Wood and Amanda Reed who would fuck with my head and my heart. Girls like Alien and Leper. Scooby Snack. And then there was Shayne. I met and befriended Lonnie Moore, and he would be the one to introduce me to my wife. I'd meet Shayne in Vegas and make her my bride, all because of one turn of events.

In the alternate reality where no one finds out who Nik Richie is, that doesn't happen. It's entirely possible I never would have met anyone. So sometimes a mistake can make you. Or it can go a little bit further and make a marriage. A family.

We have a daughter.

Her name is Press.

My wife Shayne Dahl Lamas-Richie with newborn Press Dahl Lamas-Richie.

To Press

You were born on 11/11/11.

It was shortly after I appeared on *Anderson Cooper* the first time, which is the reason why I opted to do it via satellite. In the event that you decided you wanted to be born, the last thing I wanted was to be stuck on a talk show and miss it. I had actually been telling everyone on my radio show that November 11th was the day you were coming out, and somehow I think you knew I wanted that. You cooperated. You were 6 pounds, 6 ounces. Healthy. Perfect. No blood. I was so worried there was going to be blood and there wasn't. You had big Hollywood eyes and rosy cheeks. Perfect skin. Even the nurse joked around about how "this baby already has makeup on." I looked at you and it was like looking at a little me, and I remember thinking, *Oh great, she's going to be an ugly Persian baby.*

But then we sat down together, you and I, and I started to see your mom in your features. You were a good balance of the two of us. After the nurses cleaned you up and wrapped you in blankets, we sat there for about a good hour and I just looked at you. Held you. You had that baby smell I had kept hearing about, and it was quiet. I don't remember anything ever being so quiet. It's like we were on our own little planet where there were no TV shows or websites or drama. Just us. Quiet. Your mom slept and we got acquainted. I talked to you. I didn't have that life-altering moment that other parents talk about. You didn't instantly change me or my world, but I remember thinking, *Okay, now I've got to get my shit together. I've got two girls to take care of now.*

It was time for me to grow up. My soul didn't change but I matured. I had another reason to be successful, however, it wasn't a selfish one this time. It wasn't about me or what I wanted. You were the person in my life that I needed to take care of, and I knew you wouldn't be able to take care of yourself if I failed. I was needed, and I had never had that before. To you, I wasn't Nik or Hooman or Corbin. You weren't even aware of these people. I was just Dad. And you were Press.

We named you Press because you were the daughter of two affluent people, but we wanted you to have your own gravity. To us, the name had its own distinction. Should you ever want to be an actress or artist or singer, we wanted you to have that. As I've illustrated, names can mean much more than what people call you. Sometimes they carry grandeur, infamy, elegance. One day you'll grow up to be somebody. We know that. In a way, it's already started.

The day after you were born, *TMZ* posted your baby photo for the world to see. Not even a day old and you were already making headlines. Reporters and journalists wrote about you. Press Richie already brought back more Google search results than most adults. You were famous without even knowing what fame was. And we loved you to pieces.

I used to videotape myself on trips and out at these clubs. I'd get footage of whatever suite I was staying in. It was my way of sharing myself with the world, but then I started doing it with you. On Easter you sneezed three times, scowled, and then gave me a smile. On New Year's you cooed at the camera and chewed your fingers. I was uploading these to YouTube, sharing my daughter with the world, but I was also chronicling your life. You can go back and watch yourself grow up, and so can I. Everyone can.

The world is changing, and it'll be much different by the time you're old enough to read this. All of us will be different, including your mom and myself. If we seem overprotective, it's because we know what's out there. If you feel like we don't understand what you're going through in life, we do. We've both been where you are. We can give you the advice to get through it.

And there are going to be some people that try to tell you who your father was, the kind of person he used to be. They'll say he was a bad guy who hurt a lot of people. They'll say he created something that served as an avenue for gossip and lies and lawsuits. Perhaps there's some validity in that. I've always thought that my breed of honesty was something most people weren't ready for. Or they didn't want it because it made them examine themselves. The point is that you'll grow up in an age in which everyone is a public figure. You'll be able to research yourself and your parents. You'll be able to see every little thing that was said about your family, and some of it won't be nice. Some of it will be hurtful.

We'll handle it.

In the end, it's all just talk. Words.

Even if what you read here changes the way you look at me, just remember what your mother said on our first date: *The past is the past.* It's behind us now.

You've got a very bright future, Pressy.

My daughter Press Dahl Lamas-Richie at one year of age.

Exit

I've been saying for years that everyone has dirt.

Everybody lies. Cheats. Everyone has a secret of some kind they don't want the world to know about. Even me, the guy who runs this operation, has a past I'm not completely proud of. Everyone has dirt, but the degree of it varies from person to person. Sometimes it's a girl that Photoshops herself into someone she's not. Other times it's a guy selling drugs in a club. No one is perfect. Literally every individual you encounter in life has done something wrong. Your friends. Your family. Celebrities. Non-celebrities. And yes, even Sarah Jones.

David Gingras and I are in the middle of the appeals process when it happens. The story breaks that Sarah had sex with one of her students on Dixie Heights High property. By this point, she's already resigned from her teaching post at the high school, citing "personal reasons." It doesn't go into any further detail than that. "Personal reasons" is all she says, but one can assume she means Nik Richie and the ongoing lawsuit that she has with him. Or her failed relationship that she mentioned (but didn't really want to talk about) on *Anderson Cooper.* What comes over the wire is that she got indicted on charges of first-degree sexual abuse. The boy is sixteen, a student athlete. Allegedly, the relationship between the two occurred between October 1st and December 31st. Both Sarah Jones and her mother[81] get charged for tampering with electronic evidence.

So this story breaks and the world is shocked because everyone thought they had it right. I don't really know which was easier: betting on Sarah Jones or betting against Nik Richie. I think it's easy to see someone, a teacher, a crying girl, and want to pat them on the shoulder. Defend them. Fight for them. It's easy to get suckered into the "poor me" act, and a lot of people did. Anderson Cooper fell for it. So did Chris Cuomo and

---

81 Ironically, a principal at another school in Kentucky.

the guys over at *20/20*. Pretty much every major news outlet, even the ones that traditionally report neutrally, sided with Sarah and her crusade to take down Nik Richie. All they did was illustrate the point I've been making for years: everyone, even someone as seemingly virtuous as Sarah Jones, has dirt.

Sometimes it never comes to light.

In Sarah's case, it did. Nationally.

Everywhere is reporting this story about Sarah and the young boy, and there's a lot of chatter about how this makes her case against me null and void since most of it's based on character. Reputation. Essentially, you can't say a site ruined you if you were fucking sixteen-year-old boys. None of the people are apologizing to me, but the air has shifted. Nik Richie might not be as bad as everyone thought. Maybe he has a point. And then Nancy Grace jumps all over it because she was one of the few people that didn't twist her ankle hopping on the Sarah Jones bandwagon. Unlike Anderson and *20/20*, she doesn't make that mistake. She does an hour-long special on Sarah Jones and the sex scandal, and this is literally the only time in the history of television that Nik Richie has been shown in a favorable light. Nancy gives me a little bit of grief about the "Why are all high school teachers freaks in the sack?" line, but the majority of the episode is all about Sarah and how fucked-up this is.

I'm still not the good guy. I'm still not a role model or the person you want your kids to grow up to be. This time, in this moment, the perceived villain gets to play hero. This game of being Nik Richie and running *The Dirty* has always been about small victories. Minor steps in the right direction. A little luck. A fucking great lawyer. A new wave of social media that was wanted, demanded, but not everyone was ready for. The formula of Reality Internet was simple enough in theory, but the application and maintaining its survival is a complicated algorithm. Sometimes a mistake had to be made in order to keep it going. An identity had to be compromised. The last fifteen years of my life have been an odd sort of domino effect, and it all comes to a head with Sarah Jones.

People now understand that dirt is everywhere, and it turns up in the places you least expect it. Sarah and I will have our time in court, and the result of it doesn't really matter in the end because there's always someone else. There's always another Sarah Jones. There's always another lawsuit waiting to happen, someone out to take me down. Maybe it's a politician or a social worker or the manager of a clothing store. They could be anyone.

The pattern is cyclical.

For every new lawsuit, there's another celebrity scandal. For every Leper and Alien, there's another *Dirty* Celeb just waiting to happen. A younger, blonder Scooby Snack. An even more pretentious Freddy Fags. Out with the old, in with the new. They'll keep cropping up and they'll keep being posted. There's always another. Another club, another better Vegas venue. Another promoter. Another DJ. The scene was around before Nik Richie, and it'll keep going long after I'm gone.

One day I'll stop.

Either under my own accord or should the domino effect take the wrong turn. I'll bow out eventually. *The Dirty* isn't how it was when it first started. It's a job. A paycheck. If I do an appearance, I'm not getting obliterated and figuring out which chicks I want to bang. I've got my wife. I've got my daughter. I've found my stability and the comfort zone that exists between being Nik and Hooman. It's the delicate balance of father, husband, and online persona. It's a balance that took a lot of trial and error to find. A lot of fuckups and missteps.

And sometimes you'll hear me say, "Never chase."

I say it a lot actually, but the meaning is lost on people from time to time. Essentially, it means to let life happen. Let the dominos fall. Don't spend your life chasing fame and money and the shit that doesn't matter. The road will lead you where it wants to lead you, so don't chase the trivial. Don't try to be something you're not. If you take a wrong turn, if you fail or make a mistake, it's fine. You can move on from it. You can recover. New beginnings happen all the time.

The past is the past.

Nik and Shayne Lamas-Richie in Cabo San Lucas renewing their love for each other.

Niktionary

+2 Factor: when a chick gets a boob job it increases her value two points on a ten-point scale

+2's: fake boobs

30k Milli: a guy who claims he makes millions, but really only makes around $30k a year and spends all his money on stuff he can't afford; a poser

6 head (5 head): when a person has a enormous forehead (measured in inches)

Affliction: a brand of clothing worn by losers

Afro-brow: hairy eyebrows

Air biscuit: fart

Anti-petite: no way near small

Aquaf*gs: underwater f*gs

Babushka: a big, giant, Harlem Globetrotter-like afro, that explodes out of the panties of a Crabby Patty when panty security has been breached

Beak: nose like a large bird

Beat: disgustingly ugly

Bissues: b*tch with issues

Blanimal: a black animal

Blast (putting someone on blast): putting someone in the spotlight and/or exposing them; talking crap about someone

Bucket seats: nice ass

Butterface: everything looks good but her face

Cadirack: not easy on the eyes, an eyesore

Caker: chick who wears way too much makeup

Cannibal: a lesbian. Because they eat their own kind

Car-Tastrophe: beat-looking people in a car

Ceptor head: looks good except her head

Cheesecake: real fruity guy

Chubble: problems fat people cause

Combustible cougar: horny for young men

Combustible face: hazardous look

Cougar in training (Baby Cougar): a girl who will grow up to be a cougar because her mom is one and/or she is starting to look and act like one

Cougars: women who are 40 or older who try to be 20 (by getting plastic surgery, wearing tons of makeup, dressing like they are 20, etc.) and usually date or "prey" on younger men

Cougar-Troll: an ugly cougar

Cougarville: place where cougars come from

Cougarwood: place where famous cougars go

Cougrrrr: very ugly cougar

Count Gutula: big stomach

Crabby Patty: p*ssy

Crash test dummy: a dumb friend that you can convince to do anything

Dale boy (Dales): a guy who claims to be straight but acts like he's gay (or really is just gay)

D-Bagalicious: sensational D-bag

D-Bag: douchebag; someone who sucks at life; a total jerk

Dirty **Army**: the group of people who are fans of thedirty.com

Dirty bird: dirty/sl*tty British chick

Don: a young female gold digger looking for a new wealthy father or sugar daddy

Douchetard: douche + retard

Drag hag: someone who hangs with drag queens

DRD: Dennis Rodman Disease; sexually transmitted disease(s)

Dreamkiller: one who kills the dreams of another

DSLs: D*ck sucking lips

Dugout driller: aggressive gay guy

Egg Roll(s): fat Asians

F*gadocious: super gay

F*gtastic: overly gay

F*gtician: professional f*g

Fake SGM: people who are not in the Scissor Gang Mafia but pretend to be by giving the scissor gang sign in pictures (and Nik will point out the reason why they are not cool enough to be in it)

Fanny packs: beat girls that have no appeal

Farm: a person's ass

Fattastrophe: group of very fat people

Fifty cake mistake: big girl who loves cake

Fifty-yarder: only looks good from fifty yards away

File you away: putting a hot guy/girl (whatever works for ya) in your mental hard drive so you can masturbate to them later

Flesbian: fake lesbian

Forgy: Short for "for the gays"

Frat rat: a girl who loves to hang out with and/or screw guys in fraternities

Freetard: a free retard

Front grill: teeth

F*ck trophy: baby/kid…"What bout that chick you met at the club the other night, did you hit that?" "Naw, she's got a f*ck trophy."

Fugly: f*cking ugly

FUPA: a fat upper pu**y area. Men can have it too.

Gaysian: a gay Asian

Gestappo's: those who oppose the Dirty Army

Gills: side fat; love-handles

Grave Diggaz: dirty nails

Grazer: chick that likes to eat a lot

Green Bay: cellulite; cottage cheese

Gregalicious: owns a Greg

Greg–Juice: self-explanatory

Greg: penis; tummy stick

Helmet Special: retard

Himstitute: tranny prostitute

Hoemerican: an American hoe

Horses (or any reference to a horse, stable, the derby, races or horse names): people with huge teeth and gums that resemble those of a horse

Insurgents: non-SGM perpetrator/ enemies of the army

ITG: short for inner thigh gap, the appropriate distance between a woman's inner thighs.

Jack Bauer: a person with a large forehead or a twenty head

Jay Leno: got a big chin

Kodiak: body of a bear

Lee push–up bra: from the makers of lee press-on nails

Long head clan: horse division (horse head)

Lotto baby: unknown father (a lot o' people hit that)

MAC forcefield: tons and tons of makeup that looks clown-like

Mad monkey: extremely drunk and out of control

Mick Jaggers: big lips

Muffin top: when a person's side or stomach fat bubbles over their waistband because their pants are too tight, forming the shape of a muffin

Multichin: multiple chins

Multi-Gregging: gang bang on one chick

Nominee: person with no money

Nomo's: a place where no homos are welcome

Noodles: referring to Asian people or descent

Nostrildahmus: huge nose pipes

Onion: nice a$$

Oscar Meyer: got a Greg

Pack of franks: fat rolls on a chick's body…"Damn! look at the pack of franks on that chick"

Paki house/hut: liquor store

Patch Adams: balding

Pearl catcher: chicks who get c*mmed on

Pebbles: an attractive, yet underage and overly sexual young girl (a.k.a. jailbait)

Pepperidge Farm: way too old

PGM ("Pinky Gang Mafia"): the rival gang of SGM whose members show their pinky finger when having a picture taken

Pickle smoocher: rubs the Greg

Pig fishing: guys who are out to just f*ck anything

Pirate: gay dude. Because they like semen on their poop deck

Poon lagoon: pu**y

Porta-Potty: An escort that is hired by the client for the specific purpose of being defecated upon (urine and/or fecal matter). The escort is payed a premium for this as it's a niche service that goes above and beyond standard intercourse. Although intercourse is often had in tandem with defecation, the porta-pottie's primary role is one of humiliation and belittlement so that the client may feel empowered.

Prop 8: gay person who wants to get married

Prosthetic Playa: fake wannabe player

Puffydumbbell: roid user

Purple crayon: a black man's Greg

Raisinets: ugly nipples

Red Cup Nation: those of us who agree that only red plastic cups should be used at parties (because all other colors are stupid)

Refund gap: the huge gap between some women's fake boobs that is so big that they should get their money back from their doctor

Ronald McDonalds: high-arching eyebrows

RVM: red vest mafia (valet attendant)

Sevenhead: means "Yes I ride the Short Bus!"

Sewerfront: waterfront in Scottsdale

SGM ("Scissor Gang Mafia"): people who make a scissor/backward peace sign when having their picture taken

She–Boys: trannies

Shim: a girl who looks like a man

Shimspital: hospital for shims

Shman: female type of man

Shopping bags: droopy boob job or +2's

Shotgun: a slutty chick. One cock and she's ready to blow

Shougar: a girl that is a cougar and a shim

Skankaholic: addicted to or being a skank; likes skanky chicks; an alcoholic skank

Ski jumper: big or long nose

Slant f*cker: guy who only likes f*ckin Asian chicks

Slim slow diet: a fat person who feels it necessary to show people her body…"Sick, see that fat girl in the bikini? Oh, she is feeling good about herself since she just got on the Slim Slow Diet."

Sloon: a chick that looks like she's mixed with snake lizard and baboon

Slug: ugly slut

Snicker Licker: white girls who only like black guys

Soldier: a member of the *Dirty* Army; a fan/supporter of thedirty.com

Sorostitute: a girl in a sorority that is easier than a prostitute

Sphere Job: a boob job

Spongebob: a nasty female that has a crabby patty instead of a vagina

Stallone: a really ugly Italian chick (or any chick for that matter)

Stay Puff: juice-muscular guy obviously on roids

Stretch Armstrong: face lift too tight

Sugar butt: a gay guy

Summer teeth: some are here, some are there

Superhighway gap: boobs miles apart

Synchronized sucking: what aquaf*gs do

Talons: ugly toes

Tenderfoot: gay or feminine

Thunderstorm: extremely large thighs; thunder thighs

Too Fat Shakur: 2-pac fat reference

Top Ramen: a person that is broke

Tranimal: animal tranny

Tranny: a girl with so much makeup caked on her face that she looks like a transvestite

Tri-tip: she can try the tip

Trough feeder: an obese female

Trout: an older man who dates younger women in trying to be younger or "swim upstream"

Trout mouth: looks like a fish

Tuna factory: chick who has nasty-lookin p*ssy lips…"That chick's got a tuna factory goin on down there."

Unbeweavable: lots of weave

WNBA: a tall female who is manly

Would you?: means "would you screw this chick?"

thedirty.com

feralhouse.com